Annual Editions: Technologies, Social Media, and Society, 23/e

Daniel Mittleman
Douglas Druckenmiller

http://create.mheducation.com

ISBN-10: 126018028X   ISBN-13: 9781260180282

Contents

Unit 6 123

Unit 7 139

Unit 8 153

Unit 9 169

Detailed Table of Contents

Unit 1: Introduction

What World Are We Building, Danah Boyd, *Data & Society: Points*, 2016
"It's easy to love or hate technology, to blame it for social ills, or to imagine that it will do what people cannot. But technology is made by people. In a society. And it has a tendency to mirror and magnify the issues that affect everyday life. The good, bad, and ugly."

The Fourth Industrial Revolution: What It Means and How to Respond, Klaus Schwab, *Foreign Affairs*, 2015
Of the many diverse and fascinating challenges we face today, the most intense and important is how to understand and shape the new technology revolution, which entails nothing less than a transformation of humankind.

The "Internet of Restaurants" Is Coming for Your Info, David M. Perry, *Pacific Standard*, 2017
"At the National Restaurant Association, many of the hot technology companies are selling surveillance, not supper."

Is Nothing about Your Life Private? Cory Franklin, *The Chicago Tribune*, 2017
"In 2010, top Google executive Eric Schmidt told The Atlantic magazine, 'Google policy is to get right up to the creepy line and not cross it. . . . We know where you are. We know where you've been. We can more or less know what you're thinking about'."

The Tech Humanist Manifesto, Kate O'Neill, *Medium*, 2017
"We need to encode technology with the best of our humanity."

Unit 2: Shift in Retail

What in the World Is Causing the Retail Meltdown of 2017? Derek Thompson, *The Atlantic*, 2017
"In the middle of an economic recovery, hundreds of shops and malls are shuttering. The reasons why go far beyond Amazon."

How Online Shopping Makes Suckers of Us All, Jerry Useem, *The Atlantic*, 2017
"Will you pay more for those shoes before 7 p.m.? Would the price tag be different if you lived in the suburbs? Standard prices and simple discounts are giving way to far more exotic strategies, designed to extract every last dollar from the consumer."

Imagining the Retail Store of the Future, Elizabeth Paton, *The New York Times*, 2017
Will it have robots? No checkout counters? Virtual fitting rooms? Almost anything seems possible.

Four Ways Junk Food Brands Befriend Kids Online, Teresa Davis, *The Conversation*, 2017
"Kids are inundated with advertising for junk food on social media."

Unit 3: Impact of Technology on Work

How Technology Is Destroying Jobs, David Rotman, *MIT Technology Review*, 2013
"Automation is reducing the need for people in many jobs. Are we facing a future of stagnant income and worsening inequality?"

How Artificial Intelligence and Robots Will Radically Transform the Economy, Kevin Maney, *Newsweek*, 2016
"All those dire predictions about the automated economy sound like a sci-fi horror film from the '50s: Robots are coming to take your jobs, your homes, and your children. Except it's real. And it has a happy ending."

Preface

A NOTE TO THE READER

In vetting articles for *Technologies, Social Media, and Society* from the sea of contenders, we have tried to continue in the tradition of the previous editors. The writers are journalists, computer scientists, lawyers, economists, policy analysts, and academics, the kinds of professions you would expect to find represented in a collection on the social implications of computing. They write for newspapers, business and general circulation magazines, academic journals, professional publications and, more and more, for websites. Their writing is mostly free from both the unintelligible jargon and the breathless enthusiasm that prevents people from forming clear ideas about computing and social media policy. This is by design, of course, and we hope that after reading the selections you agree. *Annual Editions: Technologies, Social Media, and Society* is organized around important dimensions of society rather than of computing. This book's major themes are the economy, community, politics considered broadly, and the balance of the risk and reward of new technology.

The units are organized to lead us through several of the critical issues of our day. You may notice that many of these issues (nature of community and friendships, causes of unemployment, intellectual property, freedom of speech, as examples) only tangentially seem to be technology or social media issues. This, too, is by design and serves as evidence for how intertwined technology policy has become with other social and economic policy decisions in the world today.

We are living during a very exciting time, comparable to the twenty-five or so years that followed the invention of Gutenberg's printing press. The principal modes for communication and collaboration in our society are changing faster than we know how to make public policy or evolve culture to deal with them. As such, business models, property rules, international treaty rules, and a myriad of other economic and social norms are experiencing both evolution and revolution, often with unanticipated or controversial outcomes. At the same time, these technological advances are empowering masses of people around the world who just a generation ago had little or no access to real opportunity. And technological advances are making available incredible new gains in medicine and productivity.

A word of caution. Each article has been selected because it is topical, interesting, and (insofar as the form permits) nicely written. To say that an article is interesting or well-written, however, does not mean that it is right. This is as true of both the facts presented in each article and the point of view of the author. We hope you will approach these articles as you might a good discussion among friends. You may not agree with all opinions, but you will come away nudged in one direction or another by reasoned arguments, holding a richer, more informed view of important issues.

This book includes several features we hope will be helpful to students and professionals. Included with each article are Learning Outcomes, Critical Thinking study/discussion questions, and Internet References. The Internet References include links to articles and videos that guide a deeper dive into the topic at hand. The use of videos further supports multiple learning styles among the students using this reader.

Though some of the critical thinking questions can be answered from within the article, many more invite further investigation, in essence, allowing each reader to construct their own understanding of the article topic. We hope the articles we gathered for this volume, along with the materials provided with them, initiate further discussion and further interest in these controversial issues of our day. They are intended to get the discussion flowing, not to provide definitive answers.

We want *Annual Editions: Technologies, Social Media, and Society* to spark your interest for exploring some of the most important discussions of the time: those about the promises and risks engendered by new developments in information technology and social media.

Editors

Danny Mittleman is an Associate Professor in the College of Computing and Digital Media at DePaul University. He teaches coursework in Virtual Collaboration, Social Media, and Social Impact of Technology. Dr. Mittleman is the author of over 55 academic publications, and several dozen more conference and invited presentations. His research focuses on the design of virtual and physical spaces for work collaboration, as well as the design of collaborative work process. He has spoken on these topics at NASA, The World Bank, the Federal Reserve,

NCSA, the Department of Defense, and multiple Fortune 500 corporations. Today all of his free time—and then some—are devoted toward raising his triplet sons.

Douglas A. Druckenmiller is a Professor of Information Systems in the School of Computer Sciences at Western Illinois University. He teaches coursework in Global Virtual Teams, Strategic Information Systems, and Computer Science Ethics. His research focuses on collaborative systems and virtual teaming technologies. He has more than 35 years of collaboration engineering experience, and has published several journal articles in the area of group decision support and problem formulation in journals such as *The Journal of Management Information Systems* (JMIS), *The Journal of the Association of Information Systems (JAIS), The International Journal of Intelligence, Technology and Planning, FUTURES,* and *Journal of Information Systems Education.*

Academic Advisory Board

Members of the Academic Advisory Board are instrumental in the final selection of articles for each edition of ANNUAL EDITIONS. Their review of articles for content, level, and appropriateness provides critical direction to the editors and staff. We think that you will find their careful consideration well reflected in this volume.

Unit 1

UNIT

Prepared by: Daniel Mittleman, *DePaul University* and
Douglas Druckenmiller, *Western Illinois University*

Introduction

No new technology is all good or all bad. Every new technology has both positive and negative consequences—and we can see this by examining any one of them. To demonstrate, let's consider the case of a big new technology that came of age about 120 years ago—the invention and mass adoption of the automobile.

The automobile permitted us to travel faster and farther than previously possible by horse. It was possible, on average to travel about 25 miles a day by horse. In fact, if you check the distances between Spanish missions along the California coast, you will find them to be about 25 miles apart—one day of travel. Even early automobiles on virtually nonexistent roads were able to cover those 25 miles in about two hours. That meant it was possible to travel 100, perhaps 200, miles in a day.

So, the automobile—once Henry Ford mass produced them and lowered the price in 1908—heralded the end of the horse-drawn carriage. This change, for many, was positive; it certainly changed man's relationship to the horse. The automobile created or advanced whole new fields of work from highway construction to petroleum engineering. It created jobs for gas station attendants, parking valets, mechanics, and car salesmen. But it eliminated many jobs for blacksmiths, stable boys, and street sweeps.

More than that, the automobile opened up the practicality of suburban living, shopping malls, and super highways. It presaged much of what we now think of as *Americana* such as carpooling, road trips, and drive through restaurants. But at the same time, it fed America's appetite for oil, which has contributed to hostilities in the Middle East, oil spills in Alaska and the Gulf of Mexico, oil pipeline controversies, and climate change.

What follows this introduction is a book of readings: a collection of recent newspaper, magazine, and journal articles as well as extended blog posts from notable authors. It is possible to step through the collected articles reading each as a disconnected essay, much as you might read a typical monthly magazine having only a loose theme, if any at all, connecting the articles.

You might decide you like some of the articles: they amuse you, they stimulate you to think, or they contain information you can put to practical use. And you might decide you dislike other articles that bore you, or don't seem relevant to your interests, or both. In truth, you could read the articles in this book in just that fashion. But to do so would miss the point of the whole exercise of the course you are currently taking.

What this book—and presumably your course—is about is the evaluation of recent technological advances on our economics, our politics, our culture, and on us. These readings address a myriad of intertwined issues about social media, privacy, security, and business. Getting one's head around the ideas from these articles—and the implications that stem from the ideas—is not a simple matter.

What differentiates this book—this reader—from a magazine, and what differentiates you reading this material inside a course rather than on your own, is the use of a framework or model to help make sense of the complex issues these articles discuss.

Here is a model I hope you will consider suggested by Neil Postman about a generation ago. It consists of five ideas:

1. **All technological change is a trade-off.** That is, every new technology introduces advantages and disadvantages.
2. **Every technological change creates winners and losers.** Advantages and disadvantages of new technologies are never distributed evenly among the world's populace.
3. **Embedded within each new technology is at least one underlying new idea.** Often this idea is not immediately apparent; sometimes it is fairly abstract. But the idea is always there and its impact may turn out to dwarf the technology itself.
4. **Technological change is not additive, it is ecological.** That is, a new technology cannot simply be added to our world; its adoption changes our world.
5. **Adopted technologies become mythic.** The existence of new technologies, once they diffuse to regular use, are taken for granted as though they have always been there and they cannot possibly be removed.

These ideas can be applied as a framework to evaluate every technological change discussed in this reader. As you read each article consider the following questions:

- What are the advantages and disadvantages this new technology presents?
- Who are the winners and losers as this technology diffuses into regular use?
- What grand idea(s) underlies this new technology and how does this idea impact our economic, social, cultural, or political institutions?
- How is diffusion of this technology changing structures, patterns, or norms in our world?

Perhaps some articles do not focus on the technology itself, but on the ideas, patterns, or outcomes already occurring. Even so, applying Postman's framework is an excellent approach to making sense of the reading.

In the case of the automobile, Postman's ideas provide a skeleton for analysis. The automobile clearly had its advantages: faster travel led to more mobility and greater opportunity for many. On the other hand, it has contributed to air pollution and a breakdown of urban neighborhoods. Postman suggests that embedded in every new technology is one or more powerful abstract ideas. Early automobile pioneers might have imagined American suburbia, but they could not foresee it as it has evolved. Nor could they have predicted the global political ramifications that the demand for a consistent, low-priced oil and gas supply would portend. Clearly the automobile changed our world. But it did so not by adding a new tool to it, rather by enabling enormous shifts in societal structures.

In this Unit, you are going to read Klaus Schwab's description of The Fourth Industrial Revolution. Schwab reminds us the first industrial revolution, brought about by the 18th century development of the steam engine, both mechanized factory production and modernized transportation through powered ships and railroads. The second revolution resulted from our ability to harness electrical power in the late 19th century. With electricity we were able to develop mass production factories, and were able to communicate instantaneously over long distance via telegraph and telephone. The third industrial revolution was the introduction of computers in the latter half of the 20th century. This enabled us to build an information society as we developed the ability to capture, process, and store vast quantities of information.

At first glance, the fourth industrial revolution looks like the third. It too uses computers to process data, but there is an important difference. What differentiated the third industrial revolution from the second is that in the second, wealth stemmed from one's ability to build and run vast factories. The more goods one could produce, the richer one could become. In the third, wealth stemmed from one's ability to acquire and use information. The more information one had, the better—and perhaps faster—one could compete. Information held value.

That is no longer true. Today information is so available and abundant, it wants to be free. One can use Google or Wikipedia, or any number of other online resources to look up an amazing amount of information. Most of us receive way more email, text messages, tweets, and assorted other pings everyday than we can possibly read. In fact we probably receive way more interesting and useful information every day that we can possibly read. So information does not hold the value it once held.

Rather, value now accrues from the ability to combine, analyze, synthesize, and filter the most useful information. And command of artificial intelligence tools that can do that is where value and wealth reside. As just one example, many of us desire a self-driving car because not only will it talk to other cars, traffic signals, and an array of sensors helping the car to transport you faster and safer than you can do yourself, but it will give you back more time in your day to visit Facebook, Snapchat, Twitter, or some more useful information source to read and filter information valuable to you.

Notice that each revolution—in fact, each trigger technology within the revolution—can be evaluated using Postman's five ideas. As you read, think about what you are reading in light of Postman's ideas. Each of the articles that follow focus on one particular slice of fourth industrial generation technology.

"The 'Internet of Restaurants' Is Coming for Your Info," follows Bruce Schneier through the Tech Pavilion at the 2017 National Restaurant Show, the major restaurant industry convention. Schneier discusses fourth industrial generation technologies that match customers to restaurant (almost like a dating app might do it). These technologies, and the businesses that emerge around them, have created a new industry. Read closely for how these new businesses make money and think about: is that money coming from the restaurants or the diners? Who benefits from these matches, and is it worth the cost? Then think about how wealth is created by aggregating the information collected. Ask yourself why this article's author chose to walk the convention floor with Schneier, a renowned Internet security and privacy expert, rather than with a restaurant industry expert. Finally, apply Postman's ideas to this industry.

In "What World Are We Building," Danah Boyd, a leading social media researcher known for her work about teenager use of social media, discusses her observations of how use of these media products impact the human social networks of their users. The ideas Postman postulates are powerful here, as the winners and losers among users of social media technologies are unclear.

Finally, in "Is Nothing About Your Life Private" we are introduced to a medical research project conducted by DeepMind, an artificial intelligence company owned by Google. DeepMind contracted with a large British healthcare firm to collect and aggregate patient data so that artificial intelligence could be employed to predict which patients would contract kidney disease in the future. The idea being if the disease is found early, it can be treated less expensively, less invasively, and result in a higher cure rate. These are noble goals, but what might go wrong when the largest big data company in the world possesses and stores in the cloud vast amounts of very personal and private medical data? And, what would Postman predict?

As you build familiarity of using Postman's ideas in this Unit, we hope you will continue to apply them as you wade deeper into this book.

Prepared by: Daniel Mittleman, *DePaul University* and
Douglas Druckenmiller, *Western Illinois University*

Article

What World Are We Building

Danah Boyd

Learning Outcomes

After reading this article, you will be able to:

- Identify biases in search engine results.

- Evaluate the role cultural prejudices play in big data and how that influences prediction.

- Distinguish between intentional and unintentional discrimination in machine learning.

1. Internet

I grew up in small town Pennsylvania, where I struggled to fit in. As a geeky queer kid, I rebelled against hypocritical dynamics in my community. When I first got access to the Internet, before the World Wide Web existed, I was like a kid in a candy store. Through early online communities, I met people who opened my eyes to social issues and helped me appreciate things that I didn't even understand. Looking back, I think of the Internet as my saving grace because the people that I met— the *strangers* that I met—helped me take the path that I'm on today. I fell in love with the Internet as a portal to the complex, interconnected society that we live in.

I studied computer science, wanting to build systems that connected people and broke down societal barriers. As my world got bigger, though, I quickly realized that the Internet was a platform and that what people did with that platform ran the full spectrum. I watched activists leverage technology to connect people in unprecedented ways while marketers used those same tools to manipulate people for capitalist gain. I stopped believing that technology alone could produce enlightenment.

In the late 90s, the hype around the Internet became bubbalicious, and it started to be painfully clear to me that economic agendas could shape technology in powerful ways. After the dot-com bubble burst in 2000, I was part of a network of people determined to build systems that would enable people to connect, share, and communicate. By then I was also a researcher trained by anthropologists, curious to know what people would do with this new set of tools called social media.

In the early days of social network sites, it was exhilarating watching people grasp that they were part of a large global network. Many of my utopian-minded friends started dreaming again of how this structure could be used to break down social and cultural barriers. Yet, as these tools became more popular and widespread, what unfolded was not a realization of the idyllic desires of many early developers, but a complexity of practices that resembled the mess of everyday life.

2. Inequity All Over Again

While social media was being embraced, I was doing research, driving around the country talking with teenagers about how they understood technology in light of everything else taking place in their lives. I watched teens struggle to make sense of everyday life and their place in it. And I watched as privileged parents projected their anxieties onto the tools that were making visible the lives of less privileged youth.

As social media exploded, our country's struggle with class and race got entwined with technology. I will never forget sitting in small town Massachusetts in 2007 with a 14-year-old white girl I call Kat. Kat was talking about her life when she made a passing reference to why her friends had all quickly abandoned MySpace and moved to Facebook: because it was safer, and MySpace was boring. Whatever look I gave her at that moment made her squirm. She looked down and said,

I'm not really into racism, but I think that MySpace now is more like ghetto or whatever, and . . . the people that have Facebook are more mature . . . The people who use MySpace—again, not in a racist way—but are usually more like [the] ghetto and hip-hop/rap lovers group.

As we continued talking, Kat became more blunt and told me that black people use MySpace and white people use Facebook.

Fascinated by Kat's explanation and discomfort, I went back to my field notes. Sure enough, numerous teens had made remarks that, with Kat's story in mind, made it very clear that a social division had unfolded between teens using MySpace and Facebook during the 2006–2007 school year. I started asking teens about these issues and heard many more accounts of how race affected engagement. After I posted an analysis online, I got a response from a privileged white boy named Craig:

The higher castes of high school moved to Facebook. It was more cultured, and less cheesy. The lower class usually were content to stick to MySpace. Any high school student who has a Facebook will tell you that MySpace users are more likely to be barely educated and obnoxious. Like Peet's is more cultured than Starbucks, and Jazz is more cultured than bubblegum pop, and like Macs are more cultured than PC's, Facebook is of a cooler caliber than MySpace.

This was not the first time that racial divisions became visible in my research. I had mapped networks of teens using MySpace from single schools only to find that, in supposedly "integrated" schools, friendship patterns were divided by race. And I'd witnessed and heard countless examples of the ways in which race configured everyday social dynamics which bubbled up through social media. In our supposedly post-racial society, social relations and dynamics were still configured by race.

In 2006–2007, I watched a historic practice reproduce itself online. I watched a digital white flight. Like U.S. cities in the 1970s, MySpace got painted as a dangerous place filled with unsavory characters, while Facebook was portrayed as clean and respectable. With money, media, and privileged users behind it, Facebook became the dominant player that attracted everyone. And among youth, racial divisions reproduced themselves again, shifting, for example, to Instagram (orderly, safe) and Vine (chaotic, dangerous).

Teenagers weren't creating the racialized dynamics of social media. They were reproducing what they saw everywhere else and projecting onto their tools. And they weren't alone. Journalists, parents, politicians, and pundits gave them the racist language they reiterated.

And today's technology is valued—culturally and financially—based on how much it's used by the most privileged members of our society.

3. Statistical Prejudice

Thirteen years ago I was sitting around a table with a group imagining how to build tools that would support rich social dynamics. None of us, I think, imagined being where we are now. Sure, there were those who wanted to be rich and famous, but no one thought that a social network site would be used by over a billion people and valued in the hundreds of billions of dollars. No one thought that every major company would have a "social media strategy" within a few years. No one saw that the technologies we were architecting would reconfigure the political and cultural landscape. None of us were focused on what we now call "big data."

"Big data" is amorphous and fuzzy, referencing, first, a set of technologies and practices for analyzing large amounts of data. But, these days, it's primarily a certain *phenomenon* that promises that if we just had more data, we could solve all of the world's problems. The problem with "big data" isn't whether or not we have data, but whether or not we have the ability to make meaning from and produce valuable insights with it. This is trickier than one might imagine.

One of the perennial problems with the statistical and machine learning techniques that underpin "big data" analytics is that they rely on data entered as input. When the data you input is biased, what you get out is just as biased. These systems learn the biases in our society, and they spit them back out at us.

Consider the work done by computer scientist Latanya Sweeney. One day she was searching for herself on Google when she noticed that the ads displayed were for companies offering criminal record background checks with titles like "Latanya Sweeney, Arrested?" which implied that she might have a criminal record. Suspicious, she started searching for other, more white-sounding names, only to find that the advertisements offered in association with those names were quite different. She set about to test the system more formally and found that, indeed, searching for black names was much more likely to produce ads for criminal justice-related products and services.

The story attracted a lot of media attention. But what the public failed to understand was that Google wasn't intentionally discriminating or selling ads based on race. Google was indifferent to the content of the specific ad that showed up with a name search. All it knew is that people clicked on those ads for some searches but not others, and so it was better to serve them up when the search queries had a statistical property similar to queries where a click happens. In other words, because racist viewers were more likely to click on these ads when searching for black names, Google's algorithm quickly learned to serve up these ads for names that are understood as black. Google was trained to be "racist" by its racist users.

Our cultural prejudices are deeply embedded in countless datasets, the very datasets that our systems are trained to learn on. Students of color are much more likely to have disciplinary school records than white students. Black men are far more likely to be stopped and frisked by police, arrested for drug possession or charged with felonies, even as their white counterparts engage in the same behaviors. Poor people are far more likely to have health problems, live further away from work, and struggle to make rent. Yet all of these data are used to fuel personalized learning algorithms, to inform risk-assessment tools for judicial decision-making, and to generate credit and insurance scores. And so the system "predicts" that people who are already marginalized are higher risks, thereby constraining their options and making sure they are, indeed, higher risks.

This was not what my peers set out to create when we imagined building tools that allowed you to map who you knew or enabled you to display interests and tastes.

Lest you think that I fear "big data," let me take a moment to highlight the potential. I'm on the board of Crisis Text Line, a phenomenal service that allows youth in crisis to communicate with counselors via text message. We've handled millions of conversations with youth who are struggling with depression, disordered eating, suicidal ideation, and sexuality confusion. The practice of counseling is not new, but the potential shifts dramatically when you have millions of messages about crises that can help train a system designed to help people. Because of the analytics that we do, counselors are encouraged to take specific paths to suss out how they can best help the texter. Natural language processing allows us to automatically bring up resources that might help a counselor or encourage them to pass the conversation to a different counselor who may be better suited to help a particular texter. In other words, we're using data to empower counselors to better help youth who desperately need our help. And we've done more active rescues during suicide attempts than I like to count (*so many* youth lack access to basic mental health services).

The techniques we use at Crisis Text Line are the exact same techniques that are used in marketing. Or personalized learning. Or predictive policing. Predictive policing, for example, involves taking prior information about police encounters and using that to make a statistical assessment about the likelihood of crime happening in a particular place or involving a particular person. In a very controversial move, Chicago has used such analytics to make a list of people most likely to be a victim of violence. In an effort to prevent crime, police officers approached those individuals and used this information in an effort to scare them to stay out of trouble. But surveillance by powerful actors doesn't build trust; it erodes it. Imagine that same information being given to a social worker. Even better, to a community liaison. Sometimes, it's not the data that's disturbing, but how it's used and by whom.

4. The World We're Creating

Knowing how to use data isn't easy. One of my colleagues at Microsoft Research—Eric Horvitz—can predict with startling accuracy whether someone will be hospitalized based on what they search for. What should he do with that information? Reach out to people? That's pretty creepy. Do nothing? Is that ethical? No matter how good our predictions are, figuring out how to use them is a complex social and cultural issue that technology doesn't solve for us. In fact, as it stands, technology is just making it harder for us to have a reasonable conversation about agency and dignity, responsibility, and ethics.

Data is power. Increasingly we're seeing data being used to assert power over people. It doesn't have to be this way, but one of the things that I've learned is that, unchecked, new tools are almost always empowering to the privileged at the expense of those who are not.

For most media activists, unfettered Internet access is at the center of the conversation, and that is critically important. Today we're standing on a new precipice, and we need to think a few steps ahead of the current fight.

We are moving into a world of prediction. A world where more people are going to be able to make judgments about others based on data. Data analysis that can mark the value of people as worthy workers, parents, borrowers, learners, and citizens. Data analysis that has been underway for decades but is increasingly salient in decision-making across numerous sectors. Data analysis that most people don't understand.

Many activists will be looking to fight the ecosystem of prediction—and to regulate when and where prediction can be used. This is all fine and well when we're talking about how these technologies are designed to do harm. But more often than not, *these tools will be designed to be helpful,* to increase efficiency, to identify people who need help. Their positive uses will exist alongside uses that are terrifying. What do we do?

One of the most obvious issues is the limited diversity of people who are building and using these tools to imagine our future. Statistical and technical literacy isn't even part of the curriculum in most American schools. In our society where technology jobs are highpaying and technical literacy is needed for citizenry, less than 5% of high schools offer AP computer science courses. Needless to say, black and brown youth are much less likely to have access, let alone opportunities. If people don't understand what these systems are doing, how do we expect people to challenge them?

We must learn how to ask hard questions of technology and of those making decisions based data-driven tech. And opening the black box isn't enough. Transparency of data, algorithms, and technology isn't enough. We need to *build assessment into* any system that we roll-out. You can't just put millions of dollars of surveillance equipment into the hands of the police in the hope of creating police accountability, yet, with police body-worn cameras, that's exactly what we're doing. And we're not even trying to assess the implications. This is probably the fastest roll-out of a technology *out of hope,* and it won't be the last. How do we get people to look beyond their hopes and fears and actively interrogate the trade-offs?

Technology plays a central role—more and more—in every sector, every community, every interaction. It's easy to screech in fear or dream of a world in which every problem magically gets solved. To make the world a better place, we need to start paying attention to the different tools that are emerging and learn to frame hard questions about how they should be put to use to improve the lives of everyday people.

We need those who are thinking about social justice to understand technology and those who understand technology to commit to social justice.

Critical Thinking

1. How have social class and race become entwined with technology?

2. What are the ethical concerns with data as power?

3. How do we tackle the limited diversity of the people who build the tools for our future?

Internet References

Facebook's Bias Is Built-In, and Bears Watching
https://goo.gl/KfcYEv

It's Not Just Facebook. Tech Companies Need to Open Up about Their Biases.
https://goo.gl/5LA1iU

When Big Data Becomes Bad Data
https://goo.gl/Os653I

DANAH BOYD is the founder and president of Data & Society, a Principal Researcher at Microsoft, and a Visiting Professor at New York University. Her research is focused on making certain that society has a nuanced understanding of the relationship between technology and society, especially as issues of inequity and bias emerge.

Article

Prepared by: Daniel Mittleman, *DePaul University* and
Douglas Druckenmiller, *Western Illinois University*

The Fourth Industrial Revolution

What It Means and How to Respond

Klaus Schwab

Learning Outcomes

After reading this article, you will be able to:

- Identify the four main effects that the Fourth Industrial Revolution will have on business.

- Differentiate between long-term gains of technological innovation and potential inequality, particularly in the labor market.

- Analyze the impact of new technologies and platforms on citizens ability to engage with government.

W e stand on the brink of a technological revolution that will fundamentally alter the way we live, work, and relate to one another. In its scale, scope, and complexity, the transformation will be unlike anything humankind has experienced before. We do not yet know just how it will unfold, but one thing is clear: the response to it must be integrated and comprehensive, involving all stakeholders of the global polity, from the public and private sectors to academia and civil society.

The First Industrial Revolution used water and steam power to mechanize production. The Second used electric power to create mass production. The Third used electronics and information technology to automate production. Now a Fourth Industrial Revolution is building on the Third, the digital revolution that has been occurring since the middle of the last century. It is characterized by a fusion of technologies that is blurring the lines between the physical, digital, and biological spheres.

There are three reasons why today's transformations represent not merely a prolongation of the Third Industrial Revolution but rather the arrival of a Fourth and distinct one: velocity, scope, and systems impact. The speed of current breakthroughs has no historical precedent. When compared with previous industrial revolutions, the Fourth is evolving at an exponential rather than a linear pace. Moreover, it is disrupting almost every industry in every country. And the breadth and depth of these changes herald the transformation of entire systems of production, management, and governance.

The possibilities of billions of people connected by mobile devices, with unprecedented processing power, storage capacity, and access to knowledge, are unlimited. And these possibilities will be multiplied by emerging technology breakthroughs in fields such as artificial intelligence, robotics, the Internet of Things, autonomous vehicles, 3-D printing, nanotechnology, biotechnology, materials science, energy storage, and quantum computing.

Already, artificial intelligence is all around us, from self-driving cars and drones to virtual assistants and software that translate or invest. Impressive progress has been made in AI in recent years, driven by exponential increases in computing power and by the availability of vast amounts of data, from software used to discover new drugs to algorithms used to predict our cultural interests. Digital fabrication technologies, meanwhile, are interacting with the biological world on a daily basis. Engineers, designers, and architects are combining computational design, additive manufacturing, materials engineering, and synthetic biology to pioneer a symbiosis between microorganisms, our bodies, the products we consume, and even the buildings we inhabit.

Challenges and Opportunities

Like the revolutions that preceded it, the Fourth Industrial Revolution has the potential to raise global income levels and improve the quality of life for populations around the world. To date, those who have gained the most from it have been consumers able to afford and access the digital world; technology has made possible new products and services that increase the efficiency and pleasure of our personal lives. Ordering a cab, booking a flight, buying a product, making a payment, listening to music, watching a film, or playing a game—any of these can now be done remotely.

In the future, technological innovation will also lead to a supply-side miracle, with long-term gains in efficiency and productivity. Transportation and communication costs will drop, logistics and global supply chains will become more effective, and the cost of trade will diminish, all of which will open new markets and drive economic growth.

At the same time, as the economists Erik Brynjolfsson and Andrew McAfee have pointed out, the revolution could yield greater inequality, particularly in its potential to disrupt labor markets. As automation substitutes for labor across the entire economy, the net displacement of workers by machines might exacerbate the gap between returns to capital and returns to labor. On the other hand, it is also possible that the displacement of workers by technology will, in aggregate, result in a net increase in safe and rewarding jobs.

We cannot foresee at this point which scenario is likely to emerge, and history suggests that the outcome is likely to be some combination of the two. However, I am convinced of one thing—that in the future, talent, more than capital, will represent the critical factor of production. This will give rise to a job market increasingly segregated into "low-skill/low-pay" and "high-skill/high-pay" segments, which in turn will lead to an increase in social tensions.

In addition to being a key economic concern, inequality represents the greatest societal concern associated with the Fourth Industrial Revolution. The largest beneficiaries of innovation tend to be the providers of intellectual and physical capital—the innovators, shareholders, and investors—which explains the rising gap in wealth between those dependent on capital versus labor. Technology is therefore one of the main reasons why incomes have stagnated, or even decreased, for a majority of the population in high-income countries: the demand for highly skilled workers has increased while the demand for workers with less education and lower skills has decreased. The result is a job market with a strong demand at the high and low ends but a hollowing out of the middle.

This helps explain why so many workers are disillusioned and fearful that their own real incomes and those of their children will continue to stagnate. It also helps explain why middle classes around the world are increasingly experiencing a pervasive sense of dissatisfaction and unfairness. A winner-takes-all economy that offers only limited access to the middle class is a recipe for democratic malaise and dereliction.

Discontent can also be fueled by the pervasiveness of digital technologies and the dynamics of information sharing typified by social media. More than 30 percent of the global population now uses social media platforms to connect, learn, and share information. In an ideal world, these interactions would provide an opportunity for cross-cultural understanding and cohesion. However, they can also create and propagate unrealistic expectations as to what constitutes success for an individual or a group, as well as offer opportunities for extreme ideas and ideologies to spread.

The Impact on Business

An underlying theme in my conversations with global CEOs and senior business executives is that the acceleration of innovation and the velocity of disruption are hard to comprehend or anticipate and that these drivers constitute a source of constant surprise, even for the best connected and most well informed. Indeed, across all industries, there is clear evidence that the technologies that underpin the Fourth Industrial Revolution are having a major impact on businesses.

On the supply side, many industries are seeing the introduction of new technologies that create entirely new ways of serving existing needs and significantly disrupt existing industry value chains. Disruption is also flowing from agile, innovative competitors who, thanks to access to global digital platforms for research, development, marketing, sales, and distribution, can oust well-established incumbents faster than ever by improving the quality, speed, or price at which value is delivered.

Major shifts on the demand side are also occurring, as growing transparency, consumer engagement, and new patterns of consumer behavior (increasingly built upon access to mobile networks and data) force companies to adapt the way they design, market, and deliver products and services.

A key trend is the development of technology-enabled platforms that combine both demand and supply to disrupt existing industry structures, such as those we see within the "sharing" or "on demand" economy. These technology platforms, rendered easy to use by the smartphone, convene people, assets, and data—thus creating entirely new ways of consuming goods and services in the process. In addition, they lower the barriers for businesses and individuals to create wealth, altering the personal and professional environments of workers. These new platform businesses are rapidly multiplying into many new services, ranging from laundry to shopping, from chores to parking, from massages to travel.

On the whole, there are four main effects that the Fourth Industrial Revolution has on business—on customer expectations, on product enhancement, on collaborative innovation, and on organizational forms. Whether consumers or businesses, customers are increasingly at the epicenter of the economy, which is all about improving how customers are served. Physical products and services, moreover, can now be enhanced with digital capabilities that increase their value. New technologies make assets more durable and resilient, while data and analytics are transforming how they are maintained. A world of customer experiences, data-based services, and asset performance through analytics, meanwhile, requires new forms of collaboration, particularly given the speed at which innovation and disruption are taking place. And the emergence of global platforms and other new business models, finally, means that talent, culture, and organizational forms will have to be rethought.

Overall, the inexorable shift from simple digitization (the Third Industrial Revolution) to innovation based on combinations of technologies (the Fourth Industrial Revolution) is forcing companies to reexamine the way they do business. The bottom line, however, is the same: business leaders and senior executives need to understand their changing environment, challenge the assumptions of their operating teams, and relentlessly and continuously innovate.

The Impact on Government

As the physical, digital, and biological worlds continue to converge, new technologies and platforms will increasingly enable citizens to engage with governments, voice their opinions, coordinate their efforts, and even circumvent the supervision of public authorities. Simultaneously, governments will gain new technological powers to increase their control over populations, based on pervasive surveillance systems and the ability to control digital infrastructure. On the whole, however, governments will increasingly face pressure to change their current approach to public engagement and policymaking, as their central role of conducting policy diminishes owing to new sources of competition and the redistribution and decentralization of power that new technologies make possible.

Ultimately, the ability of government systems and public authorities to adapt will determine their survival. If they prove capable of embracing a world of disruptive change, subjecting their structures to the levels of transparency and efficiency that will enable them to maintain their competitive edge, they will endure. If they cannot evolve, they will face increasing trouble.

This will be particularly true in the realm of regulation. Current systems of public policy and decision-making evolved alongside the Second Industrial Revolution, when decision-makers had time to study a specific issue and develop the necessary response or appropriate regulatory framework. The whole process was designed to be linear and mechanistic, following a strict "top down" approach.

But such an approach is no longer feasible. Given the Fourth Industrial Revolution's rapid pace of change and broad impacts, legislators and regulators are being challenged to an unprecedented degree and for the most part are proving unable to cope.

How, then, can they preserve the interest of the consumers and the public at large while continuing to support innovation and technological development? By embracing "agile" governance, just as the private sector has increasingly adopted agile responses to software development and business operations more generally. This means regulators must continuously adapt to a new, fast-changing environment, reinventing themselves so they can truly understand what it is they are regulating. To do so, governments and regulatory agencies will need to collaborate closely with business and civil society.

The Fourth Industrial Revolution will also profoundly impact the nature of national and international security, affecting both the probability and the nature of conflict. The history of warfare and international security is the history of technological innovation, and today is no exception. Modern conflicts involving states are increasingly "hybrid" in nature, combining traditional battlefield techniques with elements previously associated with nonstate actors. The distinction between war and peace, combatant and noncombatant, and even violence and nonviolence (think cyberwarfare) is becoming uncomfortably blurry.

As this process takes place and new technologies such as autonomous or biological weapons become easier to use, individuals and small groups will increasingly join states in being capable of causing mass harm. This new vulnerability will lead to new fears. But at the same time, advances in technology will create the potential to reduce the scale or impact of violence, through the development of new modes of protection, for example, or greater precision in targeting.

The Impact on People

The Fourth Industrial Revolution, finally, will change not only what we do but also who we are. It will affect our identity and all the issues associated with it: our sense of privacy, our notions of ownership, our consumption patterns, the time we devote to work and leisure, and how we develop our careers, cultivate our skills, meet people, and nurture relationships. It is already changing our health and leading to a "quantified" self, and sooner than we think it may lead to human augmentation. The list is endless because it is bound only by our imagination.

I am a great enthusiast and early adopter of technology, but sometimes I wonder whether the inexorable integration of technology in our lives could diminish some of our quintessential human capacities, such as compassion and cooperation. Our relationship with our smartphones is a case in point. Constant connection may deprive us of one of life's most important assets: the time to pause, reflect, and engage in meaningful conversation.

One of the greatest individual challenges posed by new information technologies is privacy. We instinctively understand why it is so essential, yet the tracking and sharing of information about us is a crucial part of the new connectivity. Debates about fundamental issues such as the impact on our inner lives of the loss of control over our data will only intensify in the years ahead. Similarly, the revolutions occurring in biotechnology and AI, which are redefining what it means to be human by pushing back the current thresholds of life span, health, cognition, and capabilities, will compel us to redefine our moral and ethical boundaries.

Shaping the Future

Neither technology nor the disruption that comes with it is an exogenous force over which humans have no control. All of us are responsible for guiding its evolution, in the decisions we make on a daily basis as citizens, consumers, and investors. We should thus grasp the opportunity and power we have to shape the Fourth Industrial Revolution and direct it toward a future that reflects our common objectives and values.

To do this, however, we must develop a comprehensive and globally shared view of how technology is affecting our lives and reshaping our economic, social, cultural, and human environments. There has never been a time of greater promise or one of greater potential peril. Today's decision-makers, however, are too often trapped in traditional, linear thinking, or too absorbed by the multiple crises demanding their attention, to think strategically about the forces of disruption and innovation shaping our future.

In the end, it all comes down to people and values. We need to shape a future that works for all of us by putting people first and empowering them. In its most pessimistic, dehumanized form, the Fourth Industrial Revolution may indeed have the potential to "robotize" humanity and thus to deprive us of our heart and soul. But as a complement to the best parts of human nature—creativity, empathy, stewardship—it can also lift humanity into a new collective and moral consciousness based on a shared sense of destiny. It is incumbent on us all to make sure the latter prevails.

Critical Thinking

1. How does the Fourth Industrial Revolution influence a segregated marketplace?
2. What are ways that the introduction of new technologies disrupts business?
3. How will advances in biotechnology and AI redefine what it means to be human?

Internet References

Change Is the Only Thing That's Constant: Digital Disruption Demands Adaptability
https://goo.gl/ekYCp9

The Fourth Industrial Revolution Redefines the Relationship between Business and Tech
http://www.information-age.com/technology/applications-and-development/123461886/fourth-industrial-revolution-redefines-relationship-between-business-and-tech

Why Perceived Inequality Leads People to Resist Innovation
https://goo.gl/OZPBgl

KLAUS SCHWAB is Founder and Executive Chairman of the World Economic Forum.

Prepared by: Daniel Mittleman, *DePaul University* and
Douglas Druckenmiller, *Western Illinois University*

Article

The "Internet of Restaurants" Is Coming for Your Info

At the National Restaurant Association, many of the hot technology companies are selling surveillance, not supper.

DAVID M. PERRY

Learning Outcomes

After reading this article, you will be able to:

- Understand real business examples and applications of the Internet of Things.

- Use the "Internet of Restaurants" as a case example in applying Postman's ideas for evaluating new technologies.

- Understand the tradeoff of new functionalities vs. security concerns in the introduction of new Internet technologies.

Once upon a time (1999 and the years that followed), there was a company named OpenTable that told San Francisco restaurants a story. Customers wanted, they said, to search for a restaurant on the wondrous world of the Internet, then click a button to make a reservation. Sure, a restaurant could just build its own website or keep managing reservations the old-fashioned way—with a book or spreadsheet offline—but OpenTable could do it all for them for a low set-up price, a monthly fee, and a dollar per diner. By 2009, when OpenTable went public, it had a $1.5 billion valuation, and was bought for $2.6 billion soon thereafter. At the time, it controlled 90 percent of the country's online booking market share, meaning that the service it had provided to restaurants became something like a mandatory fee. Restaurants without the service argued that they lost bookings to those that did. Those who signed up wondered why they had to give up all their customer data to this third-party company. Competitors arose, but the industry had already changed forever: Online reservations are just a cost of being in

the restaurant business these days. It's not clear, though, that more people go out to eat just because they can book online. It's a surcharge and a near monopoly, and cuts into the profit margins of the folks actually selling us food.

Bruce Schneier—a well-known technologist and security expert, a cybersecurity professor at Harvard's John F. Kennedy School of Government, and one of my closest friends—tells me about the controversy surrounding OpenTable as we wander through the Tech Pavilion of the 2017 National Restaurant Association. Every company here would be thrilled to become the next OpenTable. None of them are focused on reservations, or at least not only reservations, but are instead trying to find other gaps where they can insert some kind of online service. Some of the sales pitches are compelling: Companies offer to harvest customer data so the restaurant can better track its clientele's needs. They offer to manage every aspect of a restaurant's labor force. They offer to turn every piece of kitchen equipment into an "Internet of Things" device, a phrase now used casually in marketing, as if we all agree on its definition. Turn your restaurant into a panopticon! Schneier isn't surprised, as he's seen this sort of thing before in other industries. "Much of the 'Internet of Restaurants,'" as we agree to call it, "is extractive and disempowering while pretending to be about giving control to employees and owners," he says.

As *Pacific Standard* reported a year ago, the National Restaurant Association is the industry's massive annual gathering in Chicago's conference center, McCormick Place. It fills three huge halls (four, if you count the alcohol specific spin-off conference, BAR) with every kind of product you might need at your restaurant: food, drink, furniture, lots of shoes, shirts, branded belt buckles, toilet cleaners, kitchen machinery (ovens, pasta makers, a sushi-making robot), pots and pans, and much more. The giant producers and distributors (Coke, Sysco) hobnob with start-ups (Silk Road Catering, a family company making spice blends in Missoula, Montana; Nduja Artisans, a Chicago father and son making spicy spreadable Calabrian salami). States send agricultural delegations (Louisiana seafood, Minnesota wild rice, Wisconsin cheese). A Québecois delegation served smoked meats and presumably ran out of poutine. A large contingent of Italians poured prosecco and served buratta. Celebrity chefs did demos, taught classes, and hawked their wares from large stages.

"Much of the 'Internet of Restaurants' is Extractive and Disempowering While Pretending to be About Giving Control to Employees and Owners."

But in the back third of one of the halls, there is nary a snack to be found. Instead, the "tech pavilion" provides a space for over a hundred companies looking to sell a wide variety of technological tools to restaurants. These vary from touch-screen ordering (a rapidly accelerating market) to employee management, marketing, customer tracking, and a wide variety of ways to connect the machinery and processes of the food business to the Internet. "Point of Sale" is the big buzzword, as everyone is offering new ways to have your customers pay in an easy, electronic, and trackable way.

The gateway to the pavilion is run by Microsoft. The company has a large booth with a variety of "totems"—their word—each of which advertised various Microsoft or partner products on a big screen. For the partners, mostly small companies, this is their chance to make the big time. Some of the products are useful. "Cortana," from Microsoft, adds a tool to Bing (or to a restaurant's website) that automatically answers most questions about a menu, and learns answers to new ones, such as whether gluten-free options might be available. Sprinklr manages social media by tracking everything said about your brand online, organizing responses, and—in theory—allowing for better engagement. It feels kind of creepy, though, knowing that, if I tweet about my meal, there's a team aggregating my information and preparing a response in real time.

Inventory that tracks itself, systems that reduce food waste, and the ability for employees to swap shifts over an app all feel like useful innovations. Nextep Systems has made accessibility for deaf consumers one of their main selling points, while telling me they also had accessible keyboards attached for blind consumers. Tech, done well, can be liberating for disabled individuals.

But there's also a fundamentally creepy aspect to much of this. One of the prime ways to increase value for your brand is to use the Internet to practice surveillance of both your customers and employees. The customer side feels less invasive: Loyalty apps are pretty nice, if in fact you generally go to the same place, as is the ability to place orders electronically or make reservations with a click. The question, Schneier asks, is "who owns the data?" There's value to collecting data on spending habits, as we've seen across e-commerce. Are restaurants fully aware of what they are giving away? Schneier, a critic of data mining, points out that it becomes especially invasive through "secondary uses," when the "data is correlated with other data and sold to third parties." For example, perhaps you've entered your name, gender, and age into a taco loyalty app (12th taco free!). Later, the vendors of that app sell your data to other merchants who know where and when you eat, whether you are a vegetarian, and lots of other data that you have accidentally shed. Is that what customers really want?

Perhaps more concerning than privacy, though, is the clear use of tech to further dehumanize workers in food service and restaurants. Swapping shifts over the phone is useful, but multiple "labor management" programs also allow for intense oversight of workers. Mesh Systems, one of the partners at the Microsoft booth, explained how their employee management software can track every second of a worker's day. For them, and likely the attendees at the conference, surveillance of workers was a selling point.

Then there's the formal "Internet of Things," where the results are mixed. Mesh Systems works with equipment manufacturers to hook up equipment to the Internet. At the show, they had a high-end espresso machine that could track inventory and monitor maintenance needs. Both are likely to be useful, but the sales pitch included a suggestion the company could track your sales and "let you know whether it's the right size for the store." Maybe, the spokesperson suggested, they could track data from the sales to convince a store owner that they needed two machines, or at least a bigger (and more expensive one).

"This is a classic example of how the 'Internet of Things' benefits the companies that control the data," Schneier says. "You get the device, and the manufacturer gets both a maintenance contract and the opportunity to constantly market and upsell." Some of it might be genuinely useful. Regular maintenance of machinery, all the cool point of sale tricks, good marketing strategies, and efficient labor management are likely all useful to restaurant enterprises, at least once they reach a certain size. "But the tech industry," Schneier says, "often is all about the skim. The tech industry is often about grabbing value you didn't know you had," such as consumer data, "and then either selling to you or to others." He makes an analogy to John Deere tractors. They now have tires that track soil data, but that data belongs to the tractor company, even if the farmer is driving the vehicle over his or her own land. That model is rapidly infiltrating the food service industry.

Then there are more direct risks. In March of 2016, Cici's Pizza got hacked, surrendering credit card information from more than 135 different locations. The breach was made through their online point of sale systems, allowing criminals to steal credit card data in real time. That doesn't happen with an old-fashioned cash register. More important, I didn't see a single discussion of cybersecurity anywhere in the tech pavilion. Over email, a Microsoft spokesperson did offer me assurances: "We believe customers own the data that they put into the Microsoft Cloud. We invest heavily in our technology, people, and processes to help ensure that their data is private and protected." Still, Microsoft didn't have anyone at the show to talk about risks, just rewards. For risks, I had to find an AT&T booth tucked away against a wall. The technicians there weren't authorized to talk to the press, but they offered a world-weary smile when I asked them whether restaurants were setting themselves up to be hacked. An AT&T spokesperson told me over email that all businesses, including restaurants, do need to have a digital presence, but that restaurants should "measure all digital and connectivity efforts from a risk view." Each new app or connected device introduces risk. "Restaurants need to re-evaluate their cybersecurity plans regularly, and think of security as you build up your technology plans, rather than as an afterthought," the spokesperson said. Meanwhile, days after this year's NRA, news broke that nearly every Chipotle had been hacked.

"What I saw [at the NRA]," Schneier tells me later, "is the economics of the Internet invading the restaurant business. The economics of the Internet are inherently monopolistic. The big get bigger because they leverage enormous network effects." The Internet of Restaurants sells itself as helpful and slowly adds a little bit of extortion. Nice restaurant you have there, wouldn't want it to go out of business because you didn't hook your espresso machine up to the Internet.

Critical Thinking

1. Open Table's service adds a cost to restaurants, some of which may be passed on to consumers. What does Open Table add to the dining process (from either the restaurant or diner's perspective) that adds value to the transaction?

2. "Much of the 'Internet of Restaurants' is extractive and disempowering while pretending to be about giving control to employees and owners." What does Bruce Schneier mean when he says this?

3. Apply Postman's five ideas, as presented in the introduction, to the "Internet of Restaurants" to explore the impacts of this package of technologies.

Internet References

Rise of the Machines: Who Is the 'Internet of Things' Good for?
http://www.theguardian.com/technology/2017/jun/06/internet-of-things-smart-home-smart-city.

The Year Is 2040: Welcome to Your Favorite New Restaurant
https://www.eater.com/2015/9/14/9310919/restaurant-of-the-future

---

DAVID M. PERRY is a professor of history at Dominican University, contributing writer at Pacific Standard, and freelance journalist focused on disability, parenting, history, and education.

Prepared by: Daniel Mittleman, *DePaul University* and
Douglas Druckenmiller, *Western Illinois University*

Article

Is Nothing about Your Life Private?

CORY FRANKLIN

Learning Outcomes

After reading this article, you will be able to:

- Understand what the real claims are, and how real risks are being described. Be able to parse a story to find biases in its presentation.

- Articulate both pros and cons of aggregating medical data across databases and across companies.

- Develop an understanding of the complexity of the cost/benefits balance when data are curated by large global corporations or when data are stored in the cloud.

In 2010, top Google executive Eric Schmidt told *The Atlantic* magazine, "Google policy is to get right up to the creepy line and not cross it. . . . We know where you are. We know where you've been. We can more or less know what you're thinking about."

Whether it intended to or not, Google has now crossed the creepy line—with ominous implications for patients everywhere. It partnered in a British medical project involving more than 1 million patients that was effectively hidden from the public until recently. The project's lack of concern for privacy and informed consent was blatant exploitation of these patients, and unless greater attention is paid to digital companies entering the health-care universe, the public will be at significant risk in the future.

It began, as so many notorious medical experiments do, with ostensibly good intentions. In 2015, Royal Free NHS Foundation Trust, which operates a number of British hospitals, entered into a seemingly benign agreement with a Google subsidiary, DeepMind. In an effort to develop an app to monitor patients at risk of kidney disease, DeepMind was granted access to the health information of 1.6 million patients. The assumption was that this information would be limited to factors related to kidney disease, but there was no explicit mention in the agreement of the nature or amount of data to be collected. Within months, Google-contracted servers were amassing sensitive personal medical information with little relation to kidney disease, from emergency room treatments to details of personal drug abuse.

Until journalists prompted a government investigation, DeepMind accessed the personally identifiable medical records of a large number of patients—with no guarantee of confidentiality, formal research protocol, research approval, or individual consent. Also, neither Royal Free nor Google chose to explain why DeepMind, with virtually no health-care experience, was selected for this project. Apparently, neither British regulators nor physicians asked any substantive questions.

Only this month did Elizabeth Denham of the United Kingdom Information Commissioner's Office, the ombudsman for Great Britain's medical data, release a statement regarding a probe of the secretive DeepMind deal: "Our investigation found a number of shortcomings in the way patient records were shared for this trial. Patients would not have reasonably expected their information to have been used in this way, and the trust could and should have been far more transparent with patients as to what was happening."

An admirable, albeit belated, first step by the organization that failed to anticipate the obvious dangers of an arrangement between one of Britain's largest health-care providers and the world's dominant data mining and advertising corporation.

There is, of course, a larger issue at stake, one that Denham failed to address. Medical information is the last fragile redoubt of our rapidly eroding personal privacy.

While professing good intentions, Google has an unstated but obvious conflict of interest in data mining of large populations. Did Google have an ulterior motive in collecting medical information of such a huge patient cohort? And more important, when monolithic digital companies like Google, Microsoft, Apple, Facebook, and Amazon, that already control much of our personal and professional activity, enter the healthcare industry as they inevitably will, who will protect patients' interests?

Once these companies introduce artificial intelligence and proprietary algorithms into medical care, will there be transparency? If not, what recourse will the public have?

One author has likened Google to a one-way mirror—it knows much about us and is learning more every day, but we really know virtually nothing about it. The paramount concern of any medical research is to preserve the rights of patients and subjects, and this one-way mirror does little to ensure that.

After the U.K. Information Commissioner's investigation, DeepMind co-founder Mustafa Suleyman assured the public that new safeguards would be instituted and that the company's goal is to have a positive social impact. We expect him to say that, but the 20th century was replete with notorious studies that were kept secret or justified on the basis of their supposed societal benefit.

If the history of medical ethics has taught us anything, it is that patients do not exist to serve medical science, and that they must never be deprived of the right to control their medical treatment, regardless of researchers' stated beneficence.

Big Data is coming to medicine, and it would be wrong to deny the potential benefits of machine learning and artificial intelligence. But no matter how valuable the promise of these new approaches and how well-intentioned the motives of those responsible, without transparency, safeguards and continual oversight, the seeds of abuse and tragedy are never far away. And here in the United States, will HIPAA, the Health Insurance Portability and Accountability Act, offer sufficient protection?

Be forewarned, the story of Royal Free and Google DeepMind is a clarion call. It is the introductory chapter in a new marriage of health care and digital companies that seek to collect and control medical information.

One is reminded of the warning given to Charles Foster Kane in the film "Citizen Kane": "Only you're going to need more than one lesson, and you are going to get more than one lesson."

Critical Thinking

1. From what is reported in this essay, what private data actually compromised? What were DeepMind's plans for using these data? Did anything actually go wrong with their use of the data? What could go wrong in a situation as described here?

2. Use the "DeepMind's collection of patient data" as a case example in applying Postman's ideas for evaluating new technologies.

3. If Google's policy is "to get right up to the creep line, and not cross it," did Google cross the line with this DeepMind project? Whether you think they did or did not, where would you draw the line on this project, and why?

Internet References

Big data' Could Mean Big Problems for People's Healthcare Privacy
http://www.latimes.com/business/lazarus/la-fi-lazarus-big-data-healthcare-20161011-snap-story.html

Documents Detail DeepMind's Plan to Apply AI to NHS Data in 2015
https://techcrunch.com/2017/08/31/documents-detail-deepminds-plan-to-apply-ai-to-nhs-data-in-2015/

Healthcare Data: Public Good or Private Property?
https://www.ncbi.nlm.nih.gov/books/NBK54304/

CORY FRANKLIN is a Wilmette physician and author of "Cook County ICU: 30 Years of Unforgettable Patients and Odd Cases."

Prepared by: Daniel Mittleman, *DePaul University* and
Douglas Druckenmiller, *Western Illinois University*

Article

The Tech Humanist Manifesto

We need to encode technology with the best of our humanity.

KATE O'NEILL

Learning Outcomes

After reading this article, you will be able to:

- Develop a deeper understanding that most advances in technology can be used for good or for evil, and that humans decide which it will be.

- Develop a deeper understanding of the difference between humans and machines (robots or androids).

- Offer a personal view of what the relationship between humans and technology ought to be.

After twenty-plus years of working in web technology, digital strategy, marketing, and operations, with job titles like "intranet developer," "content manager," "head of customer experience," and even "search monkey," and after writing a book on the integration of physical and digital experiences and now working on a book on automation and artificial intelligence, I have a difficult time describing to people what I do. So I've decided to declare myself a tech humanist.

I have decided to declare myself a tech humanist.

Because what I've realized is that data and technology in all their forms are becoming integrated ever more tightly into our lives and ever more powerful, to the point where the work of making technology successful for human use is inseparable from the work of making the world better for humans. I would even argue that the work of making better technology needs to be in lockstep with the work of being a better human.

And no, I didn't grow up wanting to be a tech humanist. I mean, it's not like I read science fiction as a kid and thought

someday I would think, write, and speak about the emerging impact of data and technology on human experience.

I was a German major.

I still don't read science fiction now as an adult, by the way, although I do see the connection between the work that I do and that genre's exploration of technology and culture.

It's just that I've always preferred stories that explicitly examine human relationships. Because what interests me most is always *people*: we're such complicated systems of nerves and emotions and thoughts and impulses. We're self-aware animals, pondering our own existence, conscious of our place in the universe. (Not always conscious enough, but still.)

Cosmic primates.

I do think technology is endlessly fascinating. But I'm even more fascinated by humans and our endless complexity and capacity for nuance.

Which means when it comes to any aspect of technology, what I care most about are
the people who make the technology,
the people who use the technology,
the people who benefit from the technology and the people who suffer for the technology,
the people whose lives may somehow be changed by the technology.

What I care most about are the people whose lives may be somehow changed by technology.

And it's not because we *use* technology. In other words, it isn't just the tools.

Ravens use tools. So why am I not, say, a tech ravenist?

Unless we find out about other intelligent species with technology in the universe, humans are the best identifiable link between the dominant technology and the rest of organic life on this planet and beyond.

So our best hope for aligning the needs of all living things and all technological progress is in our own human enlightenment.

Our best hope for integrating the needs of all living things and all technological progress is in our own enlightenment.

We *need* technological progress. It will surely bring us cures for disease, interplanetary and someday even intergalactic travel, safe and efficient energy, new forms and modes of communication, as well as so much else.

But for our own sake, and for the sake of humans who come after us, we need to wrap that progress around human advancement.

And to do that, we need to foster our own enlightenment. We need a more sophisticated relationship with meaning and with what is truly meaningful, at every level:

in communication,
in pattern recognition,
in our relationships,
in our existence.

To develop technology in harmony with human advancement, we need to challenge our basest instincts and channel our best intentions. We need to genuinely want and be committed to creating the best futures for the most people.

We need to want the best futures for the most people.

Because the fact is we encode our biases into data, into algorithms, into technology as a whole. So as we develop an increasingly machine-driven future, we need to encode machines with the best of who we are. And in that way, infuse the future with our brightest hope, our most egalitarian views, our most evolved understandings.

We need to recognize the humanity in the data we mine for profit, to see that much of the time, analytics are people. That everything we do in the digitally and physically connected worlds creates a data trail. That who we project ourselves to be online—that self, that digital self—is our aspirational self, liking things and connecting with other people and wandering through the digital world in awe, and our aspirational self, our digital self deserves due privacy and protection in every way.

We need to recognize the humanity in the data we mine for profit.

We talk about "digital transformation" in business. But let's be honest: most corporate environments are anything but transformative. So we need to begin to re-imagine and yes, transform business operations and culture around new models of infrastructure, new understandings of the social contract between employer and employee, and fundamentally new ideas of value.

Because our world is increasingly integrated: online and offline, at work and at play, and we have to be wholly integrated selves, too.

And so we have to ask what the exchange of value means when it's about an integrated you in an integrated world.

We need to decide, for example, when we talk about autonomous cars: *whose* autonomy are we talking about? What are the broader implications of gaining freedom while losing control? Evolving from a society of private automobile ownership to privatized fleets of self-driving cars will give us back time, won't it? Or will it? And *yes*, it will mean life-changing possibilities for disabled and elderly people. If they can afford it. All in all, as anyone dependent on the New York City subway knows, if our mobility depends on machines we don't own and don't directly control, we are making a tradeoff. It may be a worthwhile tradeoff, it may even be an exciting tradeoff, but it is a tradeoff and we should ask meaningful questions about it.

We need to know that living in a culture with an ever-accelerating sense of time might mean having to resist an ever-narrowing horizon. That we have to try not to lose our sense of greater perspective in the FOMO frenzy. That our sense that experiences aren't real unless we share them and receive a few likes (or preferably a lot of likes) could cost us some peace of mind.

We need to begin to re-imagine our lives around new dimensions of meaningful experience.

And ask ourselves:

What different dynamics come into play when relationships are conducted across physical distances but connected by intimate virtual space, and what can make those relationships more meaningful.

What fosters communities when they're multi-faceted network nodes, and not found mostly in houses of worship and town squares, and what will make those communities more meaningful.

What "what we do for a living" will mean as jobs shift, as our understanding of contribution changes, and what will make that contribution more meaningful.

Because so much of the way we've derived our identity, our sense of accomplishment, achievement, contribution, value, self-worth, is subject to radical overhaul in the next decade and the one following that and beyond. More jobs will be automated, augmented, enhanced, and yes, eliminated. And certainly new jobs will be created, but we can't wait for them to make sense of this. We have to begin re-imagining now what meaningful contribution looks like in that context.

So we need to ask what it means to be human when the characteristics we think of as uniquely ours can be done by machines. What is the value of humanity?

We need to ask what it means to be human when the characteristics we think of as uniquely ours can be done by machines.

And see, it's not that I'm a human exceptionalist, exactly. I've been vegan for 20 years, after all, which I point out to illustrate that I don't think rights are something only humans deserve. And eventually if I'm around when machines become sentient, I'll probably care about AI rights and ethics, too. I can't help it: I'm a sucker for equality.

So it's not that I think humans are so special that we deserve protecting and coddling, except that . . . just maybe we *are*, and just maybe we *do*.

I just think that whatever it is—humanity—it's worth advocating for. Whatever combination of fascination and flaws it was that produced Shakespeare, Gloria Steinem, Paris, pizza, the Brooklyn Bridge, beer, Nelson Mandela, denim, Mary Tyler Moore, coffee, chocolate chip ice cream . . .

I could go on and on, but I don't even know if any of that is really the best of humanity, or even the best of what humanity has achieved. And what lies ahead of us are even greater challenges. So I don't know what the best of humanity has been and at some level I don't really care.

I just think we have to be at our best *now*. And somehow striving for our best, somehow making something lasting, and most of all working to make the best future for the most people—I think that *is* the best of what humanity can be and has to be.

And we need to start making it our mission to give it, to be it, to encode it, to build it in our culture, in our data models, our work environments, our relationships, and all throughout the technology that is interwoven in our lives. It's not science fiction; the future really does depend on it.

Critical Thinking

1. O'Neill says, "our best hope for aligning the needs of all living things and all technological progress is in our own human enlightenment." What does she mean by this? What does she mean by human enlightenment? Do you agree with the sentiment in this quote?

2. O'Neill raises several dozen of trade-offs and questions in this article. Which three resonate most with you? What are your initial answers to them, and why?

3. O'Neill raises many issues; she asks many questions without answering any. She calls this her "Tech Humanist Manifesto." In far fewer words than she used, what do you think her manifesto is? [Look up "manifesto" if you don't know what the term means.]

Internet References

Does Technology Replace Humanity?
  https://www.huffingtonpost.com/gil-laroya/does-technology-replace-h_b_424073.html
Technological Humanism
  http://ieeexplore.ieee.org/stamp/stamp.jsp?arnumber=5322537
Technology Is Not Threatening Our Humanity—We Are
  https://hbr.org/2015/10/technology-is-not-threatening-our-humanity-we-are
The Case For Humanism In Tech
  https://richardmacmanus.com/2017/01/31/the-case-for-humanism-in-tech/

KATE O'NEILL, founder of KO Insights, is an author, speaker, and "tech humanist" consultant solving strategic problems in how data and technology can shape more meaningful human experiences. Her latest book is *Pixels and Place: Connecting Human Experience Across Digital and Physical Spaces.*

O'Neill, Kate, "The Tech Humanist Manifesto," *Medium*, July 29, 2017. Used with permission of Kate O'Neill.

Unit 2

UNIT

Prepared by: Daniel Mittleman, *DePaul University* and
Douglas Druckenmiller, *Western Illinois University*

Shift in Retail

On average in 2016, Facebook users spent 50 minutes on the platform each day, up from 40 minutes in 2014. As a leisure activity, that is more time than any other pursuit outside of TV and movies. More than reading, exercise, and almost as much as much as eating and drinking. Your time is their money. Facebook's net income in the first quarter of 2016? $1.5 billion.[1]

Facebook has more than 1.7 billion monthly active users worldwide.[2] It is no surprise advertisers are looking for ways to capture that audience. In fact advertisers on Facebook grew 33 percent from 3,000,000 in March 2016 to 4,000,000 in September 2016.[3] As more and more users access technology via smartphones and tablets, the advertising industry has shifted to digital, spending more than $64 billion in 2015—up nearly 60 percent from 2014.[4]

The information age (mid-20th century to perhaps the beginning of the 21st century) was brought about by mass adoption of computing technologies. It became possible to accumulate vast wealth by building software tools and databases to access and organize information better than others. The scarce resource that drove this economy was information, and the knowledge to use it effectively.

Several commentators have suggested that the information age was short lived; that we are moving in to a new age already. But few have captured just what differentiates this new age from the information age. Clearly information is no longer a scarce resource. All of us can Google almost any information we need. Most of us are bombarded with way too much information on a daily basis in the form of e-mail, text messages, tweets, and Facebook status updates. A few of us are able to find the time to consume more than a small fraction of the information we would find interesting or useful. So, if information is no longer scare, what is it that is scarce?

Google's value propositions may provide a clue. Yes, Google provides us with information. But so do Microsoft, Apple, and others. What Google does is provide us with this information within a user experience intended to minimize our attention resources. That is, it is not the information that is scarce; rather is our time and our ability to focus on, parse through, and prioritize all the information being pushed our way. When Google helps us with that, we come back for more. And most of us will happily accept their ads on the page if we perceive real value from their services.

Google's search engine prioritizes results of our searches guessing at which pages will be most useful. Google's Gmail filters our incoming e-mail messages guessing at which ones are important. Google Maps and Earth help us navigate the physical world—and even make shopping recommendations if we request them. Google Docs, Pixlr, and YouTube (all Google products) help us organize multimedia resources in the cloud. In each case, the tool provides information, but more importantly, it organizes, filters, and prioritizes to permit us to consume information using less attention resources.

Amazon.com's growth into a retail giant can be characterized by excellence on multiple dimensions. One, they have taken a long view of a supply chain, running at a loss over their first six years of operations, not because of poor sales or management, but because they reinvested would-be profits into supply-chain infrastructure. They built large automated warehouse and distribution facilities, with far greater capacity than the needed at the time. Because of this long-term investment they can now deliver product faster, cheaper, and more reliably than almost anyone else. Faster, better, and cheaper is hard to beat.

Two, they have focused on customer personalization. Amazon has invested in ecommerce technology in the same manner they invested in supply-chain technology. By doing so, they have crafted a site effectively individualized to every shopper. Unless you have taken action (such as blocking cookies) to mask your identity from Amazon, their website will build you a customized homepage based on their knowledge of your past purchase and borrowing behaviors. They constantly strive to improve their algorithms to provide a better shopping experience (better for both Amazon and you in the sense you see products you are interested in).

[1] http://www.nytimes.com/2016/05/06/business/facebook-bends-the-rules-of-audience-engagement-to-its-advantage.html?_r=0
[2] https://zephoria.com/top-15-valuable-facebook-statistics/
[3] http://www.nbcnews.com/tech/social-media/facebook-added-1-million-advertisers-last-six-months-n655516
[4] http://www.gmrsalesandservice.com/advertising-trends-for-2016-a-shift-from-traditional-to-online/

And, three, they have been ambitious in moving into new retail markets while not locking into any particular business acquisition strategy. They have bought retailers and folded the stores into Amazon's brand; they have partnered with established retailers serving as storefront and/or distribution channel for the partnership. Each model has been employed when deemed optimal. And this has enabled Amazon to grow inventory well beyond books and digital media, where they got their start.

Some questions to consider in this unit:

- How does data gathered from social media influence marketing?
- How effective is social media as an advertising platform?

Article

Prepared by: Daniel Mittleman, *DePaul University* and
Douglas Druckenmiller, *Western Illinois University*

What in the World Is Causing the Retail Meltdown of 2017?

In the middle of an economic recovery, hundreds of shops and malls are shuttering. The reasons why go far beyond Amazon

DEREK THOMPSON

Learning Outcomes

After reading this article, you will be able to:

- Identify the primary factors driving the changes in retail shopping.

- Be able to identify factors other than digital shopping driving the trend.

- Discuss other digital technologies such as self-driving vehicles that will impact the future of retail.

From rural strip-malls to Manhattan's avenues, it has been a disastrous two years for retail.

There have been nine retail bankruptcies in 2017—as many as all of 2016. J.C. Penney, RadioShack, Macy's, and Sears have each announced more than 100 store closures. Sports Authority has liquidated, and Payless has filed for bankruptcy. Last week, several apparel companies' stocks hit new multi-year lows, including Lululemon, Urban Outfitters, and American Eagle, and Ralph Lauren announced that it is closing its flagship Polo store on Fifth Avenue, one of several brands to abandon that iconic thoroughfare.

A deep recession might explain an extinction-level event for large retailers. But GDP has been growing for eight straight years, gas prices are low, unemployment is under 5 percent, and the last 18 months have been quietly excellent years for wage growth, particularly for middle- and lower-income Americans.

So, what the heck is going on? The reality is that overall retail spending continues to grow steadily, if a little meagerly.

But several trends—including the rise of e-commerce, the over-supply of malls, and the surprising effects of a restaurant renaissance—have conspired to change the face of American shopping.

Here are three explanations for the recent demise of America's storefronts.

1. People Are Simply Buying More Stuff Online than They Used To

The simplest explanation for the demise of brick-and-mortar shops is that Amazon is eating retail. Between 2010 and last year, Amazon's sales in North America quintupled from $16 billion to $80 billion. Sears' revenue last year was about $22 billion, so you could say Amazon has grown by three Sears in six years. Even more remarkable, according to several reports, half of all U.S. households are now Amazon Prime subscribers.

But the full story is bigger than Amazon. Online shopping has done well for a long time in media and entertainment categories, like books and music. But easy return policies have made online shopping cheap, easy, and risk-free for consumers in apparel, which is now the largest e-commerce category. The success of start-ups like Casper, Bonobos, and Warby Parker (in beds, clothes, and glasses, respectively) has forced physical-store retailers to offer similar deals and convenience online.

What's more, mobile shopping, once an agonizing experience of typing private credit card digits in between pop-up ads, is getting easier thanks to apps and mobile wallets. Since 2010, mobile commerce has grown from 2 percent of digital spending to 20 percent.

People used to make several trips to a store before buying an expensive item like a couch. They would go once to browse options, again to narrow down their favorites, and again to finally pull the trigger on a blue velvet love seat. On each trip, they were likely to make lots of other small purchases as they wandered around. But today many consumers can do all their prep online, which means less ambling through shopping centers and less making incidental purchases at adjacent stores ("I'm tired, let's go home . . . oh wait, there's a DSW right there, I need new sneakers").

There will always be a place for stores. People like surveying glitzy showrooms and running their fingers over soft fabrics. But the rise of e-commerce not only moves individual sales online, but also builds new shopping habits, so that consumers gradually see the living room couch as a good-enough replacement for their local mall.

2. America Built Way Too Many Malls

There are about 1,200 malls in America today. In a decade, there might be about 900. That's not quite the "the death of malls." But it is decline, and it is inevitable.

The number of malls in the United States grew more than twice as fast as the population between 1970 and 2015, according to Cowen and Company's research analysts. By one measure of consumerist plentitude—shopping center "gross leasable area"—the United States has 40 percent more shopping space per capita than Canada, five times more the United Kingdom, and 10 times more than Germany. So it's no surprise that the Great Recession provided such a devastating blow: Mall visits declined 50 percent between 2010 and 2013, according to the real-estate research firm Cushman and Wakefield, and they've kept falling every year since.

In a long and detailed paper this week on the demise of stores, Cowen and Company research analysts offered several reasons for the "structural decay" of malls following the Great Recession. First, they said that stagnating wages and rising health-care costs squeezed consumer spending on fun stuff, like clothes. Second, the recession permanently hurt logo-driven brands, like Hollister and Abercrombie, that thrived during the 1990s and 2000s, when coolness in high-school hallways was defined by the size of the logo emblazoned on a polo shirt. Third, as consumers became bargain-hunters, discounters, fast-fashion outlets, and club stores took market share from department stores, like Macy's and Sears.

Finally, malls are retail bundles, and when bundles unravel, the collateral damage is massive. (For example, look at pay TV, where ESPN has bled millions of subscribers in the last few years as one of its key demographics, young men, abandon

the cable bundle that is critical to ESPN's distribution.) In retail, when anchor tenants like Macy's fail, that means there are fewer Macy's stragglers to amble over to American Eagle. Some stores have "co-tenancy" clauses in malls that give them the right to break the lease and leave if an anchor tenant closes its doors. The failure of one or more department stores can ultimately shutter an entire mall.

3. Americans Are Shifting their Spending from Materialism to Meals Out with Friends

Even if e-commerce and overbuilt shopping space conspired to force thousands of retail store closings, why is this meltdown happening while wages for low-income workers are rising faster than any time since the 1990s?

First, although rising wages are obviously great for workers and the overall economy, they can be difficult for low-margin companies that rely on cheap labor—like retail stores. Cashiers and retail salespeople are the two largest job categories in the country, with more than 8 million workers between them, and the median income for both occupations is less than $25,000 a year. But recently, new minimum-wage laws and a tight labor market have pushed up wages for the poorest workers, squeezing retailers who are already under pressure from Amazon.

Second, clothing stores have declined as consumers shifted their spending away from clothes toward traveling and dining out. Before the Great Recession, people bought a lot of stuff, like homes, furniture, cars, and clothes, as retail grew dramatically in the 1990s. But something big has changed. Spending on clothes is down—its share of total consumer spending has declined by 20 percent this century.

What's up? Travel is booming. Hotel occupancy is booming. Domestic airlines have flown more passengers each year since 2010, and last year U.S. airlines set a record, with 823 million passengers. The rise of restaurants is even more dramatic. Since 2005, sales at "food services and drinking places" have grown twice as fast as all other retail spending. In 2016, for the first time ever, Americans spent more money in restaurants and bars than at grocery stores.

There is a social element to this, too. Many young people are driven by the experiences that will make the best social media content—whether it's a conventional beach pic or a well-lit plate of glistening avocado toast. Laugh if you want, but these sorts of questions—"what experience will reliably deliver the most popular Instagram post?"— really drive the behavior of people ages 13 and up. This is a big deal for malls, says Barbara Byrne Denham, a senior economist at Reis, a real-estate analytics firm. Department stores have failed as anchors, but better food, entertainment, and even fitness options might bring teens and families back to struggling malls, where they might wander into brick-and-mortar stores that are currently at risk of closing.

There is no question that the most significant trend affecting brick-and-mortar stores is the relentless march of Amazon and other online retail companies. But the recent meltdown for retail brands is equally about the legacy of the Great Recession, which punished logo-driven brands, put a premium on experiences (particularly those that translate into social media moments), and unleashed a surprising golden age for restaurants.

Finally, a brief prediction. One of the mistakes people make when thinking about the future is to think that they are watching the final act of the play. Mobile shopping might be the most transformative force in retail—today. But self-driving cars could change retail as much as smartphones.

Once autonomous vehicles are cheap, safe, and plentiful, retail and logistics companies could buy up millions, seeing that cars can be stores and streets are the ultimate real estate. In fact, self-driving cars could make shopping space nearly obsolete in some areas. CVS could have hundreds of self-driving minivans stocked with merchandise roving the suburbs all day and night, ready to be summoned to somebody's home by smartphone. A new luxury-watch brand in 2025 might not spring for an Upper East Side storefront, but maybe its autonomous showroom vehicle could circle the neighborhood, waiting to be summoned to the doorstep of a tony apartment building.

Autonomous retail will create new conveniences and traffic headaches, require new regulations, and inspire new business strategies that could take even more businesses out of commercial real estate. The future of retail could be even weirder yet.

Critical Thinking

1. Why would non-digital factors affect changes in retail shopping?
2. What factors not discussed in the article could affect the future of retail shopping?
3. How can retail businesses adapt to changing retail trends?

Internet References

Brick-and-Mortar Retailers May be Locked in a Death Spiral Against the Likes of Amazon
https://goo.gl/rwa1yd

Shopping Then and Now: Five Ways Retail Has Changed and How Businesses Can Adapt.
https://goo.gl/ZifP43

Today's Must Reads for Entrepreneurs: Are Retail Stores Dying
https://goo.gl/cGC8ev

DEREK THOMPSON is a senior editor at *The Atlantic*, where he writes about economics, labor markets, and the media. He is the author of *Hit Makers*.

Article

Prepared by: Daniel Mittleman, *DePaul University* and
Douglas Druckenmiller, *Western Illinois University*

How Online Shopping Makes Suckers of Us All

Will you pay more for those shoes before 7 p.m.? Would the price tag be different if you lived in the suburbs? Standard prices and simple discounts are giving way to far more exotic strategies, designed to extract every last dollar from the consumer.

JERRY USEEM

Learning Outcomes

After reading this article, you will be able to:

- Understand how retailers are using online shopping data to set individual price points.

- Disuss fundamental online pricing strategies and algorithms used to implement them.

- Articulate the pros and cons of differential product and service pricing.

As Christmas approached in 2015, the price of pumpkin-pie spice went wild. It didn't soar, as an economics textbook might suggest. Nor did it crash. It just started vibrating between two quantum states. Amazon's price for a one-ounce jar was either $4.49 or $8.99, depending on when you looked. Nearly a year later, as Thanksgiving 2016 approached, the price again began whipsawing between two different points, this time $3.36 and $4.69.

We live in the age of the variable airfare, the surge-priced ride, the pay-what-you-want Radiohead album, and other novel price developments. But what was this? Some weird computer glitch? More like a deliberate glitch, it seems. "It's most likely a strategy to get more data and test the right price," Guru Hariharan explained, after I had sketched the pattern on a whiteboard.

The right price—the one that will extract the most profit from consumers' wallets—has become the fixation of a large and growing number of quantitative types, many of them economists who have left academia for Silicon Valley. It's also the preoccupation of Boomerang Commerce, a five-year-old start-up founded by Hariharan, an Amazon alum. He says these sorts of price experiments have become a routine part of finding that right price—and refinding it, because the right price can change by the day or even by the hour. (Amazon says its price changes are not attempts to gather data on customers' spending habits, but rather to give shoppers the lowest price out there.)

It may come as a surprise that, in buying a seasonal pie ingredient, you might be participating in a carefully designed social-science experiment. But this is what online comparison shopping hath wrought. Simply put: Our ability to know the price of anything, anytime, anywhere, has given us, the consumers, so much power that retailers—in a desperate effort to regain the upper hand, or at least avoid extinction—are now staring back through the screen. They are comparison shopping *us*.

They have ample means to do so: the immense data trail you leave behind whenever you place something in your online shopping cart or swipe your rewards card at a store register, top economists and data scientists capable of turning this information into useful price strategies, and what one tech economist calls "the ability to experiment on a scale that's unparalleled in the history of economics." In mid-March, Amazon alone had 59 listings for economists on its job site, and a website dedicated to recruiting them.

Not coincidentally, quaint pricing practices—an advertised discount off the "list price," two for the price of one, or simply "everyday low prices"—are yielding to far more exotic strategies.

"I don't think anyone could have predicted how sophisticated these algorithms have become," says Robert Dolan, a marketing professor at Harvard. "I certainly didn't." The price of a can of soda in a vending machine can now vary with the temperature outside. The price of the headphones Google recommends may depend on how budget-conscious your web history shows you to be, one study found. For shoppers, that means price—not the one offered to you right now, but the one offered to you 20 minutes from now, or the one offered to me, or to your neighbor—may become an increasingly unknowable thing. "Many moons ago, there used to be one price for something," Dolan notes. Now the simplest of questions—*what's the true price of pumpkin-pie spice?*—is subject to a Heisenberg level of uncertainty.

Which raises a bigger question: Could the Internet, whose transparency was supposed to empower consumers, be doing the opposite?

If the marketplace was a war between buyers and sellers, the 19th-century French sociologist Gabriel Tarde wrote, then price was a truce. And the practice of setting a fixed price for a good or a service—which took hold in the 1860s—meant, in effect, a cessation of the perpetual state of hostility known as haggling.

As in any truce, each party surrendered something in this bargain. Buyers were forced to accept, or not accept, the one price imposed by the price tag (an invention credited to the retail pioneer John Wanamaker). What retailers ceded—the ability to exploit customers' varying willingness to pay—was arguably greater, as the extra money some people would have paid could no longer be captured as profit. But they made the bargain anyway, for a combination of moral and practical reasons.

The Quakers—including a New York merchant named Rowland H. Macy—had never believed in setting different prices for different people. Wanamaker, a Presbyterian operating in Quaker Philadelphia, opened his Grand Depot under the principle of "One price to all; no favoritism." Other merchants saw the practical benefits of Macy's and Wanamaker's prix fixe policies. As they staffed up their new department stores, it was expensive to train hundreds of clerks in the art of haggling. Fixed prices offered a measure of predictability to bookkeeping, sped up the sales process, and made possible the proliferation of printed retail ads highlighting a given price for a given good.

Companies like General Motors found an up-front way of recovering some of the lost profit. In the 1920s, GM aligned its various car brands into a finely graduated price hierarchy:

"Chevrolet for the hoi polloi," *Fortune* magazine put it, "Pontiac . . . for the poor but proud, Oldsmobile for the comfortable but discreet, Buick for the striving, Cadillac for the rich." The policy—"a car for every purse and purpose," GM called it—was a means of customer sorting, but the customers did the sorting themselves. It kept the truce.

Customers, meanwhile, could recover some of their lost agency by clipping coupons—their chance to get a deal denied to casual shoppers. The new supermarket chains of the 1940s made coupons a staple of American life. What the big grocers knew—and what behavioral economists would later prove in detail—is that while consumers liked the assurance the truce afforded (that they would not be fleeced), they also retained the instinct to best their neighbors. They loved deals so much that, to make sense of their behavior, economists were forced to distinguish between two types of value: acquisition value (the perceived worth of a new car to the buyer) and transaction value (the feeling that one lost or won the negotiation at the dealership).

The idea that there was a legitimate "list price," and that consumers would occasionally be offered a discount on this price—these were the terms of the truce. And the truce remained largely intact up to the turn of the present century. The reigning retail superpower, Walmart, enforced "everyday low prices" that did not shift around.

But in the 1990s, the Internet began to erode the terms of the long peace. Savvy consumers could visit a Best Buy to eyeball merchandise they intended to buy elsewhere for a cheaper price, an exercise that became known as "showrooming." In 1999, a Seattle-based digital bookseller called Amazon.com started expanding into a Grand Depot of its own.

The era of Internet retailing had arrived, and with it, the resumption of hostilities.

In retrospect, retailers were slow to mobilize. Even as other corporate functions—logistics, sales-force management—were being given the "moneyball" treatment in the early 2000s with powerful predictive software (and even as airlines had fully weaponized airfares), retail pricing remained more art than science. In part, this was a function of internal company hierarchy. Prices were traditionally the purview of the second-most-powerful figure in a retail organization: the head merchant, whose intuitive knack for knowing what to sell, and for how much, was the source of a deep-seated mythos that she was not keen to dispel.

Two developments, though, loosened the head merchant's hold.

The first was the arrival of data. Thomas Nagle was teaching economics at the University of Chicago in the early 1980s when, he recalls, the university acquired the data from the grocery chain Jewel's newly installed checkout scanners. "Everyone was thrilled," says Nagle, now a senior adviser specializing in pricing at Deloitte. "We'd been relying on all these contrived surveys: 'Given these options at these prices, what would you do?' But the real world is not a controlled experiment."

The Jewel data overturned a lot of what he'd been teaching. For instance, he'd professed that ending prices with .99 or .98, instead of just rounding up to the next dollar, did not boost sales. The practice was merely an artifact, the existing literature said, of an age when owners wanted to force cashiers to open the register to make change, in order to prevent them from pocketing the money from a sale. "It turned out," Nagle recollects, "that ending prices in .99 wasn't big for cars and other big-ticket items where you pay a lot of attention. But in the grocery store, the effect was huge!"

The effect, now known as "left-digit bias," had not shown up in lab experiments, because participants, presented with a limited number of decisions, were able to approach every hypothetical purchase like a math problem. But of course in real life, Nagle admits, "if you did that, it would take you all day to go to the grocery store." Disregarding the digits to the right side of the decimal point lets you get home and make dinner.

By the early 2000s, the amount of data collected on retailers' Internet servers had become so massive that it started exerting a gravitational pull. That's what triggered the second development: the arrival, en masse, of the practitioners of the dismal science.

This was, in some ways, a curious stampede. For decades, academic economists had generally been as indifferent to corporations as corporations were to them. (Indeed, most of their models barely acknowledged the existence of corporations at all.)

But that began to change in 2001, when the Berkeley economist Hal Varian—highly regarded for the 1999 book *Information Rules*—ran into Eric Schmidt. Varian knew him but, he says, was unaware that Schmidt had become the CEO of a little company called Google. Varian agreed to spend a sabbatical year at Google, figuring he'd write a book about the start-up experience.

At the time, the few serious economists who worked in industry focused on macroeconomic issues like, say, how demand for consumer durables might change in the next year. Varian, however, was immediately invited to look at a Google project that (he recalls Schmidt telling him) "might make us a little money": the auction system that became Google AdWords. Varian never left.

Others followed. "eBay was Disneyland," says Steve Tadelis, a Berkeley economist who went to work there for a time in 2011 and is currently on leave at Amazon. "You know, pricing,

people, behavior, reputation"—the things that have always set economists aglow—plus the chance "to experiment at a scale that's unparalleled."

At first, the newcomers were mostly mining existing data for insights. At eBay, for instance, Tadelis used a log of buyer clicks to estimate how much money one hour of bargain-hunting saved shoppers. (Roughly $15 was the answer.)

Then economists realized that they could go a step further and design experiments that *produced* data. Carefully controlled experiments not only attempted to divine the shape of a demand curve—which shows just how much of a product people will buy as you keep raising the price, allowing retailers to find the optimal, profit-maximizing figure. They tried to map how the curve changed hour to hour. (Online purchases peak during weekday office hours, so retailers are commonly advised to raise prices in the morning and lower them in the early evening.)

By the mid-2000s, some economists began wondering whether Big Data could discern every individual's own *personal* demand curve—thereby turning the classroom hypothetical of "perfect price discrimination" (a price that's calibrated precisely to the maximum that *you* will pay) into an actual possibility.

As this new world began to take shape, the initial consumer experience of online shopping—so simple! and such deals!—was losing some of its sheen.

It's not that consumers hadn't benefited from the lower prices available online. They had. But some of the deals weren't nearly as good as they seemed to be. And for some people, glee began to give way to a vague suspicion that maybe they were getting ripped off. In 2007, a California man named Marc Ecenbarger thought he had scored when he found a patio set—list price $999—selling on Overstock.com for $449.99. He bought two, unpacked them, then discovered—courtesy of a price tag left on the packaging—that Walmart's normal price for the set was $247. His fury was profound. He complained to Overstock, which offered to refund him the cost of the furniture.

But his experience was later used as evidence in a case brought by consumer-protection attorneys against Overstock for false advertising, along with internal emails in which an Overstock employee claimed it was commonly known that list prices were "egregiously overstated."

In 2014, a California judge ordered Overstock to pay $6.8 million in civil penalties. (Overstock has appealed the decision.) The past year has seen a wave of similar lawsuits over phony list prices, reports Bonnie Patten, the executive director of TruthinAdvertising.org. In 2016, Amazon began to drop most mentions of "list price," and in some cases added a new reference point: its own past price.

This could be seen as the final stage of decay of the old one-price system. What's replacing it is something that most closely resembles high-frequency trading on Wall Street. Prices are never "set" to begin with in this new world. They can fluctuate hour to hour and even minute to minute—a phenomenon familiar to anyone who has put something in his Amazon cart and been alerted to price changes while it sat there. A website called camelcamelcamel.com even tracks Amazon prices for specific products and alerts consumers when a price drops below a preset threshold. The price history for any given item—Classic Twister, for example—looks almost exactly like a stock chart. And as with financial markets, flash glitches happen. In 2011, Peter A. Lawrence's *The Making of a Fly* (paperback edition) was briefly available on Amazon for $23,698,655.93, thanks to an algorithmic price war between two third-party sellers that had run amok. To understand what happened, it seemed sensible to talk to the man who helped develop the software they were using.

Guru Hariharan uncapped a dry-erase marker in a conference room at Boomerang's headquarters in Mountain View, California. He was talking about what had led retailers to this desperate place where it's necessary to change prices multiple times a day. On a whiteboard, he drew a series of lines representing the rising share of online sales for various kinds of products (books, DVDs, electronics) over time, then marked the years that major brick-and-mortar players (Borders, Blockbuster, Circuit City and RadioShack) went bankrupt. At first the years looked random. But the bankruptcies all clustered within a band where online sales hit between 20 and 25 percent. "In this range, there's a crushing point," Hariharan said, clapping his hands together for emphasis. "There's a bloodbath happening."

Beyond this crushing point, traditional retailers with both a brick-and-mortar and an online presence feel compelled to compete purely on price. Hariharan talked wistfully of the days when he'd walk into RadioShack and have a salesperson direct him to the exact connector cable he needed. But once retailers enter the crushing zone, expenses like staff, training, and customer support typically are slashed. Profit margins keep falling nonetheless—why go to the store at all if no one there can help you?—and a death spiral ensues. (RadioShack traced just this path before filing for bankruptcy in 2015.)

"It didn't have to be that way," Hariharan said. Now he's helping retailers fight back.

We can't process every piece of price information thrown our way. So we judge a store's prices based on a handful of products we know well. Grocers have recognized this for decades, which is why they keep the price of eggs and milk consistently low, making their profits on other goods whose markups we don't notice as easily.

When he was at Amazon, Hariharan, who has a degree in machine learning, helped invent and patent the Amazon Selling Coach, a system that helps third-party vendors optimize their inventory and prices. He and his team at Boomerang have built a massive system that tracks prices and has informed billions of pricing decisions for clients ranging from Office Depot to GNC to U.S. Auto Parts. But its software engine isn't built to match the lowest price out there. (That, Hariharan notes, would be a simple algorithm.) It's built to manage consumers' *perception* of price. The software identifies the goods that loom largest in consumers' perception and keeps their prices carefully in line with competitors' prices, if not lower. The price of everything else is allowed to drift upward.

Amazon long ago mastered this tactic, Hariharan says. In one instance, Boomerang monitored the pricing shifts of a popular Samsung television on Amazon over the six-month period before Black Friday. Then, on Black Friday itself, Amazon dropped the TV's price from $350 all the way to $250, undercutting competitors by a country mile. Boomerang's bots also noticed that in October, Amazon had hiked the price of some HDMI cables needed to connect the TV by about 60 percent, likely armed with the knowledge, Hariharan says, that online consumers do not comparison shop as zealously for cheaper items as they do for expensive ones.

What's interesting is how other retailers are now beginning to adapt. To show me this, a Boomerang employee opened up the dashboard seen by the firm's clients. Scrolling through a menu of premade algorithms, he selected a rule, "Beat Competitor by 10%," for certain items meeting the following criteria:

If (comp_price>cost) and (promo_flag = false) then set price = comp_price*0.90

That is: *If the competitor's price is greater than the cost of making the item, and the competitor isn't running a onetime promotion, then undercut the competitor by 10 percent.* The rule was implemented with a click, and onscreen, I could see a healthy drop in the client's Price Perception Index.

But that's not the end of the story. The price cuts will register on competitors' pricing sonars. Whether or not to respond in kind depends, in part, on how *their* algorithms interpret the signal. Is this the first shot in a pricing war? Or is the retailer just trying to clear inventory from its warehouse? In practice, it's hard to tell. So an innocuous, temporary price cut may set off a machine-against-machine price war that, if left unchecked, could quickly devastate a retailer's bottom line. Boomerang clients are prompted to select "Guardrails"—further rules that provide a check on the initial set of rules—and establish a certain amount of human oversight. Faisal Masud, the chief technology officer at Staples, one of Boomerang's first customers, thinks human involvement makes sense only in rare cases. "We want to make sure the software makes the decisions, not the human being," he says. "It's all automatic. Otherwise you're losing."

The complexity of retail pricing today has driven at least one of Boomerang's clients into game theory—a branch of mathematics that, it's safe to say, has seldom found practical use in shopping aisles. Hariharan says, with a smile: "It lets you say, 'What is the dominant competitor's reaction to me? And if I know the reaction to me, what is my first, best move?' Which is the Nash equilibrium." Yes, that's John Nash, the eponymous Beautiful Mind, whose brilliant contributions to mathematics now extend to the setting of mop prices.

Where does all this end?

One scenario is: in simplicity.

The apparel start-up Everlane, for instance, is betting that it can capitalize on consumer backlash to retailers' ever more vaguely underhanded tactics. The company spells out the cost of making each of its products and the profit it earns on each. Recently it informed customers that the cost of cashmere from Inner Mongolia had dropped. It was dropping the price of its cashmere sweaters by $25, because they now cost less to make. "Radical transparency," Everlane founder and CEO Michael Preysman calls the approach.

On another occasion, Everlane decided to clear clothing and shoe inventory by giving customers three choices of what to pay. The lowest price covered the cost of making and shipping the items. The middle price also covered the overhead of selling them. And the highest provided Everlane a profit.

Lest someone wonder, *Would framing price as a moral dilemma be the ultimate pricing ploy?*, the answer is no: 87 percent of customers chose the lowest price, Preysman reports. (Eight percent picked the middle price; 5 percent chose the highest.) The point, Preysman stresses, was to give customers a glimpse of how stuff gets made, how workers get paid, and other things not typically visible on a shoebox or a sweater tag.

"The theory of Everlane, I think, is still a theory we have to prove," Preysman says. Companies have "trained customers in the United States to be as addicted to sales as possible. It has become a core piece of the retail-industrial complex and it is very, very difficult to unwind. So reeducation is hard when you play in a market where people play these games on a daily basis."

But a different scenario follows from the possibility that consumers don't really want clarity. They are content to be fooled into paying more if they can keep the belief that they're paying less; that they have the agency and agility to find special, unbeatable deals, only for them. This would amount to a rejection of the new truce that Everlane is extending. And it would open the way for retailers and economists to grab their holy grail.

Perfect price discrimination was, again, supposed to exist only as a classroom thought experiment. But it posits that a seller knows the walk-away price of every single buyer and hence, by offering a price just barely below it, can extract every last farthing of potential profit from each of them.

In the past, retailers have used demographic data to try to deduce walk-away price. In 2000, some people thought Amazon was doing this when customers noticed they were being charged different prices for the same DVDs. Amazon denied it. This was the result of a random price test, CEO Jeff Bezos explained in a news release. "We've never tested and we never will test prices based on customer demographics."

But demographics are actually a crude way of personalizing prices, the Brandeis economist Benjamin Shiller argued in a recent paper, "First-Degree Price Discrimination Using Big Data." If Netflix were to use only demographic factors, such as people's race, household income, and zip code, to personalize subscription prices, his model predicted, it could boost its profits by .3 percent. But if Netflix also used people's web-browsing history—the percentage of web use on Tuesdays, the number of visits to RottenTomatoes.com, and some 5,000 other variables—it could boost its profits by 14.6 percent.

Netflix was not doing any of this; it hadn't even provided Shiller with the data he used (which he obtained from a third party). But Shiller demonstrated that personalized pricing was feasible.

Are other companies doing this? Four researchers in Catalonia tried to answer the question with dummy computers that mimicked the web-browsing patterns of either "affluent" or "budget conscious" customers for a week. When the personae went "shopping," they weren't shown different prices for the same goods. They were shown different goods. The average price of the headphones suggested for the affluent personae was four times the price of those suggested for the budget-conscious personae. Another experiment demonstrated a more direct form of price discrimination: Computers with addresses in greater Boston were shown lower prices than those in more-remote parts of Massachusetts on identical goods.

In their paper, "Detecting Price and Search Discrimination on the Internet," the researchers suggested that consumers could benefit from a price-discrimination watchdog system that would continuously monitor for customized prices (although it's unclear who would build or operate this). Another paper—this one co-authored by Google's Hal Varian—argues that if personalized pricing becomes too aggressive, shoppers will become more "strategic," selectively withholding or disclosing information in order to obtain the best price.

Which, to Bonnie Patten of TruthinAdvertising.org, seems like a whole lot of work. It's already "so complicated," she told me. "Everything is 50 percent off, but they have all these exclusions where it doesn't count, and then everyone is trying to calculate 20 percent of 50 percent in their heads." She already has a full-time job, was her point. And three kids.

"As a general matter," she went on, "I find it so difficult to determine the actual price of the product that when I'm shopping for my kids, my new technique is to make all my decisions at the cashier. I pick up lots of clothes. I completely ignore all pricing until I get to the register. And then if something is too much, I say, 'I don't want it.'"

This struck me as sensible in the extreme. And how did she shop for herself? "I do not shop," Patten said.

In what sense?, I asked, confused.

"I just gave up," she said. "I just stopped shopping."

I thought about this after we hung up. Maybe it was a function of her job, which let her see too much. Maybe she was a certain type—"survival shopper" was the label she used—who simply didn't experience the thrill of finding a pair of $30 moccasins for $8. Such thoughts helped stay the alternative explanation, the one Gabriel Tarde called "the madness of doubt": that there's a finite amount of uncertainty we can absorb, a limit to how much we can check the ticker to see whether the Swiffer's price is up or down this morning; that somewhere in us is a shut-off point, and that Patten had hit it.

Critical Thinking

1. Comparison shopping using the Internet seemed to give shoppers the upper hand in finding the lowest price. Explain what is meant by "They are comparison shopping us."

2. What are retail company's ethical obligations to its customers: honesty, full information, or maximizing revenue opportunities?

3. Companies use algorithms to set market priceing. Amazon, for example, may show different shoppers a different price for the exact same item based on what it knows about the shopper's demographics, shopping history, and browsing patterns. In what situations do you think differential pricing is or isn't ethical?

Internet References

3 Predictions for the Future of Retail—From the CEO of Walmart
https://goo.gl/dLxxzB

Ethics in Internet Selling and Advertising—The Better Way forward
https://goo.gl/DMk5pA

Four Ways Junk Food Brands Befriend Kids Online
https://goo.gl/ss3PDU

JERRY USEEM has covered business and economics for *The New York Times*, *Fortune*, and other publications.

Article

Prepared by: Daniel Mittleman, *DePaul University* and
Douglas Druckenmiller, *Western Illinois University*

Imagining the Retail Store of the Future

ELIZABETH PATON

Learning Outcomes

After reading this article, you will be able to:

- Discuss the technological trends that are transforming the retail customer experience.

- Identify the social factors of retail shopping that will remain important for customers.

- Distinguish between the experience of online and offline retail shopping and the integration of both experiences in the retail space of the future.

LONDON—What will the store of the future look like? Will we be served by fleets of gleaming robots, using built-in facial recognition technology to adjust each sales pitch to a person's current mood or past spending preferences? Will there be voice-activated personal assistants, downloading the availability, color and fit of any and every garment to your smartphone? Three-D printing stations? No checkout counters when you leave? Could there even be floating, holographic product displays on the shop floor that change when a customer walks by?

Perhaps shoppers will make all their purchases from their own home, using virtual fitting rooms via virtual reality headsets. Drones will then drop deliveries in the backyard or on the front steps.

As fanciful as these innovations may sound, none are hypothetical. All exist, are being tested and could be rolled out in as little as a decade. But is this the sort of shopping experience that customers really want?

Scores of leading retailers and fashion brands increasingly say no. And in an ever-more-volatile and unpredictable shopping environment, where long-term survival is dictated by anticipating and catering to consumers' desires (often before they themselves even know what they want), the race to find out how and where people will do their spending has started to heat up.

On Wednesday, for example, Farfetch—the global online marketplace for independent luxury boutiques—held a daylong event at the Design Museum in London. There, in front of 200 fashion industry insiders and partners, José Neves, the founder of Farfetch, unveiled "The Store of the Future," a suite of new technologies developed by his company to help brands and boutiques bridge the worlds of online and offline.

Nevertheless, in a telephone call last week, Mr. Neves said: "I am a huge believer in physical stores. They are not going to vanish and will stay at the center of the seismic retail revolution that is only just getting started."

A corresponding report released by Bain & Company this week suggests that he might be right; although 70 percent of high-end purchases are influenced by online interactions, the consultancy maintains that stores will continue to play a critical role, with 75 percent of sales still occurring in a physical location by 2025.

What may change, however, is a store's primary purpose. Forget e-commerce, or bricks and mortar, or even omnichannel sales; according to Mr. Neves, the new retail era is one anchored in "augmented retail," a blend of the digital and physical allowing a shopper to shift seamlessly between the two realms.

"Customers don't wake up and think, I will be online this morning or offline later; we are rarely purely one or the other anymore and tend to jump constantly between two worlds without noticing," Mr. Neves said. "Harnessing this behavior is a major challenge for retailers and brands and why we are doing this event. It is in our interests to give our partners first-hand access to information about changing behaviors and new technology, so everyone is 'future-proofed' as to what might come next."

Holition is an augmented-reality consultancy and software provider based in London that has worked with some well-known retail brands. Last fall it worked with the British cosmetics company Charlotte Tilbury on a "magic mirror" concept, a virtual makeup selling tool that allows users to try on different looks that are digitally superimposed onto their faces in 40 seconds. They can then send the selection of photos

to their email address, ready to be referred to later or shared socially. And they then can buy products, available from glamorous makeup artists milling around nearby.

"Technology is still often a barrier in the retail place, with smartphones, iPads and screens getting in the way of what the consumer wants to see, touch and feel 80 percent of the time," said Jonathan Chippindale, Holition's chief executive.

"The holy grail now for retailers is creating digital empathy. No one can really guess what the future will look like. But those who are using technology and data to create bespoke shopping experiences that recognize every person is different, and with different needs, are more likely to come out on top."

Tom Chapman, a founder of MatchesFashion.com, agreed. It was originally a bricks and mortar boutique; now 95 percent of the British fashion retailer's sales—which hit 204 million pounds (about $253 million) in 2016—are online. But Mr. Chapman said boutiques and physical events remained vital "marketing opportunities," with a more specialized inventory selection and the opportunity for customers to do more than buy merchandise; for example, the MatchesFashion.com "In Residence" series offers talks, film screenings, and designer meet-and-greets, along with social media lessons, exercise classes, and floristry sessions.

"You need to be accessible to your customer wherever she wants to find you," Mr. Chapman said, "and we have seen that a sizable proportion want human interaction and access that goes far beyond a credit card transaction."

"Stores cannot just be row after row of product rail anymore," he added. "To survive, they have to tell stories—rooted in a sense of community and entertainment—and have points of view that makes the owner stand out."

Rachel Shechtman, the founder of Story, a store in Manhattan, has taken that concept further than most. The store, opened in 2011, was created to present its point of view like a magazine, one that gets a complete makeover with a new design, range of products and marketing message every four to eight weeks.

Story has multiple revenue streams. One is with sponsors, who can use the store to create "living advertorials" with singular themes, and where companies can then promote items to consumers as they shop; brands, corporations and retailers pay $500,000 and up for a "feature" slot. Features have included "His Story," sponsored by Braun, Old Spice and Gillette, with a hot towel shave station offering free shaves daily, and a "Making Things" story, sponsored by General Electric, with MakerBot 3-D printers and injection molding machines.

"If time is the ultimate luxury and people want a higher return on investment of their time, you need to give them a reason to be in a physical space," said Ms. Shechtman, who has

worked with more than 4,000 brands and who consults for a range of big-box retailers.

The US department store Lord & Taylor is doubling down on that approach, with the unveiling of its 30,000-square-foot Dress Address last month, the largest dress floor in the country. Along with featuring designers like Oscar de la Renta, Cushnie et Ochs, Naeem Khan and Marchesa, there will be a special section called "The Gallery" with a full-service concierge, as well as a pop-up store concept. The first pop-up will be Cameron Silver's Decades; brands will change every eight weeks. While technology may play a role, it is largely behind the scenes, adding delivery speed and a broader choice to customers if they want it.

"Not everyone wants a high touch or overly complicated experience," said Liz Rodbell, president of Lord & Taylor and its parent group, Hudson's Bay department stores. "When women buy occasion-wear for a major celebration, it is an incredibly valuable and intimate retail opportunity. They want an extensive and rich assortment of options, and they want a human connection. They want a dress that makes a memory, and that's what we aim to give them."

Still, there is no question that a certain demographic of consumers—particularly those under 35—are demanding the ability to have any product they want, whenever they want it.

Last week, Yoox Net-a-Porter, in partnership with Valentino, started "Next Era"—access to the biggest Valentino store in the world, but one that won't be on any street, plaza or avenue. Scheduled to open early next year, the initiative will give customers online access to any product they want from any Valentino store or logistics center globally, as well as those of Yoox Net-a-Porter, with rapid delivery, a smartphone-centric interface and artificial-intelligence-powered services such as on-site personalization.

And this week, the rival Farfetch unveiled F90, a delivery service for Gucci in which Farfetch will facilitate the delivery and return of products directly from the Gucci store to a customer in 90 minutes across 10 cities.

"Timely delivery of product remains the top of all criteria for luxury consumers," Mr. Neves of Farfetch said. "They want storytelling and theater of course, but they also want their chosen item, in the right color, size and in their hands as quickly as possible.

"Ultimately the use of data to transform stores will separate those who make it to the next step and those who won't."

Critical Thinking

1. In your experience what is the most effective combination of online and offline retail exeriences.

2. What will be the impact of augmented reality technology on the retail experience?

3. Will new virtual technologies and augemtented reality increase or decrease the need for retail space. How will this change the design of retail spaces?

Internet References

Retail for Consumer Industries: Thinking Outside the (Brick-and-Mortar) Box
https://goo.gl/Xvwg6m

Six Retail Business Models of the Future
https://goo.gl/Xvwg6m

What Does the Store of the Future Look Like?
https://goo.gl/PDJFqT

ELIZABETH PATON is a reporter for the *The New York Times Styles* section, covering the fashion and luxury sectors in Europe. Her areas of industry focus and interest include business, tech and sustainability, along with *Fashion Week* coverage from London, Milan, and Paris.

Article

Prepared by: Daniel Mittleman, *DePaul University* and
Douglas Druckenmiller, *Western Illinois University*

Four Ways Junk Food Brands Befriend Kids Online

Teresa Davis

Learning Outcomes

After reading this article, you will be able to:

- Understand reasons why children are more vulnerable to advertising than adults.

- Describe four strategies that brands use to interact with kids online.

If a stranger offered a child free lollies in return for their picture, the parent would justifiably be angry. When this occurs on Facebook, they may not even realise it's happening.

There was outrage after a recent report in The Australian suggesting that the social media company can identify when young people feel emotions like "anxious," "nervous," or "stupid." Although Facebook has denied offering tools to target users based on their feelings, the fact is that a variety of brands have been advertising to young people online for many years.

We're all familiar with traditional print and television advertising, but persuasion is harder for children and parents to detect online. From using cartoon characters to embody the brand, to games that combine advertising with interactive content ("advergames"), kids are exposed to a pervasive ecosystem of marketing on social media.

The blurring of the line between advertising, entertainment, and socialising has never been greater, or more difficult to fight.

Kids Are Vulnerable to Junk Food Advertising

Junk food advertising aimed at both adults and children is nothing new, but research shows that young people are particularly vulnerable.

Their minds are more susceptible to persuasion, given that the part of their brain that controls impulsivity and decision-making is not always fully developed until early adulthood. As a result, children are likely to respond impulsively to interactive and attractive content.

While the issue of advertising junk food to children through television and other broadcast media gets a lot of attention, less is understood about how children are consuming such marketing online.

How Brands Interact Online

We examined how six "high-fat-sugar-salt" food brands approached consumers at an interactive, direct and social level online in 2012 to 2013 (although the practice continues).

Analysing content on official Facebook pages, website advergames and free branded apps, we coded brand placements as primary, secondary, direct, or implied brand mentions.

While the content may not be explicitly targeted at children, the colours, skill level of the games, and the prizes are attractive to younger people. The responses on Facebook in particular show that young consumers often interact with these posts, sharing comments and reposting.

We found food brands being presented online and interactively in four main ways: as "the prize," "the entertainer," the "social enabler," and as "a person."

1. The Prize

The fast-food company Hungry Jack's Shake and Win app has been offered since 2012. By "shaking" the app, it tells you, using your smartphone GPS, which Hungry Jack's outlet is closest and where you can redeem your "free" offer or discount.

In this way, it combines several interactive elements to push the user toward immediate consumption with the brand coded as a reward.

2. The Entertainer

Free branded video game apps or advergames are also used to engage young consumers, disguising advertising as entertainment.

In the 2012 Chupa Chups game Lol-a-Coaster (which is not currently available on the Australian iTunes store), for example, we found a lollipop appeared as part of game play up to 200 times in one minute. The game is simple to play, full of fun primary colours and sounds, and the player is socialised to associate the brand with positive emotion.

Chuck's Lol-A-Coaster: an interactive game for Chupa Chups.

3. The Social Enabler

Brands often leverage Facebook's "tagging" capability to spread their message, adding a social element. When a company suggests that you tag your family and friends on Facebook with their favourite product flavour, for example, the young consumer is not only using the brand to connect with others, but letting the brand connect to their own Facebook network. For a brand like Pringles, this increases their reach on social media.

4. The Person

Some brands also use a humanised character, like Chupa Chups's Chuck, to voice the brand and post messages to consumers on Facebook.

Often this character interacts with the consumer in a very human way, asking them about their everyday lives, aspirations, and fears. This creates the possibility of a long-term brand relationship and brand loyalty.

Brands Need to Clean Up their Act

Using Facebook, advergames, and other online platforms, food marketers can create deeper relationships with kids than ever before. Going far beyond a televised advertisement, they are able to create an entire "brand ecosystem" around the child online.

The latest National Health Survey found that around one in four Australian kids aged 5–17 were overweight or obese. Food marketers promoting unhealthy options to kids online should be held to account.

In Australia, the food marketing industry is mostly self-regulating. Brands are meant to abide by a code of practice which, if breached, holds them account through a complaints-based system.

While some companies have also pledged, via an Australian Food and Grocery Council code, not to target child audiences using interactive games unless offering a healthy choice, the current system is too slow and weak to be a real deterrent. That needs to change.

While online food marketing may be cheap for the corporations, the price that society pays when it comes to issues such as childhood obesity is immeasurable.

Critical Thinking

1. Why are children more vulnerable to advertising than adults? What responsibilities should advertisers have to these vulnerabilities?

2. What strategies do brands use to interact wtih children online? For each strategy, discuss your evaluation of its ethics.

3. Who should be responsible for policing online advertising to children? To what extent does responsibility lay with corporations (the brands), parents, industry standards boards, or the government? Why?

Internet References

Does Technology Change the Ethics of Marketing to Children?
 https://www.fastcompany.com/3008070/does-technology-change-ethics-marketing-children

Hidden Ads on Social Media and Games Could be Influencing Your Kids' Diets
 https://www.huffingtonpost.com/entry/these-hidden-ads-may-be-influencing-your-kids-diets-for-the-worse_us_581ca89ae4b0aac62483b803

Report of the APA Task Force on Advertising and Children
 https://www.apa.org/pubs/info/reports/advertising-children.aspx

TERESA DAVIS is an Associate Professor at the University of Sydney.

Unit 3

UNIT

Prepared by: Daniel Mittleman, *DePaul University* and
Douglas Druckenmiller, *Western Illinois University*

Impact of Technology on Work

There exists a two-faced relationship between technology innovation and work. Technologies are the tools and processes used to increase work productivity. That is, technology helps people accomplish more with the same, or less, effort. Innovation is the development of new technologies that enable ever increasing work productivity.

Each generation of information technology innovation—from mainframe computers in the 1960s, to mini-computers in the 1970s, to desktop computers in the 1980s, to the Internet and WWW in the 1990s, to Web 2.0 and mobile computing in the 2000s, and to Web 3.0 and a triple convergence of big data, analytics and artificial intelligence today—has promised—and sometimes delivered—greater productivity gains in the workplace. These gains have enabled new industries and new markets; they have engendered corporate giants out of garage-based startups; and they have created a new generation of billionaires.

But concurrent with the decade of technological innovation, overall workplace productivity has been largely stagnant. Production and service workers aren't earning significantly more money. And recent technology innovations are threatening their jobs either because communication technologies now makes it easier to shift their jobs overseas, or because new automation and robotic gains make semi-skilled human labor less necessary.

These two faces of technology innovation are not new this generation. Every generation for at least the last two hundred years has grappled with the paradox of technological advancement.[1] Is it more of the same this generation, or is something new and different happening?

Since the onset of the industrial revolution about two centuries ago, we have witnessed a steady decline in the average workweek from about 69 hours a week in 1830 to about 38 hours a week today in the United States.[2]

And this is not the total story as the concepts of vacation time, sick days, personal days, and holidays, when factored into the average, brings real hours worked down well below 35 per week. We consider full-time work to be about half as much as our ancestors did 190 years ago. And that leaves us with much more free time than our great, great, great, great, grandparents had.

Until about 40 years ago wages increased at about the same rate as workplace productivity. That is, as innovation led to better work technologies, the gains were passed along commensurately to the worker. Since then, productivity has continued to grow at the same rate, but worker compensation has stagnated.[3] Until that point in time, workers were able to enjoy an ever decreasing workweek because their increased compensation reflected the productivity gains that enabled the shorter week.

Ezra Klein suggests that perhaps we have been thinking about the relationship between productivity wealth wrongly. He "imagine[s] a world in which wages look flat but workers feel richer because their paychecks are securing them wonders beyond their previous imagination."[4] He suggests that our personal gains from productivity may not be in dollars, but in additional leisure time, higher quality life experiences, and opportunities not previously afforded us. An immediate personal example of his argument is that a generation ago, to compile the chart shown in reference 2, I would have had to walk to the

---

[1] It goes back farther than 200 years. The Guttenberg Press in the early 16th century both enabled enormous advances in human knowledge and economic gains, but also precipitated enormous changes to existing social and political systems. Some, such as the monks who previously maintained almost total control over the production and dissemination of knowledge, lost that control and some of their standing in the political and social order of the day.

[2] Table shown is compiled from statistics from several studies and data repositories. See: https://ourworldindata.org/working-hours/, https://eh.net/encyclopedia/hours-of-work-in-u-s-history/, and http://stats.oecd.org/Index.aspx?DataSetCode=ANHRS.

[3] See: http://www.epi.org/publication/understanding-the-historic-divergence-between-productivity-and-a-typical-workers-pay-why-it-matters-and-why-its-real/

[4] See: http://www.vox.com/a/new-economy-future/technology-productivity, which is also included in Unit 6.

library and spend a half day gathering data from paper-bound almanacs and government reports, then spend several more hours constructing and printing the chart. Today, I was able to google the information from my office and cut and paste it directly into Excel, which has a function that quickly produces the chart. I was able to save four to six hours of time that I can now use for additional research—or as leisure time. But an alternative argument is that, enjoying leisure time and hedonistic adventures are well and fine, but the bills have to get paid. And many workers are worried about their bottom line.

The power balance between employer and employee has shifted. Now, workers experience a shorter week without commensurate economic gains. Perhaps this shift represents a real lessening of the value of the employee *vis a vis* the technologies being innovated to support that employee. Perhaps, we are reaching the tipping point where soon many of those employees will not be needed at all.

Whether or not this proposition is true, it appears many workers believe it to be true and hence the angst that manifested among many this recent presidential election.

If people are working less, what are they doing with the rest of their time?

Some people are retooling—going back to school to become or stay current with technological change. Some people are using the time for leisure activities. And some people are finding new ways to make money in the social economy. Consider Uber, and Lyft, Airbnb, and eBay as examples of new forms of social commerce that empower an individual with little capital resources, but moderate time resources to become an entrepreneur. More

of this could occur and empower the populace to more control over their own time and their own financial security.

That is a vision of a rosy, almost utopian, future. There also exists a dystopian vision to consider.

Uber is public and clear that their long-term plans do not include human drivers. Already, much of the management function (matchmaking drivers and riders) is handled by software algorithm. Uber has invested heavily in self-driving cars and hopes to convert its fleet over as that technology matures—which looks to happen well within the next decade. Uber is not alone: Apple, Google, Tesla, and many of the traditional automobile manufacturers have self-driving cars under development. And, Otto, a startup led by engineers out of Apple, Tesla, and Google, is building self-driving semi tractor-trailers that could largely eliminate the need for long-haul truck drivers within a decade.

Robots are already replacing assembly-line workers. Retail stores are installing more and more customer-controlled checkout lanes, lessening the need for checkout clerks. And retail sales continue to shift away from brick and mortar stores toward e-commerce sites such as Amazon, further cutting into the demand for retail workers. E-commerce fulfillment has become more automated with robots filling and packing boxes at large warehouses, shipped to trucks that may be self-driving (or retail drones that fly a package directly to one's doorstep).

If unskilled and semi-skilled jobs are harder to come by, what becomes of the strata of the population who have traditionally filled those jobs? What is their role in a future—automation rich—economy?

Article

Prepared by: Daniel Mittleman, *DePaul University* and
Douglas Druckenmiller, *Western Illinois University*

How Technology Is Destroying Jobs

David Rotman

Learning Outcomes

After reading this article, you will be able to:

- Articulate the arguments both for why technology innovation causes unemployment and why it does not.

- Understand what workplace robots are and how the growth in their use may affect employment today.

Given his calm and reasoned academic demeanor, it is easy to miss just how provocative Erik Brynjolfsson's contention really is. Brynjolfsson, a professor at the MIT Sloan School of Management, and his collaborator and coauthor Andrew McAfee have been arguing for the last year and a half that impressive advances in computer technology—from improved industrial robotics to automated translation services—are largely behind the sluggish employment growth of the last 10 to 15 years. Even more ominous for workers, the MIT academics foresee dismal prospects for many types of jobs as these powerful new technologies are increasingly adopted not only in manufacturing, clerical, and retail work but in professions such as law, financial services, education, and medicine.

That robots, automation, and software can replace people might seem obvious to anyone who's worked in automotive manufacturing or as a travel agent. But Brynjolfsson and McAfee's claim is more troubling and controversial. They believe that rapid technological change has been destroying jobs faster than it is creating them, contributing to the stagnation of median income and the growth of inequality in the United States. And, they suspect, something similar is happening in other technologically advanced countries.

Perhaps the most damning piece of evidence, according to Brynjolfsson, is a chart that only an economist could love. In economics, productivity—the amount of economic value created for a given unit of input, such as an hour of labor—is a crucial indicator of growth and wealth creation. It is a measure of progress. On the chart Brynjolfsson likes to show, separate lines represent productivity and total employment in the United States. For years after World War II, the two lines closely tracked each other, with increases in jobs corresponding to increases in productivity. The pattern is clear: as businesses generated more value from their workers, the country as a whole became richer, which fueled more economic activity and created even more jobs. Then, beginning in 2000, the lines diverge; productivity continues to rise robustly, but employment suddenly wilts. By 2011, a significant gap appears between the two lines, showing economic growth with no parallel increase in job creation. Brynjolfsson and McAfee call it the "great decoupling." And Brynjolfsson says he is confident that technology is behind both the healthy growth in productivity and the weak growth in jobs.

It's a startling assertion because it threatens the faith that many economists place in technological progress. Brynjolfsson and McAfee still believe that technology boosts productivity and makes societies wealthier, but they think that it can also have a dark side: technological progress is eliminating the need for many types of jobs and leaving the typical worker worse off than before. Brynjolfsson can point to a second chart indicating that median income is failing to rise even as the gross domestic product soars. "It's the great paradox of our era," he says. "Productivity is at record levels, innovation has never been faster, and yet at the same time, we have a falling median income and we have fewer jobs. People are falling behind because technology is advancing so fast and our skills and organizations aren't keeping up."

Brynjolfsson and McAfee are not Luddites. Indeed, they are sometimes accused of being too optimistic about the extent and speed of recent digital advances. Brynjolfsson says they began writing *Race Against the Machine,* the 2011 book in which they laid out much of their argument, because they wanted to explain the economic benefits of these new technologies (Brynjolfsson spent much of the 1990s sniffing out evidence that information technology was boosting rates of productivity). But it became clear to them that the same technologies making many jobs safer, easier, and more productive were also reducing the demand for many types of human workers.

Anecdotal evidence that digital technologies threaten jobs is, of course, everywhere. Robots and advanced automation have been common in many types of manufacturing for decades. In the United States and China, the world's manufacturing powerhouses, fewer people work in manufacturing today than in 1997, thanks at least in part to automation. Modern automotive plants, many of which were transformed by industrial robotics in the 1980s, routinely use machines that autonomously weld and paint body parts—tasks that were once handled by humans. Most recently, industrial robots like Rethink Robotics' Baxter more flexible and far cheaper than their predecessors, have been introduced to perform simple jobs for small manufacturers in a variety of sectors. The website of a Silicon Valley startup called Industrial Perception features a video of the robot it has designed for use in warehouses picking up and throwing boxes like a bored elephant. And such sensations as Google's driverless car suggest what automation might be able to accomplish someday soon.

A less dramatic change, but one with a potentially far larger impact on employment, is taking place in clerical work and professional services. Technologies like the Web, artificial intelligence, big data, and improved analytics—all made possible by the ever increasing availability of cheap computing power and storage capacity—are automating many routine tasks. Countless traditional white-collar jobs, such as many in the post office and in customer service, have disappeared. W. Brian Arthur, a visiting researcher at the Xerox Palo Alto Research Center's intelligence systems lab and a former economics professor at Stanford University, calls it the "autonomous economy." It's far more subtle than the idea of robots and automation doing human jobs, he says: it involves "digital processes talking to other digital processes and creating new processes," enabling us to do many things with fewer people and making yet other human jobs obsolete.

It is this onslaught of digital processes, says Arthur, that primarily explains how productivity has grown without a significant increase in human labor. And, he says, "digital versions of human intelligence" are increasingly replacing even those jobs once thought to require people. "It will change every profession in ways we have barely seen yet," he warns.

McAfee, associate director of the MIT Center for Digital Business at the Sloan School of Management, speaks rapidly and with a certain awe as he describes advances such as Google's driverless car. Still, despite his obvious enthusiasm for the technologies, he doesn't see the recently vanished jobs coming back. The pressure on employment and the resulting inequality will only get worse, he suggests, as digital technologies—fueled with "enough computing power, data, and geeks"—continue their exponential advances over the next several decades. "I would like to be wrong," he says, "but when all these science-fiction technologies are deployed, what will we need all the people for?"

New Economy?

But are these new technologies really responsible for a decade of lackluster job growth? Many labor economists say the data are, at best, far from conclusive. Several other plausible explanations, including events related to global trade and the financial crises of the early and late 2000s, could account for the relative slowness of job creation since the turn of the century. "No one really knows," says Richard Freeman, a labor economist at Harvard University. That's because it's very difficult to "extricate" the effects of technology from other macroeconomic effects, he says. But he's skeptical that technology would change a wide range of business sectors fast enough to explain recent job numbers.

Employment trends have polarized the workforce and hollowed out the middle class.

David Autor, an economist at MIT who has extensively studied the connections between jobs and technology, also doubts that technology could account for such an abrupt change in total employment. "There was a great sag in employment beginning in 2000. Something did change," he says. "But no one knows the cause." Moreover, he doubts that productivity has, in fact, risen robustly in the United States in the past decade (economists can disagree about that statistic because there are different ways of measuring and weighing economic inputs and outputs). If he's right, it raises the possibility that poor job growth could be simply a result of a sluggish economy. The sudden slowdown in job creation "is a big puzzle," he says, "but there's not a lot of evidence it's linked to computers."

To be sure, Autor says, computer technologies are changing the types of jobs available, and those changes "are not always for the good." At least since the 1980s, he says, computers have increasingly taken over such tasks as bookkeeping, clerical work, and repetitive production jobs in manufacturing—all of which typically provided middle-class pay. At the same time, higher-paying jobs requiring creativity and problem-solving skills, often aided by computers, have proliferated. So have low-skill jobs: demand has increased for restaurant workers, janitors, home health aides, and others doing service work that is nearly impossible to automate. The result, says Autor, has been a "polarization" of the workforce and a "hollowing out" of the middle class—something that has been happening in numerous industrialized countries for the last several decades. But "that is very different from saying technology is affecting the total number of jobs," he adds. "Jobs can change a lot without there being huge changes in employment rates."

What's more, even if today's digital technologies are holding down job creation, history suggests that it is most likely a temporary, albeit painful, shock; as workers adjust their skills and entrepreneurs create opportunities based on the new technologies, the number of jobs will rebound. That, at least, has always been the pattern. The question, then, is whether today's computing technologies will be different, creating long-term involuntary unemployment.

At least since the Industrial Revolution began in the 1700s, improvements in technology have changed the nature of work and destroyed some types of jobs in the process. In 1900, 41 percent of Americans worked in agriculture; by 2000, it was only 2 percent. Likewise, the proportion of Americans employed in manufacturing has dropped from 30 percent in the post-World War II years to around 10 percent today—partly because of increasing automation, especially during the 1980s.

While such changes can be painful for workers whose skills no longer match the needs of employers, Lawrence Katz, a Harvard economist, says that no historical pattern shows these shifts leading to a net decrease in jobs over an extended period. Katz has done extensive research on how technological advances have affected jobs over the last few centuries—describing, for example, how highly skilled artisans in the mid-19th century were displaced by lower-skilled workers in factories. While it can take decades for workers to acquire the expertise needed for new types of employment, he says, "we never have run out of jobs. There is no long-term trend of eliminating work for people. Over the long term, employment rates are fairly stable. People have always been able to create new jobs. People come up with new things to do."

Still, Katz doesn't dismiss the notion that there is something different about today's digital technologies—something that could affect an even broader range of work. The question, he says, is whether economic history will serve as a useful guide. Will the job disruptions caused by technology be temporary as the workforce adapts, or will we see a science-fiction scenario in which automated processes and robots with superhuman skills take over a broad swath of human tasks? Though Katz expects the historical pattern to hold, it is "genuinely a question," he says. "If technology disrupts enough, who knows what will happen?"

Dr. Watson

To get some insight into Katz's question, it is worth looking at how today's most advanced technologies are being deployed in industry. Though these technologies have undoubtedly taken over some human jobs, finding evidence of workers being displaced by machines on a large scale is not all that easy. One reason it is difficult to pinpoint the net impact on jobs is that automation is often used to make human workers more efficient, not necessarily to replace them. Rising productivity means businesses can do the same work with fewer employees, but it can also enable the businesses to expand production with their existing workers, and even to enter new markets.

Take the bright-orange Kiva robot, a boon to fledgling e-commerce companies. Created and sold by Kiva Systems, a startup that was founded in 2002 and bought by Amazon for $775 million in 2012, the robots are designed to scurry across large warehouses, fetching racks of ordered goods and delivering the products to humans who package the orders. In Kiva's large demonstration warehouse and assembly facility at its headquarters outside Boston, fleets of robots move about with seemingly endless energy: some newly assembled machines perform tests to prove they're ready to be shipped to customers around the world, while others wait to demonstrate to a visitor how they can almost instantly respond to an electronic order and bring the desired product to a worker's station.

A warehouse equipped with Kiva robots can handle up to four times as many orders as a similar unautomated warehouse, where workers might spend as much as 70 percent of their time walking about to retrieve goods. (Coincidentally or not, Amazon bought Kiva soon after a press report revealed that workers at one of the retailer's giant warehouses often walked more than 10 miles a day.)

Despite the labor-saving potential of the robots, Mick Mountz, Kiva's founder and CEO, says he doubts the machines have put many people out of work or will do so in the future. For one thing, he says, most of Kiva's customers are e-commerce retailers, some of them growing so rapidly they can't hire people fast enough. By making distribution operations cheaper and more efficient, the robotic technology has helped many of these retailers survive and even expand. Before founding Kiva, Mountz worked at Webvan, an online grocery delivery company that was one of the 1990s dot-com era's most infamous flameouts. He likes to show the numbers demonstrating that Webvan was doomed from the start; a $100 order cost the company $120 to ship. Mountz's point is clear: something as mundane as the cost of materials handling can consign a new business to an early death. Automation can solve that problem.

Meanwhile, Kiva itself is hiring. Orange balloons—the same color as the robots—hover over multiple cubicles in its sprawling office, signaling that the occupants arrived within the last month. Most of these new employees are software engineers: while the robots are the company's poster boys, its lesser-known innovations lie in the complex algorithms that guide the robots' movements and determine where in the warehouse products are stored. These algorithms help make the system adaptable. It can learn, for example, that a certain product is seldom ordered, so it should be stored in a remote area.

Though advances like these suggest how some aspects of work could be subject to automation, they also illustrate that humans still excel at certain tasks—for example, packaging various items together. Many of the traditional problems in robotics—such as how to teach a machine to recognize an object as, say, a chair—remain largely intractable and are especially difficult to solve when the robots are free to move about a relatively unstructured environment like a factory or office.

Techniques using vast amounts of computational power have gone a long way toward helping robots understand their surroundings, but John Leonard, a professor of engineering at MIT and a member of its Computer Science and Artificial Intelligence Laboratory (CSAIL), says many familiar difficulties remain. "Part of me sees accelerating progress; the other part of me sees the same old problems," he says. "I see how hard it is to do anything with robots. The big challenge is uncertainty." In other words, people are still far better at dealing with changes in their environment and reacting to unexpected events.

For that reason, Leonard says, it is easier to see how robots could work *with* humans than on their own in many applications. "People and robots working together can happen much more quickly than robots simply replacing humans," he says. "That's not going to happen in my lifetime at a massive scale. The semiautonomous taxi will still have a driver."

One of the friendlier, more flexible robots meant to work with humans is Rethinks Baxter. The creation of Rodney Brooks, the company's founder, Baxter needs minimal training to perform simple tasks like picking up objects and moving them to a box. It's meant for use in relatively small manufacturing facilities where conventional industrial robots would cost too much and pose too much danger to workers. The idea, says Brooks, is to have the robots take care of dull, repetitive jobs that no one wants to do.

It's hard not to instantly like Baxter, in part because it seems so eager to please. The "eyebrows" on its display rise quizzically when it's puzzled; its arms submissively and gently retreat when bumped. Asked about the claim that such advanced industrial robots could eliminate jobs, Brooks answers simply that he doesn't see it that way. Robots, he says, can be to factory workers as electric drills are to construction workers: "It makes them more productive and efficient, but it doesn't take jobs."

The machines created at Kiva and Rethink have been cleverly designed and built to work with people, taking over the tasks that the humans often don't want to do or aren't especially good at. They are specifically designed to enhance these workers' productivity. And it's hard to see how even these increasingly sophisticated robots will replace humans in most manufacturing and industrial jobs anytime soon. But clerical and some professional jobs could be more vulnerable. That's because the marriage of artificial intelligence and big data is beginning to give machines a more humanlike ability to reason and to solve many new types of problems.

Even if the economy is only going through a transition, it is an extremely painful one for many.

In the tony northern suburbs of New York City, IBM Research is pushing super-smart computing into the realms of such professions as medicine, finance, and customer service. IBM's efforts have resulted in Watson, a computer system best known for beating human champions on the game show *Jeopardy!* in 2011. That version of Watson now sits in a corner of a large data center at the research facility in Yorktown Heights, marked with a glowing plaque commemorating its glory days. Meanwhile, researchers there are already testing new generations of Watson in medicine, where the technology could help physicians diagnose diseases like cancer, evaluate patients, and prescribe treatments.

IBM likes to call it cognitive computing. Essentially, Watson uses artificial-intelligence techniques, advanced natural-language processing and analytics, and massive amounts of data drawn from sources specific to a given application (in the case of health care, that means medical journals, textbooks, and information collected from the physicians or hospitals using the system). Thanks to these innovative techniques and huge amounts of computing power, it can quickly come up with "advice"—for example, the most recent and relevant information to guide a doctor's diagnosis and treatment decisions.

Despite the system's remarkable ability to make sense of all that data, it's still early days for Dr. Watson. While it has rudimentary abilities to "learn" from specific patterns and evaluate different possibilities, it is far from having the type of judgment and intuition a physician often needs. But IBM has also announced it will begin selling Watson's services to customer-support call centers, which rarely require human judgment that's quite so sophisticated. IBM says companies will rent an updated version of Watson for use as a "customer service agent" that responds to questions from consumers; it has already signed on several banks. Automation is nothing new in call centers, of course, but Watson's improved capacity for natural-language processing and its ability to tap into a large amount of data suggest that this system could speak plainly with callers, offering them specific advice on even technical and complex questions. It's easy to see it replacing many human holdouts in its new field.

Digital Losers

The contention that automation and digital technologies are partly responsible for today's lack of jobs has obviously touched a raw nerve for many worried about their own employment. But this is only one consequence of what Brynjolfsson and McAfee see as a broader trend. The rapid acceleration of technological progress, they say, has greatly widened the gap between economic winners and losers—the income inequalities that many economists have worried about for decades. Digital technologies tend to favor "superstars," they point out. For example, someone who creates a computer program to automate tax preparation might earn millions or billions of dollars while eliminating the need for countless accountants.

New technologies are "encroaching into human skills in a way that is completely unprecedented," McAfee says, and many middle-class jobs are right in the bull's-eye; even relatively high-skill work in education, medicine, and law is affected. "The middle seems to be going away," he adds. "The top and bottom are clearly getting farther apart." While technology might be only one factor, says McAfee, it has been an "underappreciated" one, and it is likely to become increasingly significant.

Not everyone agrees with Brynjolfsson and McAfee's conclusions—particularly the contention that the impact of recent technological change could be different from anything seen before. But it's hard to ignore their warning that technology is widening the income gap between the tech-savy and everyone else. And even if the economy is only going through a transition similar to those it's endured before, it is an extremely painful one for many workers, and that will have to be addressed somehow. Harvard's Katz has shown that the United States prospered in the early 1900s in part because secondary education became accessible to many people at a time when employment in agriculture was drying up. The result, at least through the 1980s, was an increase in educated workers who found jobs in the industrial sectors, boosting incomes and reducing inequality. Katz's lesson: painful long-term consequences for the labor force do not follow inevitably from technological changes.

Brynjolfsson himself says he's not ready to conclude that economic progress and employment have diverged for good. "I don't know whether we can recover, but I hope we can," he says. But that, he suggests, will depend on recognizing the problem and taking steps such as investing more in the training and education of workers.

"We were lucky and steadily rising productivity raised all boats for much of the 20th century," he says. "Many people, especially economists, jumped to the conclusion that was just the way the world worked. I used to say that if we took care of productivity, everything else would take care of itself; it was the single most important economic statistic. But that's no longer true." He adds, "It's one of the dirty secrets of economics: technology progress does grow the economy and create wealth, but there is no economic law that says everyone will benefit." In other words, in the race against the machine, some are likely to win while many others lose.

Critical Thinking

1. Define productivity and explain why when technology innovation makes one employee more productive it does not automatically cost other employees their jobs.
2. Brynjolfsson demonstrates that something new happened around 2001 so that increased productivity no longer led to a growth in the number of jobs. Generate at least three independent hypotheses as to why there appeared a sudden change in this relationship at that point in time.

Internet References

Andrew McAfee: Are Droids Taking Our Jobs?
    www.ted.com/talks/andrew_mcafee_are_droids_taking_our_jobs.html
Robots at Work: Toward a Smarter Factory
    www.wfs.org/futurist/2013-issues-futurist/may-june-2013-vol-47-no-3/robots-work-toward-smarter-factory
Should We Fear "The End of Work"?
    www.pbs.org/newshour/businessdesk/2013/07/should-we-fear-the-end-of-work.html

Article   Prepared by: Daniel Mittleman, *DePaul University* and
                                    Douglas Druckenmiller, *Western Illinois University*

How Artificial Intelligence and Robots Will Radically Transform the Economy

KEVIN MANEY

Learning Outcomes

After reading this article, you will be able to:

- Discuss both the opportunities and threats AI affords us.

- Discuss how new technology replaces one set of jobs with another set of jobs, and provide examples of when this has happened.

- Articulate how new technologies instill fear in segments of society and how that fear manifests.

Next time you stop for gas at a self-serve pump, say hello to the robot in front of you. Its life story can tell you a lot about the robot economy roaring toward us like an EF5 tornado on the prairie.

Yeah, your automated gas pump killed a lot of jobs over the years, but its biography might give you hope that the coming wave of automation driven by artificial intelligence (AI) will turn out better for almost all of us than a lot of people seem to think.

The first crude version of an automated gas-delivering robot appeared in 1964 at a station in Westminster, Colorado. Short Stop convenience store owner John Roscoe bought an electric box that let a clerk inside activate any of the pumps outside. Self-serve pumps didn't catch on until the 1970s, when pump-makers added automation that let customers pay at the pump, and over the next 30 years, stations across the nation installed these task-specific robots and fired attendants. By the 2000s, the gas attendant job had all but disappeared. (Two states, New Jersey and Oregon, protect full-service gas by law.)

That's hundreds of thousands of jobs vaporized—there are now 168,000 gas stations in the United States. The loss of those jobs was undoubtedly devastating for the individuals who had

them, but the broader impact has been pretty positive for the rest of us.

As has happened throughout the history of automation, some jobs got destroyed by automated gas pumps, but new and often better jobs were created. Attendants went away, but to make the sophisticated pumps, companies like Wayne Fueling Systems in Texas, Bennett Pump Co. in Michigan and Gilbarco Veeder-Root in North Carolina hired software coders, engineers, sales staff, and project managers. Station owners took their extra profits and turned their stations into mini-marts, which needed clerks, and built more gas stations, which needed more pumps from Wayne, Bennett or Gilbarco, and those companies then hired more people.

Consumers spent less money on gas because they weren't paying for someone else to pump it. That left them more money for iPhones or fish tacos ordered on Seamless, creating more new kinds of employment.

A generation of gas station attendants got smoked, but the automation sent some clear signals that relying on such unskilled jobs isn't a great career plan. Those signals led to more parents encouraging their kids to go to college. In 1970, 14 percent of men held four-year college degrees, and 8 percent of women did. By 2015, that was up to 32 percent of men and women. So over time, we took hundreds of thousands of people out of the pool of those who might want a gas station attendant job and pushed them up, toward the professional job market, adding a lot of value to society and their wallets. While technology is partly responsible for years of middle-class wage stagnation, it has mostly hurt the less educated and helped the more educated.

Economists have shown time and again that automation helps overall standards of living rise, literacy rates improve, average life span lengthen and crime rates fall. After waves of automation—the Industrial Revolution, mechanization, computerization—we're way better off in almost every way. As Matt Ridley details in his book *The Rational Optimist*, in 1900, the average American spent $76 out of every $100 on food, clothing and shelter; today, he or she spends $37. To buy a Model T in 1908 took about 4,700 hours of work; today, the average person has to work about 1,000 hours to buy a car that's a thousand times better than a Model T. The United Nations estimates that poverty was reduced more in the past 50 years than in the previous 500. If progress has been less kind to the lower end of the workforce, it still helps that segment live better than before, at least by making products more affordable and better at the same time.

And now, even with software automating all kinds of work, there are signs that the technology is creating more jobs than it destroys. U.S. census data released in September showed the largest annual drop in poverty since 1999. Nearly 3 million jobs were created from 2014 to 2015. Donald Trump won the presidential election by promising to bring jobs "back" to America—a promise believed by many who feel left behind by technology-driven shifts. Yet all evidence suggests that the jobs lie ahead, created by moving forward.

It's hard to see how anyone could argue that we'd be better off today if Roscoe had never installed his automated device.

Rage and Impotence

This is the scary part of the story.

The world's top tech companies are in a race to build the best AI and capture that massive market, which means the technology will get better fast—and come at us as fast. IBM is investing $1 billion in its Watson; Amazon is banking on Alexa; Apple has Siri. Google, Facebook, and Microsoft are devoting their research labs to AI and robotics. In September, Salesforce. com announced its adding AI, called Einstein, to its business software. Its value, CEO Marc Benioff said at the launch, will be in "helping people do the things that people are good at and turning more things over to machines."

AI will lead us into the mother of all tech revolutions. The last time anything came close was around 1900, when the automobile, telecommunications, the airplane, and mass electrification all came together at once, radically changing the world from the late 1800s to the 1920s. Such times are particularly frightening. "A society that had established countless routines and habits, norms and regulations, to fit the conditions of the previous revolution, does not find it easy to assimilate the new one," wrote economist Carlota Perez in *Technological Revolutions and Financial Capital*, her classic book. "A sense of impotence and frustration accumulates and a growing incongruence is experienced between the new and the old paradigm."

That's what we're feeling today as a panoply of powerful technologies come crashing together. AI is the most important, the "ur-force," as tech philosopher Kevin Kelly calls it. Emerging right along with AI are robotics, virtual reality, blockchain, 3-D printing and other wonders. Each would be huge by itself. Together, they will swirl into that roaring EF5 tornado, blowing down the industries and institutions in its path.

We've networked the entire world, put computing devices in the hands of 3 billion individuals, and created the largest pool in history of educated people working in economies that encourage innovation. Over the past decade, we've built a global computing cloud and moved our shopping, friendships, work, entertainment, and much else about life online. In this hyperconnected global market, waves of automation can get invented and deployed warp-speed faster than at any time before.

The speed will be difficult to handle. New inventions usually permeate society only when people are ready for them. In research my coauthors and I did for our book *Play Bigger*, we found that the ideal time for a tech startup to go public is when it is between 6 and 10 years old. After searching for a reason, we concluded that even in today's whiz-bang tech environment, it takes at least six years for a strange new business idea (think streaming music in 2006, when Spotify was founded) to catch fire. Most people's brains can't adjust any faster.

Today's AI-driven revolution is coming so fast that we have trouble even imagining how it will turn out. Jeff Hawkins, founder of AI and brain research company Numenta (and inventor of the Palm Pilot), tells me that AI today is at a point similar to computing in the early 1950s, when pioneers first laid down the basic ideas of electronic computers. Less than 20 years later, computers made possible airline reservation systems and bank ATMs and helped NASA put men on the moon—outcomes no one could have foreseen from the early '50s. Guessing the impact of AI and robots in a decade or two is proving even harder.

"Twenty years from now, this technology will be one of the major drivers of innovation and technology, if not the major one," Hawkins says. "But you want specific predictions? It's impossible."

The Unemployment Line Starts Here

Truck driver is the most common job in the world—3.5 million of them in the United States alone. Over the summer, the Dutch government ran a successful test of driverless trucks crossing Europe. Uber recently paid $680 million to buy Otto, a startup working on auto-drive trucks and founded by former Google AI specialists. Consulting company McKinsey has predicted that within eight years, one-third of all trucks on the road will drive themselves. In maybe 15 years, *truck driver* will, like *gas station attendant*, be an anachronism.

Uber invested in Otto not just to operate trucks but because Uber wants to run fleets of self-driving cars. In September, it began testing such a fleet in Pittsburgh. Canada's postal service wants to send drones instead of vans to deliver rural mail. Millions of driver jobs of all kinds could swirl down AI's drain before Trump finishes his four-year term.

Within maybe five years, AI will be better than humans at diagnosing medical images and better than legal assistants at researching case law, Surya Ganguli, a leading AI scientist at Stanford University, tells me. Hawkins says we will eventually make machines that are great mathematicians. "Mathematicians try to figure out proofs and mathematical structure and see elegance in high-dimensional spaces in their heads," he says. "That's not a 'human' thing. You can build an intelligent machine that is designed for that. It actually lives in a mathematical space, and its native behaviors are mathematical behaviors. And it can run a million times faster than a human and never get tired. It can be designed to be a brilliant mathematician."

If you do something predictable and rote, then sometime in the next 10 years you'll probably feel like a gas pump jockey, circa 1980. One by one, companies will eliminate or marginalize your work. It will happen to the least educated first and fastest, hitting drivers, waiters, factory workers and office administrators.

Then the robotization of work will eat into more knowledge-based jobs. Low-level accounting will get eaten by software. So will basic writing: Bloomberg already uses AI to write company earnings reports. Robots today can be better stock traders than humans. It won't be long before you'll be able to contact an AI doctor via your smartphone, talk to it about your symptoms, use your camera to show it anything it wants to see and get a triage diagnosis that tells you to either take a couple of Advil or get to a specialist.

Versions of AI have been around for decades. Google's search engine is so accurate because it is built on AI and learns from billions of searches. AI is how Facebook directs items you most likely want to see to your news feed. But for AI to be powerful enough to drive a truck or diagnose patients, it needs a few things that are just now exploding onto the scene. One is enormous amounts of data. Now that we do so many things online, every action gets recorded and stored, adding valuable data that can fuel AI. The Internet of Things is putting sensors on people, in cars, in nature. To analyze that data and feed it into AI software takes enormous computing power, which has now become available and affordable to even a tiny garage startup through cloud companies like Amazon Web Services.

Put it all together, and we'll soon be at a point when AI can get built to do almost anything, including, possibly, your job.

That realization has set off a panic that is going viral faster than the latest Kim Kardashian butt photo. A research paper from Oxford University proclaimed that machines will take over nearly half of all work done by humans. Some technologists have said 90 percent of the population will end up out of work. There are smart, seemingly rational people who believe the United States should institute a "guaranteed basic income" so that the masses who won't be able to find work can avoid depredation. In September, to help soothe the public and forestall intervention from government, most of the giants in AI formed a group called the Partnership on AI. "We passionately believe in the potential for [AI] to transform in a positive way our world," Google's Mustafa Suleyman said, Yoda-like, at the time.

"The concern is not that robots will take human jobs and render humans unemployable," Jason Furman, chairman of the Council of Economic Advisers, said in a recent talk. The worry is that the speed of AI's encroachment on jobs "could lead to sustained periods of time with a large fraction of people not working."

President Barack Obama recently weighed in about AI. "If properly harnessed, it can generate enormous prosperity and opportunity," he said as guest editor of Wired. "But it also has some downsides that we're gonna have to figure out in terms of not eliminating jobs. It could increase inequality. It could suppress wages."

In the long run, we'll find equilibrium. But the transition in the short term will suck for a lot of people you know. And maybe for you.

How I Learned to Stop Worrying and Love AI

And yet, there's a happily ever after in here. Somewhere.

I talked recently with Ryan Detert, who started a company called Influential, which is built on AI from IBM's Watson. The AI scours social media to find "influencers" who have a large number of followers and analyzes the online personality of those individuals. Then the company can work with brands—Kia and Corona are among its clients—to find influencers who match the traits of their target audiences. The brands then pay the influencers to tout the products. This is creating an entirely new job of brand influencer, not to mention new kinds of jobs at Influential and companies like it.

Over and over again, the robot economy will invent work we can't even dream of today, much as the Internet gave birth to unforeseen careers. Nobody's grandmother was a search engine optimization specialist. Today, that job pays pretty well.

Along the way, AI will also help people learn how to prosper in the age of AI. Sal Khan started Khan Academy by developing online tutorial videos for math and science students. In its next phase, the organization is deploying AI in its lessons. The AI gets to know the student and understand how the person is learning so it can go over old material or add more challenging stuff. Khan's vision includes helping masses of people continually learn new skills that will make them more relevant in fast-changing job markets.

AI will be better than anything today at helping you find whatever new jobs it creates. AI will power software that gets to know you, your skills and your desires and will constantly monitor job openings and freelance opportunities all over the planet for you. The U.S. Department of Labor says there are about 8 million unemployed people and 4.5 million open jobs. An AI matching system can bring those numbers down dramatically by making sure more people find work.

Successful people in the AI age will focus on work that takes advantage of unique human strengths, like social interaction, creative thinking, decision-making with complex inputs, empathy and questioning. AI cannot think about data it doesn't have. It predicts what you want to see on Facebook based on what you've already liked. It can't predict that you might like something that's entirely different. Only humans can think that way. As Kelly says, the most valuable people in an age of push-button answers will be the people who ask the most interesting questions.

AI's proponents say it will collaborate with us, not compete against us. AI software in a conference room could listen to the conversation in a business meeting while constantly searching the internet for information that might be relevant, then serve it up when asked. "It can bring in knowledge of the outside world that the humans might not be aware of," says Ganguli, and that means the humans can make better decisions.

About a year ago, I saw cancer researcher M. Soledad Cepeda give a talk about AI in her work. She said AI software can analyze in two seconds the amount of data and text that a research assistant would need two weeks to plow through. That frees up the assistants to do more thoughtful work and speeds up the scientists' search for cures.

In that way, by acting as our collaborator, AI will give us a chance at cracking our most pressing problems. It promises to help us end cancer, ease climate change, manage bursting cities and get our species to Mars. Of course, we don't know if we'll succeed at any of that, but one certainty is that we can't do it without AI. So if you're still standing at that gas pump filling your tank, here's what the robot, based on its decades of experience, will tell you about the new robot economy: The one thing worse for the human race than developing AI would be stopping the development of AI.

If this is a fairy tale about work and jobs, AI is both the bad witch and good witch—destroyer and creator. In such stories, good almost always wins. But in the middle of the story, the characters don't know that. And that's where we are now: face to face with the monster for the first time, doing everything we can to get through the scary forest alive.

Critical Thinking

1. Apply Postman's five ideas to the self-serve gas pump. Winners and losers are spelled out in the article, but how do the other ideas inform this technology change?

2. Author Maney suggests the job of truck driver is going the way of the gas station attendant. Do you agree? If it does, apply Postman's five ideas to the technology of self-driving trucks to predict the wider societal impacts of this new technology.

3. Carlota Perez wrote about the "sense of impotence and frustration" that is experienced during periods of [fast] [overwhelming] [multi] technological change. What specific pushbacks are we experiencing today as we [travel along] the current technology surge?

Internet References

Chill: Robots Won't Take All Our Jobs
https://www.wired.com/2017/08/robots-will-not-take-your-job/

Robots and AI Are Going to Make Social Inequality Even Worse, Says New Report.
https://www.theverge.com/2017/7/13/15963710/robots-ai-inequality-social-mobility-study

Robots Stealing Human Jobs Isn't the Problem. This Is.
https://www.usatoday.com/story/money/2017/06/29/ai-stealing-human-jobs-isnt-problem-is/412217001/

KEVIN MANEY is a best-selling author, award-winning columnist, and musician still waiting for his big break.

Article

Prepared by: Daniel Mittleman, *DePaul University* and
Douglas Druckenmiller, *Western Illinois University*

Cognitive Collaboration: Why Humans and Computers Think Better Together

Jim Guszcza, Harvey Lewis, and Peter Evans-Greenwood

Learning Outcomes

After reading this article, you will be able to:

- Define "intelligence augmentation" and provide examples of its use.

- Understand differences between general intelligence and narrow intelligence.

- Understand what abilities AI and humans each bring toward solving complex problems.

A Science of the Artificial

Although artificial intelligence (AI) has experienced a number of "springs" and "winters" in its roughly 60-year history, it is safe to expect the current AI spring to be both lasting and fertile. Applications that seemed like science fiction a decade ago are becoming science fact at a pace that has surprised even many experts.

The stage for the current AI revival was set in 2011 with the televised triumph of the IBM Watson computer system over former *Jeopardy*! game show champions Ken Jennings and Brad Rutter. This watershed moment has been followed rapid-fire by a sequence of striking breakthroughs, many involving the machine learning technique known as *deep learning*. Computer algorithms now beat humans at games of skill, master video games with no prior instruction, 3D-print original paintings in the style of Rembrandt, grade student papers, cook meals, vacuum floors, and drive cars.[1]

All of this has created considerable uncertainty about our future relationship with machines, the prospect of technological unemployment, and even the very fate of humanity. Regarding the latter topic, Elon Musk has described AI "our biggest existential threat." Stephen Hawking warned that "The development of full artificial intelligence could spell the end of the human race." In his widely discussed book *Superintelligence*, the philosopher Nick Bostrom discusses the possibility of a kind of technological "singularity" at which point the general cognitive abilities of computers exceed those of humans.[2]

Discussions of these issues are often muddied by the tacit assumption that, because computers outperform humans at various circumscribed tasks, they will soon be able to "outthink" us more generally. Continual rapid growth in computing power and AI breakthroughs notwithstanding, this premise is far from obvious.

Furthermore, the assumption distracts attention from a less speculative topic in need of deeper attention than it typically receives: the ways in which machine intelligence and human intelligence *complement* one another. AI has made a dramatic comeback in the past five years. We believe that another, equally venerable, concept is long overdue for a comeback of its own: *intelligence augmentation*. With intelligence augmentation, the ultimate goal is not building machines that think like humans, but designing machines that help humans think better.

The History of the Future of AI

Any sufficiently advanced technology is indistinguishable from magic.

—Arthur C. Clarke's Third Law[3]

AI as a scientific discipline is commonly agreed to date back to a conference held at Dartmouth University in the summer of 1955. The conference was convened by John McCarthy, who coined the term "artificial intelligence," defining it as the science of creating machines "with the ability to achieve goals in the world."[4] The Dartmouth Conference was attended by a who's who of AI pioneers, including Claude Shannon, Alan Newell, Herbert Simon, and Marvin Minsky.

Interestingly, Minsky later served as an adviser to Stanley Kubrick's adaptation of the Arthur C. Clarke novel *2001: A Space Odyssey*. Perhaps that movie's most memorable character was HAL 9000: a computer that spoke fluent English, used commonsense reasoning, experienced jealousy, and tried to escape termination by doing away with the ship's crew. In short, HAL was a computer that implemented a very general form of human intelligence.

The attendees of the Dartmouth Conference believed that, by 2001, computers would implement an artificial form of human intelligence. Their original proposal stated:

The study is to proceed on the basis of the conjecture that *every aspect of learning or any other feature of intelligence* can in principle be so precisely described that a machine can be made to simulate it. An attempt will be made to find how to make machines use language, form abstractions and concepts, solve kinds of problems now reserved for humans, and improve themselves [emphasis added].[5]

As is clear from widespread media speculation about a "technological singularity," this original vision of AI is still very much with us today. For example, a *Financial Times* profile of DeepMind CEO Demis Hassabis stated that:

At DeepMind, engineers have created programs based on neural networks, modelled on the human brain. These systems make mistakes, but learn and improve over time. They can be set to play other games and solve other tasks, so the intelligence is general, not specific. This AI "thinks" like humans do.[6]

Such statements mislead in at least two ways. First, in contrast with the artificial *general* intelligence envisioned by the Dartmouth Conference participants, the examples of AI on offer—either currently or in the foreseeable future—are all examples of *narrow* artificial intelligence. In human psychology, general intelligence is quantified by the so-called "*g* factor" (aka IQ), which measures the degree to which one type of cognitive ability (say, learning a foreign language) is associated with other cognitive abilities (say, mathematical ability). This is not characteristic of today's AI applications: An algorithm designed to drive a car would be useless at detecting a face in a crowd or guiding a domestic robot assistant.

Second, and more fundamentally, current manifestations of AI have little in common with the AI envisioned at the Dartmouth Conference. While they do manifest a narrow type of "intelligence" in that they can solve problems and achieve goals, this does not involve implementing human psychology

or brain science. Rather, it involves machine learning: the process of fitting highly complex and powerful—but typically uninterpretable—statistical models to massive amounts of data.

For example, AI algorithms can now distinguish between breeds of dogs more accurately than humans can.[7] But this does not involve algorithmically representing such concepts as "pinscher" or "terrier." Rather, deep learning neural network models, containing thousands of uninterpretable parameters, are trained on large numbers of digitized photographs that have already been labeled by humans.[8] In a similar way that a standard regression model can predict a person's income based on various educational, employment, and psychological details, a deep learning model uses a photograph's pixels as input variables to predict such outcomes as "pinscher" or "terrier"—without needing to understand the underlying concepts.

The ambiguity between general and narrow AI—and the evocative nature of terms like "neural," "deep," and "learning"—invites confusion. While neural networks are loosely inspired by a simple model of the human brain, they are better viewed as generalizations of statistical regression models. Similarly, "deep" refers not to psychological depth, but to the addition of structure ("hidden layers" in the vernacular) that enables a model to capture complex, nonlinear patterns. And "learning" refers to numerically estimating large numbers of model parameters, akin to the "β" parameters in regression models. When commentators write that such models "learn from experience and get better," they mean that more data result in more accurate parameter estimates. When they claim that such models "think like humans do," they are mistaken.[9]

In short, the AI that is reshaping our societies and economies is far removed from the vision articulated in 1955 at Dartmouth, or implicit in such cinematic avatars as HAL and Lieutenant Data. Modern AI is founded on computer-age statistical inference—not on an approximation or simulation of what we believe human intelligence to be.[10] The increasing ubiquity of such applications will track the inexorable growth of digital technology. But they will not bring us closer to the original vision articulated at Dartmouth. Appreciating this is crucial for understanding both the promise and the perils of real-world AI.

Licklider's Augmentation

Five years after the Dartmouth Conference, the psychologist and computer scientist J. C. R. Licklider articulated a significantly different vision of the relationship between human and computer intelligence. While the general AI envisioned at Dartmouth remains the stuff of science fiction, Licklider's vision is today's science fact, and provides the most productive way to think about AI going forward.[11]

Rather than speculate about the ability of computers to *implement* human-style intelligence, Licklider believed computers would *complement* human intelligence. He argued that humans and computers would develop a symbiotic relationship, the strengths of one counterbalancing the limitations of the other:

Men will set the goals, formulate the hypotheses, determine the criteria, and perform the evaluations. Computing machines will do the routinizable work that must be done to prepare the way for insights and decisions in technical and scientific thinking. . . . The symbiotic partnership will perform intellectual operations much more effectively than man alone can perform them.[12]

This kind of human–computer symbiosis already permeates daily life. Familiar examples include:

- Planning a trip using GPS apps like Waze
- Using Google Translate to help translate a document
- Navigating massive numbers of book or movie choices using menus of personalized recommendations
- Using Internet search to facilitate the process of researching and writing an article

In each case, the human specifies the goal and criteria (such as "Take me downtown but avoid highways" or "Find me a highly rated and moderately priced sushi bar within walking distance"). An AI algorithm sifts through otherwise unmanageable amounts of data to identify relevant predictions or recommendations. The human then evaluates the computer-generated options to arrive at a decision. In no case is human intelligence mimicked; in each case, it is augmented.

Developments in both psychology and AI subsequent to the Dartmouth Conference suggest that Licklider's vision of human–computer symbiosis is a more productive guide to the future than speculations about "superintelligent" AI. It turns out that the human mind is less computer-like than originally realized, and AI is less human-like than originally hoped.

Linda, *C'est Moi*

AI algorithms enjoy many obvious advantages over the human mind. Indeed, the AI pioneer Herbert Simon is also renowned for his work on bounded rationality: We humans must settle for solutions that "satisfice" rather than optimize because our memory and reasoning ability are limited. In contrast, computers do not get tired; they make consistent decisions before and after lunchtime; they can process decades' worth of legal cases, medical journal articles, or accounting regulations with minimal effort; and they can evaluate five hundred predictive factors

far more accurately than unaided human judgment can evaluate five.

This last point hints at a transformation in our understanding of human psychology, introduced by Daniel Kahneman and Amos Tversky well after the Dartmouth Conference and Licklider's essay. Consider the process of making predictions: Will this job candidate succeed if we hire her? Will this insurance risk be profitable? Will this prisoner recidivate if paroled? Intuitively, it might seem that our thinking approximates statistical models when making such judgments. And indeed, with training and deliberate effort, it can—to a degree. This is what Kahneman calls "System 2" thinking, or "thinking slow."[13]

But it turns out that most of the time we use a very different type of mental process when making judgments and decisions. Rather than laboriously gathering and evaluating the relevant evidence, we typically lean on a variety of mental rules of thumb (heuristics) that yield narratively plausible, but often logically dubious, judgments. Kahneman calls this "System 1," or "thinking fast," which is famously illustrated by the "Linda" experiment. In an experiment with students at top universities, Kahneman and Tversky described a fictional character named Linda: She is very intelligent, majored in philosophy at college, and participated in the feminist movement and anti-nuclear demonstrations. Based on these details about Linda's college days, which is the more plausible scenario involving Linda today?

1. Linda is a bank teller.
2. Linda is a bank teller who is active in the feminist movement.

Kahneman and Tversky reported that 87 percent of the students questioned thought the second scenario more likely, even though a moment's thought reveals that this could not possibly be the case: Feminist bank tellers are a subset of all bank tellers. But adding the detail that Linda is still active in the feminist movement lends narrative coherence, and therefore intuitive plausibility, to the (less likely) second scenario.

Kahneman calls the mind "a machine for jumping to conclusions": We confuse the easily imaginable with the highly probable,[14] let emotions cloud judgments, find patterns in random noise, tell spuriously causal stories about cases of regression to the mean, and overgeneralize from personal experience. Many of the mental heuristics we use to make judgments and decisions turn out to be systematically biased. Dan Ariely's phrase "predictably irrational" describes the mind's systematic tendency to rely on biased mental heuristics.

Such findings help explain a phenomenon first documented by Kahneman's predecessor Paul Meehl in the 1950s and subsequently validated by hundreds of academic studies and industrial applications of the sort dramatized in Michael Lewis's

Moneyball: The predictions of simple algorithms routinely beat those of well-informed human experts in a wide variety of domains. This points to the need for human–computer collaboration in a way that even Licklider himself probably didn't imagine. It turns out that minds need algorithms to de-bias our judgments and decisions as surely as our eyes need artificial lenses to see adequately.

I'm Sorry, Dave. I'm Afraid I Can't Do That.

While it is easy to anthropomorphize self-driving cars, voice-activated personal assistants, and computers capable of beating humans at games of skill, we have seen that such technologies are "intelligent" in essentially the same minimal way that credit scoring or fraud detection algorithms are. This means that they are subject to a fundamental

limitation of data-driven statistical inference: Algorithms are reliable only to the extent that the data used to train them are sufficiently complete and representative of the environment in which they are to be deployed. When this condition is not met, all bets are off.

To illustrate, consider a few examples involving familiar forms of AI:

- During the *Jeopardy!* match with Watson, Jennings, and Rutter, Alex Trebek posed this question under the category "US cities": "Its largest airport is named for a World War II hero; its second largest, for a World War II battle." Watson answered "Toronto."[15]
- One of us used a common machine translating service to translate the recent news headline "Hillary slams the door on Bernie" from English into Bengali, then back again. The result was "Barney slam the door on Clinton."[16]
- In 2014, a group of computer scientists demonstrated that it is possible to "fool" state-of-the-art deep learning algorithms into classifying unrecognizable or white noise images as common objects (such as "peacock" or "baseball") with very high confidence.[17]
- On May 7, 2016, an unattended car in "autopilot" mode drove underneath a tractor-trailer that it did not detect, shearing off the roof of the car and killing the driver.[18]

None of these stories suggest that the algorithms aren't highly useful. Quite the contrary. IBM's Watson did, after all, win *Jeopardy!*; machine translation and image recognition algorithms are enabling new products and services; and even the self-driving car fatality must be weighed against the much larger number of lives likely to be saved by autonomous vehicles.[19]

Rather, these examples illustrate another point that Licklider would have appreciated: Certain strengths of human intelligence can counterbalance the fundamental limitations of brute-force machine learning.

Returning to the above examples:

- Watson, an information retrieval system, would have responded correctly if it had access to, for example, a Wikipedia page listing the above facts about Chicago's two major airports. But it is unable to use commonsense reasoning, as answering "Toronto" to a question about "US cities" illustrates.[20]
- Today's machine translation algorithms cannot reliably extrapolate beyond existing data (including millions of phrase pairs from documents) to translate novel combinations of words, new forms of slang, and so on. In contrast, a basic phenomenon emphasized by Noam Chomsky in linguistics is the ability of young children to acquire language—with its infinite number of possible sentences—based on surprisingly little data.[21]
- A deep learning algorithm must be trained with many thousands of photographs to recognize (for example) kittens—and even then, it has formed no conceptual understanding. In contrast, even small children are actually very good at forming hypotheses and learning from a small number of examples.
- Autonomous vehicles must make do with algorithms that cannot reliably extrapolate beyond the scenarios encoded in their databases. This contrasts with the ability of human drivers to use judgment and common sense in unfamiliar, ambiguous, or dynamically changing situations.

In short, when routine tasks can be encoded in big data, it is a safe bet that algorithms can be built to perform them better than humans can. But such algorithms will lack the conceptual understanding and commonsense reasoning needed to evaluate novel situations. They can make inferences from structured hypotheses but lack the intuition to prioritize which hypothesis to test in the first place. The cognitive scientist Alison Gopnik summarizes the situation this way:

One of the fascinating things about the search for AI is that it's been so hard to predict which parts would be easy or hard. At first, we thought that the quintessential preoccupations of the officially smart few, like playing chess or proving theorems—the corridas of nerd machismo—would prove to be hardest for computers. In fact, they turn out to be easy. Things every dummy can do, like recognizing objects or picking them up, are much harder. And it turns out to be much easier to simulate the reasoning of a highly trained adult expert than to mimic the ordinary learning of every baby.[22]

Just as humans need algorithms to avoid "System 1" decision traps, the inherent limitations of big data imply the need for human judgment to keep mission-critical algorithms in check. Neither of these points were as obvious in Licklider's time as they are today. Together, they imply that the case for human–computer symbiosis is stronger than ever.

Game Over?

Chess provides an excellent example of human–computer collaboration—and a cautionary tale about over-interpreting dramatic examples of computers outperforming humans. In 1997, IBM's Deep Blue beat the chess grandmaster Garry Kasparov. A major news magazine made the event a cover story titled "The brain's last stand." Many observers proclaimed the game to be over.[23]

Eight years later, it became clear that the story is considerably more interesting than "machine vanquishes man." A competition called "freestyle chess" was held, allowing any combination of human and computer chess players to compete. The competition resulted in an upset victory that Kasparov later reflected upon:

The surprise came at the conclusion of the event. The winner was revealed to be not a grandmaster with a state-of-the-art PC but a pair of amateur American chess players using three computers at the same time. Their skill at manipulating and "coaching" their computers to look very deeply into positions effectively counteracted the superior chess understanding of their grandmaster opponents and the greater computational power of other participants. Weak human + machine + better process was superior to a strong computer alone and, more remarkably, superior to a strong human + machine + inferior process. . . . Human strategic guidance combined with the tactical acuity of a computer was overwhelming.[24]

"Freestyle *x*" is a useful way of thinking about human–computer collaboration in a variety of domains. To be sure, some jobs traditionally performed by humans have been and will continue to be displaced by AI algorithms. An early example is the job of bank loan officer, which was largely eliminated after the introduction of credit scoring algorithms. In the future, it is possible that jobs ranging from long-haul truck driver to radiologist could be largely automated.[25] But there are many other cases where variations on "freestyle *x*" are a more plausible scenario than jobs simply being replaced by AI.

For example, in their report *The future of employment: How susceptible are jobs to computerization?*, the Oxford University business school professors Carl Benedikt Frey and Michael Osbourne list "insurance underwriters" as one of the top five jobs most susceptible to computerization, a few notches away from "tax preparers." Indeed, it is true that sophisticated actuarial models serve as a type of AI that eliminates the need for manual underwriting of standard personal auto or homeowners insurance contracts.

Consider, though, the more complex challenge of underwriting businesses for commercial liability or injured worker risks. There are fewer businesses to insure than there are cars and homes, and there are typically fewer predictive data elements common to the wide variety of businesses needing insurance (some are hipster artisanal pickle boutiques; others are construction companies). In statistical terms, this means that there are fewer rows and columns of data available to train predictive algorithms. The models can do no more than mechanically tie together the limited number of risk factors fed into them. They cannot evaluate the accuracy or the completeness of this information, nor can they weigh it together with various case-specific nuances that might be obvious to a human expert, nor can they underwrite new types of businesses and risks not represented in the historical data. However, such algorithms can often automate the underwriting of small, straightforward risks, giving the underwriter more time to focus on the more complex cases requiring commonsense reasoning and professional judgment.

Similar comments about job loss to AI can be made about fraud investigators (particularly in domains where fraudsters rapidly evolve their tactics, rendering historical data less relevant), hiring managers, university admissions officers, public sector case workers, judges making parole decisions, and physicians making medical diagnoses. In each domain, cases fall on a spectrum. When the cases are frequent, unambiguous, and similar across time and context—and if the downside costs of a false prediction are acceptable—algorithms can presumably automate the decision. On the other hand, when the cases are more complex, novel, exceptional, or ambiguous—in other words, not fully represented by historical cases in the available data—human–computer collaboration is a more plausible and desirable goal than complete automation.

The current debates surrounding self-driving cars illustrate this spectrum. If driving environments could be sufficiently controlled—for example, dedicated lanes accessible only to autonomous vehicles, all equipped with interoperable sensors—level 5 autonomous vehicles would be possible in the near term.[26] However, given the number of "black swan"-type scenarios possible (a never-before-seen combination of weather, construction work, a mattress falling off a truck, and someone crossing the road—analogous to the example of translating "Hillary slams the door on Bernie" into Bengali), it is unclear when it will be possible to dispense entirely with human oversight and commonsense reasoning.

Bridging the Empathy Gap

For the reasons given above, and also because of its inherent "human element," medicine is a particularly fertile domain for "freestyle *x*" collaboration. Paul Meehl realized 60 years ago that even simple predictive algorithms can outperform unaided clinical judgment.[27] Today, we have large databases of lifestyle data, genomics data, self-tracking devices, mobile phones capable of taking medical readings, and Watson-style information retrieval systems capable of accessing libraries of continually updated medical journals. Perhaps the treatment of simple injuries, particularly in remote or underserved places, will soon be largely automated, and certain advanced specialties such as radiology or pathology might be largely automated by deep learning technologies.

More generally, the proliferation of AI applications in medicine will likely alter the mix of skills that characterize the most successful physicians and health care workers. Just as the skills that enabled Garry Kasparov to become a chess master did not guarantee dominance at freestyle chess, it is likely that the best doctors of the future will combine the ability to use AI tools to make better diagnoses with the ability to empathetically advise and comfort patients. Machine learning algorithms will enable physicians to devote fewer mental cycles to the "spadework" tasks computers are good at (memorizing the *Physicians' Desk Reference*, continually scanning new journal articles) and more to such characteristically human tasks as handling ambiguity, strategizing treatment and wellness regimens, and providing empathetic counsel.

Just as it is overly simplistic to think that computers are getting smarter than humans, it is probably equally simplistic to think that only humans are good at empathy. There is evidence that AI algorithms can play a role in promoting empathy. For example, the Affectiva software is capable of inferring people's emotional states from webcam videos of their facial expressions. Such software can be used to help optimize video content: An editor might eliminate a section from a movie trailer associated with bored audience facial expressions. Interestingly, the creators of Affectiva were originally motivated by the desire to help autistic people better infer emotional states from facial expressions. Such software could be relevant not only in medicine and marketing, but in the broader business world: Research has revealed that teams containing more women, as well as team members with high degrees of social perception (the trait that Affectiva was designed to support), exhibit higher group intelligence.[28]

There is also evidence that big data and AI can help with both verbal and nonverbal communications between patients and health care workers (and, by extension, between teachers and students, managers and team members, salespeople and customers, and so on). For example, Catherine Kreatsoulas has led the development of algorithms that estimate the likelihood of coronary heart disease based on patients' own descriptions of their symptoms. Kreatsoulas has found evidence that men and women tend to describe symptoms differently, potentially leading to differential treatment. It's possible that well-designed AI algorithms can help avoid such biases.[29]

Regarding nonverbal communication, Sandy Pentland and his collaborators at MIT Media Lab have developed a wearable device, known as the "sociometer," that can measure patterns of nonverbal communication. Such devices could be used to quantify otherwise intangible aspects of communication style in order to coach health care workers on how to cultivate a better bedside manner. This work could even bear on medical malpractice claims: There is evidence that physicians who are perceived as more "likable" are sued for malpractice less often, independently of other risk factors.[30]

Algorithms Can Be Biased, Too

Another type of mental operation that cannot (and must not) be outsourced to algorithms is reasoning about fairness, societal acceptability, and morality. The naive view that algorithms are "fair" and "objective" simply because they use hard data is giving way to recognition of the need for oversight. In a broad sense, this idea is not new. For example, there has long been legal doctrine around the socially undesirable disparate impact that hiring and credit scoring algorithms can potentially have on various classes of individuals.[31] More recent examples of algorithmic bias include online advertising systems that have been found to target career-coaching service ads for high-paying jobs more frequently to men than women, and ads suggestive of arrests more often to people with names commonly used by black people.[32]

Such examples point to yet another sense in which AI algorithms must be complemented by human judgment: If the data used to train an algorithms reflect unwanted pre-existing biases, the resulting algorithm will likely reflect, and potentially amplify, these biases.

The example of judges—and sometimes algorithms—making parole decisions illustrates the subtleties involved. In light of the work of Meehl, Kahneman, and their collaborators, there is good reason to believe that judges should consult algorithms when making parole decisions. A well-known study of judges making parole decisions indicates that, early in the morning, judges granted parole roughly 60 percent of the time. This probability would shrink steadily to near zero by mid-morning break, then would shoot up to roughly 60 percent after break, shrink steadily back to zero by lunch time, jump back to 60 percent after lunch, and so on throughout the day. It seems that blood sugar level significantly affects these hugely important decisions.[33]

Cognitive Collaboration: Why Humans and Computers Think Better Together by Jim Guszcza, Harvey Lewis, and Peter Evans-Greenwood

63

Such phenomena suggest that *not* considering the use of algorithms to improve parole decisions would be morally questionable. Yet a recent study vividly reminds us that building such algorithms is no straightforward task. The journalist Julia Angwin, collaborating with a team of data scientists, reported that a widely used black-box recidivism risk scoring model mistakenly flags black defendants at roughly twice the rate as it mistakenly flags white people. A few months after Angwin's story appeared, the Wisconsin Supreme Court ruled that while judges could use risk scores, the scores cannot be a "determinative" factor in whether or not a defendant is jailed. In essence, the ruling calls for a judicial analog of freestyle chess: Algorithms must not automate judicial decisions; rather, judges should be able to use them as *tools* to make better decisions.[34]

An implication of this ruling is that such algorithms should be designed, built, and evaluated using a broader set of methods and concepts than the ones typically associated with data science. From a narrowly technical perspective, an "optimal" model is often judged to be the one with the highest out-of-sample accuracy. But from a broader perspective, a usable model must balance accuracy with such criteria as omitting societally vexed predictors, avoiding unwanted biases,[35] and providing enough transparency to enable the end user to evaluate the appropriateness of the model indication in a particular case.[36]

The winners of the freestyle chess tournament have been described as "driving" their computer algorithms in a similar way that a person drives a car. Just as the best cars are ergonomically designed to maximize the driver's comfort and control, so decision-support algorithms must be designed to go with the grain of human psychology, rather than simply bypass human psychology altogether. Paraphrasing Kasparov, humans plus computers *plus a better process* for working with algorithms will yield better results than either the most talented humans or the most advanced algorithms working in isolation. The need to design those better processes for human–computer collaboration deserves more attention than it typically gets in discussions of data science or artificial intelligence.

Designing the Future

There is a coda to our story. One of Licklider's disciples was Douglas Engelbart of the Stanford Research Institute (SRI). Two years after Licklider wrote his prescient essay, Engelbart wrote an essay of his own called "Augmenting human intellect: A conceptual framework," which focused on "increasing the capability of a man to approach a complex problem situation, to gain comprehension to suit his particular needs, and to derive solutions to problems."[37] Like Licklider's, this was a vision that involved keeping humans in the loop, not automating away human involvement.

Engelbart led the Augmentation Research Center at SRI, which in the mid-1960s invented many of the elements of the modern personal computer. For example, Engelbart conceived of the mouse while pondering how to move a cursor on a computer screen. The mouse—along with such key elements of personal computing as videoconferencing, word processing, hypertext, and windows—was unveiled at "the mother of all demos" in San Francisco in 1968, which is today remembered as a seminal event in the history of computing.[38]

About a decade after Engelbart's demo, Steve Jobs purchased the mouse patent from SRI for $40,000. Given this lineage, it is perhaps no accident that Jobs memorably articulated a vision of human–computer collaboration very close in spirit to Licklider's:

I think one of the things that really separates us from the high primates is that we're tool builders. I read a study that measured the efficiency of locomotion for various species on the planet. . . . Humans came in with a rather unimpressive showing, about a third of the way down the list, but somebody at *Scientific American* had the insight to test the efficiency of locomotion for a man on a bicycle. . . . A human on a bicycle blew the condor away, completely off the top of the charts. And that's what a computer is to me . . . it's the most remarkable tool that we've ever come up with; it's the equivalent of a bicycle for our minds.[39]

Consistent with this quote, Jobs is remembered for injecting human-centric design thinking into personal computer technology. We believe that fully achieving Licklider's vision of human–computer symbiosis will require a similar injection of psychology and design thinking into the domains of data science and AI.

Endnotes

1. Watson's triumph on *Jeopardy!* was reported by John Markoff, "Computer wins on 'Jeopardy!': Trivial, it's not," *New York Times*, February 16, 2011, www.nytimes.com/2011/02/17/science/17jeopardy-watson.html. The algorithmically generated Rembrandt was reported by Chris Baraniuk, "Computer paints 'new Rembrandt' after old works analysis," *BBC News*, April 6, 2016, www.bbc.com/news/technology-35977315. For robot chefs, see Matt Burgess, "Robot chef that can cook any of 2,000 meals at tap of button to go on sale in 2017," *Factor Tech*, April 14, 2015, http://factor-tech.com/robotics/17437-robot-chef-that-can-cook-any-of-2000-meals-at-tap-of-a-button-to-go-on-sale-in-2017/. Regarding self-driving cars, see Cecilia Kang, "No driver? Bring it on. How Pittsburgh became Uber's testing ground," *New York Times*, September 10, 2016, https://nyti.ms/2k52awS. View in article

2. Regarding technological unemployment, a recent World Economic Forum report predicted that the next four years will see more than 5 million jobs lost to AI-fueled automation

and robotics. See World Economic Forum, *The future of jobs: Employment, skills and workforce strategy for the fourth industrial revolution*, January 2016, http://www3.weforum.org/docs/WEF_Future_of_Jobs.pdf. Regarding Musk and Hawking on AI as an existential threat, see Samuel Gibbs, "Elon Musk: Artificial intelligence is our biggest existential threat," *Guardian*, October 27, 2014, www.theguardian.com/technology/2014/oct/27/elon-musk-artificial-intelligence-ai-biggest-existential-threat, and Rory Cellan-Jones, "Stephen Hawking warns artificial intelligence could end mankind," *BBC News*, December 2, 2014, www.bbc.com/news/technology-30290540. In his book *Superintelligence* (Oxford University Press, 2014), Nick Bostrom entertains a variety of speculative scenarios about the emergence of "superintelligence," which he defines as any intellect that greatly exceeds the cognitive performance of humans in virtually all domains of interest. View in article

3. The Arthur C. Clarke Foundation, "Sir Arthur's quotations," www.clarkefoundation.org/about-sir-arthur/sir-arthurs-quotations/, accessed October 24, 2016. View in article

4. In more detail: McCarthy defined artificial intelligence as "the science and engineering of making intelligent machines, especially intelligent computer programs" and defined intelligence as "the computational part of the ability to achieve goals in the world." He noted that "Varying kinds and degrees of intelligence occur in people, many animals and some machines." See John McCarthy, "What is artificial intelligence?," http://www-formal.stanford.edu/jmc/whatisai/whatisai.html, accessed October 24, 2016. View in article

5. The original proposal can be found in John McCarthy, Marvin L. Minsky, Nathaniel Rochester, and Claude E. Shannon, "A proposal for the Dartmouth Summer Research Project on Artificial Intelligence," *AI Magazine* 27, no. 4 (2006), www.aaai.org/ojs/index.php/aimagazine/article/view/1904/1802. Regarding the time frame, the proposal went on to state, "We think that a significant advance can be made in one or more of these problems if a carefully selected group of scientists work on it for a summer." (!) In hindsight, this optimism might seem surprising, but it is worth remembering that the authors were writing in the heyday of both behaviorist psychology, led by B. F. Skinner, and the logical positivist school of philosophy. Our understanding of both human psychology and the challenges of encoding knowledge in logically perfect languages has evolved considerably since the 1950s. View in article

6. "Demis Hassabis, master of the new machine age," *Financial Times*, March 11, 2016, www.ft.com/content/630bcb34-e6b9-11e5-a09b-1f8b0d268c39. This is not an isolated statement. Two days earlier, the *New York Times* carried an opinion piece by an academic who stated that "Google's AlphaGo is demonstrating for the first time that machines can truly learn and think in a human way." Howard Yu, "AlphaGo's success shows the human advantage is eroding fast," *New York Times*, March 9, 2016, www.nytimes.com/roomfordebate/2016/03/09/does-alphago-mean-artificial-intelligence-is-the-real-deal/

alphagos-success-shows-the-human-advantage-is-eroding-fast. View in article

7. Kaiming He, Xiangyu Zhang, Shaoqing Ren, and Jian Sun, "Delving deep into rectifiers: Surpassing human-level performance on ImageNet classification," February 6, 2015, https://arxiv.org/pdf/1502.01852v1.pdf. View in article

8. It is common for such algorithms to fail in certain ambiguous cases that can be correctly labeled by human experts. These new data points can then be used to retrain the models, resulting in improved accuracy. This virtuous cycle of human labeling and machine learning is called "human-in-the-loop computing." See, for example, Lukas Biewald, "Why human-in-the-loop computing is the future of machine learning," *Computerworld*, November 13, 2015, www.computerworld.com/article/3004013/robotics/why-human-in-the-loop-computing-is-the-future-of-machine-learning.html. View in article

9. In a recent IEEE interview, the Berkeley statistician and machine learning authority Michael Jordan comments that "Each neuron [in a deep learning neural net model] is really a cartoon. It's a linear-weighted sum that's passed through a nonlinearity. Anyone in electrical engineering would recognize those kinds of nonlinear systems. Calling that a neuron is clearly, at best, a shorthand. It's really a cartoon. There is a procedure called logistic regression in statistics that dates from the 1950s, which had nothing to do with neurons but which is exactly the same little piece of architecture." Lee Gomes, "Machine-learning maestro Michael Jordan on the delusions of big data and other huge engineering efforts," *IEEE Spectrum*, October 20, 2014, http://spectrum.ieee.org/robotics/artificial-intelligence/machinelearning-maestro-michael-jordan-on-the-delusions-of-big-data-and-other-huge-engineering-efforts. For technical details of how deep learning models are founded on generalized linear models (a core statistical technique that generalizes both classical and logistic regression), see Shakir Mohamed, "A statistical view of deep learning (I): Recursive GLMs," January 19, 2015, http://blog.shakirm.com/2015/01/a-statistical-view-of-deep-learning-i-recursive-glms/. View in article

10. Computer Age Statistical Inference is the title of a new monograph by the eminent Stanford statisticians Brad Efron and Trevor Hastie. This book presents a unified survey of classical (e.g., maximum likelihood, Bayes theorem), "mid-century modern" (e.g., empirical Bayes, shrinkage, ridge regression), and modern (e.g., lasso regression, tree-based modeling, deep learning neural networks) statistical methods. See Bradley Efron and Trevor Hastie, Computer Age Statistical Inference: Algorithms, Evidence, and Data Science (Cambridge University Press, 2016). View in article

11. While not a household name, Licklider occupies an important place in the history of computing, and has been called "computing's Johnny Appleseed." During his tenure as research director at the US Department of Defense's Advanced Research Projects Agency (ARPA), Licklider wrote a memo, fancifully entitled "Memorandum for members and affiliates of the intergalactic computer network," outlining a vision that led to

the creation of ARPANet, the forerunner of the Internet. See the Wikipedia page on Licklider, https://en.wikipedia.org/wiki/J._C._R._Licklider, for references. View in article

12. J. C. R. Licklider, "Man-computer symbiosis," IRE Transactions on Human Factors in Electronics, March 1960, http://worrydream.com/refs/Licklider%20-%20Man-Computer%20Symbiosis.pdf. In this essay, Licklider analogized the relationship of humans and computers with that of the fig wasp and the fig tree. View in article

13. Kahneman outlines the so-called dual process theory of psychology (System 1 versus System 2 mental operations) in his book Thinking, Fast and Slow (Farrar, Straus, and Giroux, 2013). This book contains an account of the "Linda" experiment discussed in the following paragraph. View in article

14. It is helpful to keep this point, known as the "availability heuristic," in mind when considering the likelihood of apocalyptic scenarios of AI technologies run amok. View in article

15. Michelle Castillo, "Why did Watson think Toronto is a US city on 'Jeopardy!'?," TIME, February 16, 2011, http://techland.time.com/2011/02/16/why-did-watson-think-toronto-is-a-u-s-city-on-jeopardy/. The correct answer is Chicago. View in article

16. The news story was from March 16, 2016. Repeating the experiment on October 2, 2016 yielded the same result. Note that "Barney" approximates a Bengali pronunciation of the name Bernie. View in article

17. Ahn Nguyen, Jason Yosinski, and Jeff Clune, "Deep neural networks are easily fooled: High confidence predictions for unrecognizable images" in 2015 IEEE Conference on Computer Vision and Pattern Recognition, https://arxiv.org/pdf/1412.1897.pdf. View in article

18. Bill Vlasic and Neal E. Boudette, "As US investigates fatal Tesla crash, company defends autopilot system," New York Times, July 12, 2016, https://nyti.ms/2k53Fev. View in article

19. The Obama administration recently released a set of autonomous vehicle guidelines and articulated the expectation that autonomous vehicles will "save time, money, and lives." See Cecilia Kang, "Self-driving cars gain powerful ally: The government," New York Times, September 16, 2016, https://nyti.ms/2k50mnF. View in article

20. Canadians could be forgiven for thinking this is a mistake many US citizens might also make. The Open Mind Common Sense Project, initiated by Marvin Minsky, Robert Speer, and Catherine Havasi, attempts to "crowdsource" common sense by using Internet data to build network graphs that represent relationships between concepts. See Catherine Havasi, "Who's doing common-sense reasoning and why it matters," TechCrunch, August 9, 2014, https://techcrunch.com/2014/08/09/guide-to-common-sense-reasoning-whos-doing-it-and-why-it-matters/. View in article

21. Chomsky introduced the "poverty of the stimulus argument" for why the ability to acquire language must be an innate capability "hard-wired" into the human brain. View in article

22. Alison Gopnik, "Can machines ever be as smart as three-year-olds?" edge.org, www.edge.org/response-detail/26084, accessed October 24, 2016. This point is sometimes called Moravec's Paradox after Hans Moravec, who wrote in his book Mind Children (Harvard University Press, 1990): "It is comparatively easy to make computers exhibit adult-level performance on intelligence tests or playing checkers, and difficult or impossible to give them the skills of a one-year-old when it comes to perception and mobility." View in article

23. Adrian Crockett, "What investment bankers can learn from chess," Fix the Pitch, http://fixthepitch.pellucid.com/what-investment-bankers-can-learn-from-chess/, accessed October 24, 2016. View in article

24. Garry Kasparov, "The chess master and the computer," New York Review of Books, February 11, 2010, www.nybooks.com/articles/2010/02/11/the-chess-master-and-the-computer/. View in article

25. Regarding truck drivers, see "Self-driving trucks: What's the future for America's 3.5 million truckers?," Guardian, June 17, 2016, www.theguardian.com/technology/2016/jun/17/self-driving-trucks-impact-on-drivers-jobs-us. Regarding radiologists, see Ziad Obermeyer and Ezekiel Emanuel, "Predicting the future—big data, machine learning, and clinical medicine," New England Journal of Medicine 375 (September 29, 2016): pp. 1216–1219. The authors of the latter piece comment that, because their work largely involves interpreting digitized images, "machine learning will displace much of the work of radiologists and anatomical pathologists." View in article

26. See Gill Pratt's comments in the Aspen Ideas Festival discussion, "On the road to artificial intelligence," www.aspenideas.org/session/road-artificial-intelligence. For a primer on the National Highway Traffic Safety Administration's levels for self-driving cars, see Hope Reese, "Autonomous driving levels 0 to 5: Understanding the differences," Tech Republic, January 20, 2016, www.techrepublic.com/article/autonomous-driving-levels-0-to-5-understanding-the-differences/. Briefly, level 0 means traditional cars with no driver assistance; today's cars with "autopilot" mode are considered level 2; level 4 means "fully autonomous"; and level 5 means no steering wheel—in other words, full automation with no possibility of human–computer collaboration. View in article

27. See Thinking, Fast and Slow by Daniel Kahneman. Interestingly, Kahneman comments here that Meehl was a hero of his. Michael Lewis's celebrated book Moneyball (W. W. Norton & Company, 2004) can be viewed as an illustration of the phenomenon Meehl discovered in the 1950s, and that Kahneman and Tversky's work helped explain. In a profile of Daniel Kahneman, Lewis commented that he was unaware of the behavioral economics implications of his story until he read a review of his book by the behavioral economics pioneers Richard Thaler and Cass Sunstein. See Richard Thaler and Cass Sunstein, "Who's on first," New Republic, August 2003, https://newrepublic.com/article/61123/whos-first;

and Michael Lewis, "The king of human error," *Vanity Fair*, December 2011, www.vanityfair.com/news/2011/12/michael-lewis-201112. View in article

28. For more information on Affectiva, see Raffi Khatchadourian, "We know how you feel," *New Yorker*, January 19, 2015, www.newyorker.com/magazine/2015/01/19/know-feel. For more information on measuring group intelligence and the relationship between social perception and group intelligence, see James Guszcza, "From groupthink to collective intelligence: A conversation with Cass Sunstein," *Deloitte Review* July 17, 2015, http://dupress.deloitte.com/dup-us-en/deloitte-review/issue-17/groupthink-collective-intelligence-cass-sunstein-interview.html. View in article

29. For a description of Kreatsoulis's work, see Abhinav Sharma, "Can artificial intelligence identify your next heart attack?," *Huffington Post*, April 29, 2016, www.huffingtonpost.com/abhinav-sharma/can-artificial-intelligen_2_b_9798328.html. View in article

30. For information on sociometric badges, see Alex "Sandy" Pentland's book Social Physics (Penguin Books, 2015) and his April 2012 Harvard Business Review article "The new science of building great teams," https://hbr.org/2012/04/the-new-science-of-building-great-teams. For a discussion of research linking physicians' communication styles with the likelihood of being sued for malpractice, see Aaron Carroll, "To be sued less, doctors should consider talking to patients more," *New York Times*, June 1, 2015, https://nyti.ms/2jDC86Z. View in article

31. For a brief introduction to the legal doctrine of disparate impact, see Ian Ayres, "Statistical methods can demonstrate racial disparity," *New York Times*, April 27, 2015, https://nyti.ms/1Ow2JNh. Ayres, a Yale Law School professor, has authored and co-authored several law review articles exploring the concept. View in article

32. Amit Datta, Michael Carl Tschantz, and Anupam Datta, "Automated experiments on ad privacy settings," Proceedings on Privacy Enhancing Technologies 2015, no. 1: pp. 92–112, www.degruyter.com/view/j/popets.2015.1.issue-1/popets-2015-0007/popets-2015-0007.xml; Latanya Sweeney, "Discrimination in online ad delivery," January 28, 2013, http://papers.ssrn.com/sol3/papers.cfm?abstract_id=2208240. View in article

33. "I think it's time we broke for lunch . . . ," *Economist*, April 14, 2011, www.economist.com/node/18557594. In the October 2016 *Harvard Business Review* article "Noise: How to overcome the high, hidden cost of inconsistent decision making" (https://hbr.org/2016/10/noise), Daniel Kahneman and several co-authors discuss the ubiquity of random "noise" resulting in inconsistent decisions in both business and public policy. The authors discuss the benefits of using algorithms as an intermediate source of information in a variety of contexts, including jurisprudence. They comment, "It's obvious in [the case of making parole decisions] that human judges must retain the final authority for the decisions: The public would be shocked to see justice meted out by a formula." View in article

34. Julia Angwin, Jeff Larson, Surya Mattu, and Lauren Kirchner, "Machine bias: There's software used across the country to predict future criminals. And it's biased against blacks," *ProPublica*, May 23, 2016, www.propublica.org/article/machine-bias-risk-assessments-in-criminal-sentencing. Angwin discusses the Wisconsin Supreme Court decision in "Make algorithms accountable," *New York Times*, August 1, 2016, https://nyti.ms/2k594ly. View in article

35. An academic paper that appeared after both the Angwin article and the Wisconsin Supreme Court decision proves that no realistic scoring model can simultaneously satisfy two highly intuitive concepts of "fairness." Continuing with the recidivism example: A predictive model is said to be "well-calibrated" if a particular model score implies the same probability of re-arrest regardless of race. The recidivism model studied by the Angwin team did (by design) satisfy this concept of fairness. On the other hand, the Angwin team pointed out that the false-positive rate for blacks is higher than that of whites. In other words, the model judges blacks who are not re-arrested to be riskier than whites who are not re-arrested. Given that the fact that the overall recidivism rate for blacks is higher than that of whites, it follows by mathematical necessity that a well-calibrated recidivism model will fail the Angwin team's criterion of fairness. See Jon Kleinberg, Sendhil Mullainathan, and Manish Raghavan, "Inherent trade-offs in the fair determination of risk scores," September 19, 2016, https://arxiv.org/abs/1609.05807. View in article

36. For a complementary perspective, see Kate Crawford and Ryan Calo, "There is a blind spot in AI research," Nature, October 13, 2016, www.nature.com/news/there-is-a-blind-spot-in-ai-research-1.20805. The authors comment that "Artificial intelligence presents a cultural shift as much as a technical one. . . . We need to ensure that [societal] changes are beneficial, before they are built further into the infrastructure of everyday life." In a Wired magazine interview with Barack Obama, MIT Media Lab director Joi Ito expresses the view that artificial intelligence is "not just a computer science problem," but requires input from a broader cross-section of disciplines and perspectives. Scott Dadich, "Barack Obama, neural nets, self-driving cars, and the future of the world," Wired, November 2016, www.wired.com/2016/10/president-obama-mit-joi-ito-interview/. View in article

37. Douglas C. Engelbart," Augmenting human intellect: A conceptual framework," October 1962, www.dougengelbart.org/pubs/augment-3906.html. View in article

38. Nicely dating the story is the fact that Stuart Brand, the editor of the *Whole Earth Catalog*, was the event's cameraman. See Dylan Tweney, "Dec. 9, 1968: The mother of all demos," *Wired*, December 9, 2010, www.wired.com/2010/12/1209computer-mouse-mother-of-all-demos/. This demo "also premiered 'what you see is what you get' editing, text and graphics

Cognitive Collaboration: Why Humans and Computers Think Better Together by Jim Guszcza, Harvey Lewis, and Peter Evans-Greenwood

67

displayed on a single screen, shared-screen videoconferencing, outlining, windows, version control, context-sensitive help and hyperlinks." View in article

39. Jobs made this comment in the 1990 documentary film *Memory & Imagination: New Pathways to the Library of Congress.* Clip available at "Steve Jobs, 'Computers are like a bicycle for our minds.'—Michael Lawrence Films," YouTube, posted June 1, 2006, https://youtu.be/ob_GX50Za6c. View in article

Critical Thinking

1. Elon Musk has described AI as "our biggest existential threat." Stephen Hawking warned that "The development of full artificial intelligence could spell the end of the human race." Why are Musk and Hawking concerned? Do you agree with their assessments? Explain your answer.

2. How does machine intelligence differ from human intelligence? What are the real world (and, more specifically, workplace) implications of these differences?

3. What is an example of a human and a computer doing a task better than either could do it alone?

Internet References

Humanity and AI Will Be Inseparable

https://www.theverge.com/a/verge-2021/humanity-and-ai-will-be-inseparable

Minds and Machines: Can We Work Together in the Digital Age?—Science Weekly Podcast

https://www.theguardian.com/science/audio/2017/jul/26/minds-and-machines-can-we-work-together-in-the-digital-age-science-weekly-podcast

Perfecting Your Digital Assistant

https://www.theverge.com/a/verge-2021/aaron-levie-ceo-box-interview

Jim Guszcza is the U.S. chief data scientist of Deloitte Consulting, and a member of Deloitte's Advanced Analytics and Modeling practice. Jim has extensive experience applying predictive analytics techniques in a variety of public and private sector domains.

Harvey Lewis is a data scientist with Deloitte UK. His research focuses on data, analytics, cognitive technologies, and other business disruptors.

Peter Evans-Greenwood is currently a fellow at The Centre for the edge—helping organisations embrace the digital revolution through understanding and applying what is happening on the edge of business and society.

Prepared by: Daniel Mittleman, *DePaul University* and
Douglas Druckenmiller, *Western Illinois University*

Article

Robots Stealing Human Jobs Isn't the Problem. This Is.

ALIA E. DASTAGIR

Learning Outcomes

After reading this article, you will be able to:

- Be able to discuss the "skills gap" caused by automation of jobs, and its relationship to unemployment.

- Understand the role of education, skills training, and life-long learning play in reducing "skills-gap."

- Be able to describe how automation, in the past, has destroyed jobs and whole industries, as well as how it has created new jobs and industries in its wake.

A 15-hour work week. That's what influential economist John Maynard Keynes prophesied in his famous 1930 essay "Economic Possibilities for Our Grandchildren," forecasting that in the next century technology would make us so productive we wouldn't know what to do with all our free time.

This is not the future Keynes imagined.

Many higher income workers put in 50 or more hours per week, according to an NPR/Harvard/Robert Wood Johnson Foundation poll. Meanwhile, lower-income workers are fighting to get enough hours to pay the bills, as shown in a University of Washington report on Seattle's $15 minimum wage publicized this week.

Yet some of today's best minds are making Keynes-like predictions. This month, Apple co-founder Steve Wozniak said robots will one day replace us—but we needn't worry for a few hundred years.

In May, Facebook CEO Mark Zuckerberg told Harvard's 2017 class that increased automation would strip us not only of our jobs but also of our sense of purpose.

The Problem: Skills Gap

Automation. Artificial intelligence. Machine learning. Many experts disagree on what these new technologies will mean for the workforce, the economy and our quality of life. But where they do agree is that technology will change (or completely take over) tasks that humans do now. The most pressing question, many economists and labor historians say, is whether people will have the skills to perform the jobs that are left.

"We are moving into an era of extensive automation and a period in which capitalism is just simply not going to need as many workers," said Jennifer Klein, a Yale University professor who focuses on labor history. "It's not just automating in manufacturing but anything with a service counter: grocery stores, movie theaters, car rentals . . . and this is now going to move into food service, too.

"What are we going to do in an era that doesn't need as many people? It's not a social question we've seriously addressed."

Instead of worrying about the mass unemployment a robot Armageddon could bring, we should instead shift our attention to making sure workers—particularly low-wage workers—have the skills they need to compete in an automated era, says James Bessen, an economist, Boston University law lecturer, and author of the book *Learning by Doing: The Real Connection Between Innovation, Wages, and Wealth.*

"The problem is people are losing jobs and we're not doing a good job of getting them the skills and knowledge they need to work for the new jobs," Bessen said.

Addressing this skills gap will require a paradigm shift both in the way we approach job training and in the way we approach education, he said.

"Technology is very disruptive. It is destroying jobs. And while it is creating others, because we don't have an easy way

to transition people from one occupation to another, we're going to face increased social disruption," he said.

In this new age, Bessen said, we can't treat learning as finite.

"We need to move to a world where there is lifelong learning," he said. "You have to get rid of this idea that we go to school once when we're young and that covers us for our career. . . . Schools need to teach people how to learn, how to teach themselves if necessary."

Universal Basic Income

A universal basic income (UBI) has been proposed as one possible solution to the loss of jobs caused by automation. A UBI would give everyone a fixed amount of money, regularly, no matter what. Proponents say not only would it help eradicate poverty, but it would be especially useful for people whose jobs are eliminated by automation, giving them the flexibility to learn new skills required in a new job or industry, without having to worry about how they'd eat or pay rent.

Some also suggest it would breed innovation. In his Harvard speech, Zuckerberg told the audience: "We should have a society that measures progress not just by economic metrics like GDP, but by how many of us have a role we find meaningful. We should explore ideas like universal basic income to give everyone a cushion to try new things."

Several countries are exploring or experimenting with a UBI, including Kenya, Finland, the Netherlands, and Canada.

Concerns About Automation Aren't New

Americans have been worrying about automation wiping out jobs for centuries, and in some occupations, automation has drastically reduced the need for human labor.

- In 1900, 41 percent of American workers were employed in agriculture, but by 2000, automated machinery brought that number down to just 2 percent, MIT professor David Autor wrote in the *Journal of Economic Perspectives* in 2015.
- The arrival of the automobile ushered out horses, reducing the need for blacksmiths and stable hands.
- In the 21st century, computers are increasingly performing tasks humans once did.

But the relationship between automation and employment is complex. When automation replaces human labor, it can also reduce cost and improve quality, which, in turn, increases demand.

Such was the case in textiles. In the early 19th century, 98 percent of the work of a weaver became automated , but the number of textile workers actually grew.

"At the beginning of the 19th century, it was so expensive that . . . a typical person had one set of clothing," Bessen said. "As the price started dropping because of automation, people started buying more and more, so that by the 1920s the average person was consuming 10 times as much cloth per capita per year."

More demand for cloth meant a greater need for textile workers. But that demand, eventually, was satisfied.

When ATMs were introduced in the 1970s, people thought they would be a death knell for bank tellers. The number of tellers per bank did fall, but because ATMs reduced the cost of operating a bank branch, more branches opened, which in turn hired more tellers. U.S. bank teller employment rose by 50,000 between 1980 and 2010. But the tasks of those tellers evolved from simply dispensing cash to selling other things the banks provided, like credit cards and loans. And the skills those tellers had that the ATMs didn't—like problem solving—became more valuable.

When computers take over some human tasks within an occupation, Bessen's research shows those occupations grow faster, not slower.

"AI is coming in and it's going to make accountants that much better, it's going to make financial advisers that much better, it's going to make health care providers that much more effective, so we're going to be using more of their services at least for the next 10 or 20 years," Bessen said.

These examples, though, are of occupations where automation replaces some part of human labor. What about when automation completely replaces the humans in an entire occupation? So far, that's been pretty rare. In a 2016 paper, Bessen looked at 271 detailed occupations used in the 1950 Census and found that while many occupations no longer exist, in only one case was the demise of an occupation attributed mostly to automation: the elevator operator.

A 2017 report from the McKinsey Global Institute found that less than 5 percent of occupations can be completely automated.

What's in Store

History has taught us a lot about how automation disrupts industries, though economists admit they can't account for the infinite ways technology may unsettle work in the future.

When a new era of automation does usher in major economic and social disruption—which Bessen doesn't predict will happen for at least another 30 to 50 years—it's humans that will ultimately decide the ways in which robots get to change the world.

"It's not a threat as much as an opportunity," he said. "It's how we take advantage of it as individuals and a society that will determine the outcome."

Critical Thinking

1. Dastigir says, "the relationship between automation and employment is complex." Describe the complexities she is alluding to.
2. What is meant by "skills-gap"? What are strategies that can be considered to reduce "skills-gap"?
3. Technology certainly has made us more productive over the past 200 years. Why do you think Keynes was wrong almost 90 years ago when he predicted we would have a 15 hour work week and too much free time today? How does this inform the idea we will have a shorter work week in the future?

Internet References

The Future Is Automated. Here's How We Can Prepare For It
https://www.weforum.org/agenda/2017/01/the-future-is-automated-here-s-how-we-can-prepare-for-it/

The Optimist's Guide to the Robot Apocalypse
https://qz.com/904285/the-optimists-guide-to-the-robot-apocalypse/

To Close the Skills Gap, Start With the Learning Gap
https://www.brookings.edu/opinions/to-close-the-skills-gap-start-with-the-learning-gap/

ALIA E. DASTAGIR is a culture writer at *USA TODAY*.

Unit 4

UNIT

Prepared by: Daniel Mittleman, *DePaul University* and
Douglas Druckenmiller, *Western Illinois University*

Big Data, Analytics, and AI

The triple convergence of big data, analytics, and artificial intelligence (AI) is a rapidly changing computing revolution engaging every industry in a profound transformation. A recent McKinsey report[1] notes that the application of these innovations are currently unevenly spread among industry leaders and are realizing only a fraction of their potential benefits. While the digital divide between leaders and followers is large, research shows that companies that more fully utilize the technology are more profitable and achieve that profitability three times faster. This digital divide also exists between countries, regions, and economic sectors. The divide exists because of the difficulties in deciding just how to apply the technology within an organizational context. According to the report, most businesses indicate they are only somewhat effective at employing the new technology.

Applications in AI are not new, but recent developments such as deep learning are accelerating change with implications for society and the economy. Most recently companies such as Facebook, Google, and IBM have invested in deep learning technologies. Facebook is pursuing advanced image analysis, Google's technology, DeepMind, has made impressive showings with AlphaGo defeating a world class "Go" champion, and IBM's Watson technology has come of age with many applications in healthcare and traditional business fields.

Forrester Research predicts these emerging Cognitive Intelligence (CI) applications will bring about an "Insights Revolution."[2] The gap between advanced data analytics and how to use data resources to drive business innovation is being bridged by the new developments in AI and deep learning.

Thus the technology is fundamentally changing the competitive landscape. Increasing globalization of the workforce, disruption of markets by new entrants, and emergence of new economies is accelerating competition with older established companies and economic sectors. Though currently unevenly distributed, data-analytics and AI applications provide fundamental changes in what data are collected and how it is used. These transformations make possible new technologies like microtargeting which is affecting many segments such as labor, education, travel, marketing, and politics.

This chapter explores the societal impacts and the challenges of employing a technology which is not fully transparent. We fundamentally can't tell how AI systems arrive at their conclusions and trusting such systems is inherently dangerous. Microtargeting applied to politics is a fundamental challenge to our democratic systems. Can our democracy survive? Privacy concerns and biased systems are major challenges of these new technologies. How can they be addressed?

[1] McKinsey & Company (15 May 2017). What's now and next in analytics, AI, and automation. *McKinsey & Company*. Retrieved from http://www.mckinsey.com/global-themes/digital-disruption/whats-now-and-next-in-analytics-ai-and-automation

[2] Forrester Research(19 Jul. 2017). *Go.forrester.com*. Retrieved from https://go.forrester.com/wp-content/uploads/Forrester_Predictions_2017_Artificial_Intelligence_Will_Drive_The_Insights_Revolution.pdf

Article

Prepared by: Daniel Mittleman, *DePaul University* and
Douglas Druckenmiller, *Western Illinois University*

Customized or Creepy: How Websites Tow the Line with User Data

A Princeton "web census" sheds new light on how websites are customizing and testing content for different users and audience segments.

STEVEN MELENDEZ

Learning Outcomes

After reading this article, you will be able to:

- Identify pros and cons to customization of Internet content.

- Distinguish between first- and third-party cookies.

- Discuss Facebook and Cornell University's manipulation of users' news feeds.

Two visitors to the same news site see different headlines on the same article. Two potential donors see different suggested giving amounts on a charity website. A software vendor with free and premium versions keeps a list of "countries that are likely to pay."

Those are some recent findings from the Princeton University Center for Information Technology Policy's Web Transparency and Accountability Project, which conducts a monthly "web census," tracking privacy-related practices across the Internet. Essentially, the project team sends an automated web-crawling bot to visit about 1 million websites and monitor how they, in turn, monitor their visitors.

Showing different versions of a site to different people isn't inherently creepy, nor is monitoring what they do while visiting a website—without some basic monitoring and user segmentation, there would be no recommended products on Amazon or Netflix and no way for international websites to figure out which language users prefer.

And yet, some types of customization just make Internet users uncomfortable, and some may even risk crossing ethical boundaries. And so, without further ado, here's a mostly unscientific guide to web-tracking practices in the wild, on a scale of 1 (not particularly creepy) to 5 (pretty creepy).

First-Party Cookies

If you've visited any European websites in the past few years, you've probably seen a little pop-up warning explaining that the sites use cookies—small text files stored by your browser with information about your activity on the site.

Under EU regulations, sites are required to let you know if they use cookies and allow you to opt out of having your browser store the files.

But despite the ubiquitous warnings, basic, first-party cookies, which are stored by a particular website you're visiting and served back with each page on the site you load, really aren't all that creepy.

First, sites are generally out in the open about their use of cookies—if there's no European-style pop up, they're often disclosed in reasonably plain English in privacy policies—and it's easy to find instructions on viewing and deleting stored cookies in any major browser or on using private browsing modes to avoid storing them from browsing session to browsing session.

More importantly, first-party cookies are by definition tied to a particular website. They're just a convenient way for programmers to keep track of information, like your user name or what's in your shopping cart, that you've already provided to the site, often with the assumption that they'd store it.

A/B Testing

One reason different users see different editions of the same site or app is A/B testing—a practice where different users are purposely shown different versions of a site in order to measure which one is more effective.

The practice is a cornerstone of many modern, agile development practices, and of data-oriented business philosophies like Eric Ries's "Lean Startup" methodology. It's used by websites to test everything from quick color scheme tweaks to radically revamped algorithms for ordering social networking feeds. And modern Internet users are often accustomed to sites varying slightly from user to user, says Pete Koomen, cofounder and CTO of Optimizely, Optimizely, a San Francisco company that provides tools for customer segmentation and A/B testing.

"I actually think that at this point this is part and parcel of most users' expectation of how the web works," he says.

And yet, for particular sites, even sophisticated users can be unaware that there are multiple versions of the user experience, says Lisa Barnard, an assistant professor of strategic communication at Ithaca College who's studied online marketing. And they can be disturbed to learn that even seemingly static content like news headlines can vary from user to user as part of an experiment.

"I teach students who are digital natives, they understand how this stuff works, and every time I tell them about A/B testing, they're shocked," Barnard says. "They realize that something's happening [with targeted ads] because they know that they're seeing something they were looking at before, but with something like A/B testing of headlines on a news site, there's no tip off."

And once they find out it's been happening without their knowledge, they're not always happy, she says.

Among the information the Princeton researchers gather in their web census is the complete set of JavaScript code embedded in each page, explains project research engineer Dillon Reisman in a recent blog post. And on many sites, that includes code from Optimizely to implement A/B tests.

The team even built a Google Chrome extension—cheekily called Pessimizely—that can, depending on a website's configuration, make it possible to see which segments of a particular web page are being tested and tweaked with Optimizely and how the page's audience is being segmented.

Reisman emphasizes that there's absolutely nothing wrong with using Optimizely, which boasts more than 6,000 corporate customers. But, he says, the findings still point to general unresolved questions about how transparent Internet companies ought to be about how they're tracking visitor data and conducting user experiments, even if the practices themselves aren't inherently negative.

To be clear, Optimizely doesn't track users from website to website, explains Koomen.

"When a customer uses Optimizely to run experiments on their site, they only see the results of those experiments for their site alone," he says.

For researchers and the public at large, Optimizely actually provides an unusually good look at how websites can vary from visitor to visitor, says Reisman. Customers can configure it to make testing variations and customer segment names visible for better integration with third-party tools, and the web census project and Pessimizely extension are able to access that data as well.

Reisman says he'd generally like to see companies more explicitly spell out all of the tracking, testing, and personalized tweaking they do, perhaps in their privacy policies.

"I'm grateful that data's there, because it's so rare that you get to see what websites are doing when they're A/B testing, and this actually is a very unique opportunity," he says.

Third-Party Tracking Cookies

A little more off-putting are third-party cookies: cookies set by a website other than the site you're visiting, which can help advertising companies and others track your behavior across the Internet.

Advertisers say these and other more complex tools for tracking users from site to site allow for better targeting of ads based on your browser history, but several studies have found consumers can find this more stalkerish than helpful.

A study by Barnard, the Ithaca College professor, found last year that ads that track users across websites can be perceived as "creepy" and sometimes make customers less likely to buy.

"They feel like companies know too much about them, and that they're tracking them around the Internet," Barnard says. "There's something about that tracking that makes people uncomfortable, and, kind of, the uncertainty of how much these companies know about them and how they're using it."

And a Consumer Reports survey found most consumers unwilling to trade personal information for targeted ads and unconvinced such ads brought them more value. For those users, many popular browsers now contain built-in features to block third-party cookies.

Consumer Data Collection Tools

Cookies are data files stored by your browser, which means that if you're aware of them and willing to do a little legwork, you can control if and when they're stored.

But they're not the only way for advertisers and website owners to track visitors from site to site. Clever—or creepy—programmers have found other ways to monitor your travels around the web that can be harder to detect and control.

The researchers behind the Princeton web census found websites using a variety of "device fingerprinting" techniques that allow them to identify visitors based on characteristics of their computers or phones, without having to store any data. For instance, websites—and advertisers—can examine the list of fonts installed on a computer or the exact output produced by a system's audio or image processing software, which can vary from system to system.

It's hard not to view these techniques, which are generally designed to circumvent users' desired tracking restrictions, as intrusive. Luckily, at least one of the techniques, using characteristics of HTML graphics canvas elements to track users, appears to be on the decline after some public backlash, the researchers report.

"First, the most prominent trackers have by and large stopped using it, suggesting that the public backlash following that study was effective," they write. "Second, the overall number of domains employing it has increased considerably, indicating that knowledge of the technique has spread and that more obscure trackers are less concerned about public perception."

Still, while more legitimate websites may shy away from these techniques, it's likely there will be a cat-and-mouse game for some time between shadier trackers and researchers who reveal their techniques.

Psychological Experiments

In 2012, researchers at Facebook and Cornell University tweaked a selection of users' news feeds, showing them either a week of all positive stories or all negative stories. The immediate result? People who saw positive posts created more positive content of their own; people who saw negative stories posted more negative messages.

But the broader result was widespread condemnation of the project from across the Internet, including from the scientific community. Doing experiments with vague-at-best consent through website terms of service, with an eye toward influencing people's emotional state, was widely denounced as unsavory, unethical, and potentially even dangerous.

"Deception and emotional manipulation are common tools in psychological research, but when they're done in an academic setting they are heavily reviewed and participants have to give consent," says data ethicist Jake Metcalf, a founding partner at ethics consultancy Ethical Resolve.

The company has since adopted and published new research vetting guidelines, influenced by those used in academic studies, and says it hopes they can be informative to other companies doing similar work.

"It is clear now that there are things we should have done differently," Facebook CTO Mike Schroepfer acknowledged in a statement after the study came to light.

Surprising Price Variations

Last year, investigative journalism site ProPublica reported that prices of online test prep services booked through the *Princeton Review*'s website could vary by more than $1,000 dollars based on users' zip codes. One result, according to the report, was that Asian users were more likely to be offered higher prices for tutoring services than non-Asians. The Princeton Review emphasized in a statement this was not its intent and that prices were based on "differential costs" and "competitive attributes" of different regional markets.

And in 2012, the *Wall Street Journal* reported that office supply chain Staples offered different prices to users in different zip codes and pointed out numerous other examples of online stores offering different prices, or discount offers, based on users' location, device type, or other information, often to users' frustration.

Also that year, the paper famously reported that travel booking site Orbitz was showing different lists of hotels on the first page of search results to Mac and Windows users, specifically showing higher-priced options for Apple users, who were found to be bigger spenders (though the company has emphasized particular hotels were priced the same for all users).

While differential pricing isn't generally illegal, as long as there's no discrimination against a protected class like a racial or religious group, it still often makes customers uncomfortable and anxious about whether they've truly gotten the best deal available.

"When that type of story comes out, people get upset," says Barnard. "It's that uncertainty that, I think, makes people really uncomfortable."

Critical Thinking

1. How transparent should companies be about the ways in which they track you online or experiment with customization?

2. Why would a company use A/B testing and how does it work?

3. Make a case for which is worse: emotional manipulation or differential pricing.

Internet References

How Marketers Are Driving Growth Through Personalized Content
https://goo.gl/F6JiCd

Why a Personalized Web Robs Us of the Internet's Rich Diversity
https://goo.gl/41dv1n

What Does Netflix's Algorithm Want?
https://goo.gl/UghwRK

STEVEN MELENDEZ is an independent journalist living in New Orleans.

Will Democracy Survive Big Data and Artificial Intelligence? by Dirk Helbing et al.

77

Prepared by: Daniel Mittleman, *DePaul University* and
Douglas Druckenmiller, *Western Illinois University*

Article

Will Democracy Survive Big Data and Artificial Intelligence?

DIRK HELBING ET AL.

Learning Outcomes

After reading this article, you will be able to:

- Dicuss the advantages created by the development Big Data and artificial intelligence.

- Articulate the primary dangers presented by Big Data and artificial intelligence.

- Explain the term "nudging" and how this is a form of governmental paternalism.

W e are in the middle of a technological upheaval that will transform the way society is organized. We must make the right decisions now.

> **"Enlightenment is man's emergence from his self-imposed immaturity. Immaturity is the inability to use one's understanding without guidance from another."**
>
> —Immanuel Kant, "What is Enlightenment?" (1784)

The digital revolution is in full swing. How will it change our world? The amount of data we produce doubles every year. In other words: in 2016, we produced as much data as in the entire history of humankind through 2015. Every minute we produce hundreds of thousands of Google searches and Facebook posts. These contain information that reveals how we think and feel. Soon, the things around us, possibly even our clothing, also will be connected with the Internet. It is estimated that in 10 years' time there will be 150 billion networked measuring sensors, 20 times more than people on Earth. Then, the amount of data will double every 12 hours. Many companies are already trying to turn this Big Data into Big Money.

Everything will become intelligent; soon we will not only have smart phones, but also smart homes, smart factories, and smart cities. Should we also expect these developments to result in smart nations and a smarter planet?

The field of artificial intelligence is, indeed, making breathtaking advances. In particular, it is contributing to the automation of data analysis. Artificial intelligence is no longer programmed line by line, but is now capable of learning, thereby continuously developing itself. Recently, Google's DeepMind algorithm taught itself how to win 49 Atari games. Algorithms can now recognize handwritten language and patterns almost as well as humans and even complete some tasks better than them. They are able to describe the contents of photos and videos. Today 70 percent of all financial transactions are performed by algorithms. News content is, in part, automatically generated. This all has radical economic consequences: in the coming 10 to 20 years around half of today's jobs will be threatened by algorithms. About 40 percent of today's top 500 companies will have vanished in a decade.

It can be expected that supercomputers will soon surpass human capabilities in almost all areas—somewhere between 2020 and 2060. Experts are starting to ring alarm bells. Technology visionaries, such as Elon Musk from Tesla Motors, Bill Gates from Microsoft, and Apple cofounder Steve Wozniak, are warning that super-intelligence is a serious danger for humanity, possibly even more dangerous than nuclear weapons.

Is This Alarmism?

One thing is clear: the way in which we organize the economy and society will change fundamentally. We are experiencing the largest transformation since the end of the Second World War; after the automation of production and the creation of self-driving cars the automation of society is next. With this, society is at a crossroads, which promises great opportunities, but also considerable risks. If we take the wrong decisions it could threaten our greatest historical achievements.

In the 1940s, the American mathematician Norbert Wiener (1894–1964) invented cybernetics. According to him, the behavior of systems could be controlled by the means of suitable feedbacks. Very soon, some researchers imagined controlling the economy and society according to this basic principle, but the necessary technology was not available at that time.

Today, Singapore is seen as a perfect example of a data-controlled society. What started as a program to protect its citizens from terrorism has ended up influencing economic and immigration policy, the property market and school curricula. China is taking a similar route. Recently, Baidu, the Chinese equivalent of Google, invited the military to take part in the China Brain Project. It involves running so-called deep learning algorithms over the search engine data collected about its users. Beyond this, a kind of social control is also planned. According to recent reports, every Chinese citizen will receive a so-called "Citizen Score," which will determine under what conditions they may get loans, jobs, or travel visa to other countries. This kind of individual monitoring would include people's Internet surfing and the behavior of their social contacts (see "Spotlight on China").

With consumers facing increasingly frequent credit checks and some online shops experimenting with personalized prices, we are on a similar path in the West. It is also increasingly clear that we are all in the focus of institutional surveillance. This was revealed in 2015 when details of the British secret service's "Karma Police" program became public, showing the comprehensive screening of everyone's Internet use. Is Big Brother now becoming a reality?

Programmed Society, Programmed Citizens

Everything started quite harmlessly. Search engines and recommendation platforms began to offer us personalised suggestions for products and services. This information is based on personal and meta-data that has been gathered from previous searches, purchases and mobility behaviour, as well as social interactions. While officially, the identity of the user is protected, it can, in practice, be inferred quite easily. Today,

algorithms know pretty well what we do, what we think and how we feel—possibly even better than our friends and family or even ourselves. Often the recommendations we are offered fit so well that the resulting decisions feel as if they were our own, even though they are actually not our decisions. In fact, we are being remotely controlled ever more successfully in this manner. The more is known about us, the less likely our choices are to be free and not predetermined by others.

But it won't stop there. Some software platforms are moving toward "persuasive computing." In the future, using sophisticated manipulation technologies, these platforms will be able to steer us through entire courses of action, be it for the execution of complex work processes or to generate free content for Internet platforms, from which corporations earn billions. *The trend goes from programming computers to programming people.*

These technologies are also becoming increasingly popular in the world of politics. Under the label of "nudging," and on massive scale, governments are trying to steer citizens toward healthier or more environmentally friendly behaviour by means of a "nudge"—a modern form of paternalism. The new, caring government is not only interested in what we do, but also wants to make sure that we do the things that it considers to be right. The magic phrase is "big nudging," which is the combination of Big Data with nudging. To many, this appears to be a sort of digital scepter that allows one to govern the masses efficiently, without having to involve citizens in democratic processes. Could this overcome vested interests and optimize the course of the world? If so, then citizens could be governed by a data-empowered "wise king," who would be able to produce desired economic and social outcomes almost as if with a digital magic wand.

Preprogrammed Catastrophes

But one look at the relevant scientific literature shows that attempts to control opinions, in the sense of their "optimization," are doomed to fail because of the complexity of the problem. The dynamics of the formation of opinions are full of surprises. Nobody knows how the digital magic wand, that is to say the manipulative nudging technique, should best be used. What would have been the right or wrong measure often is apparent only afterwards. During the German swine flu epidemic in 2009, for example, everybody was encouraged to go for vaccination. However, we now know that a certain percentage of those who received the immunization were affected by an unusual disease, narcolepsy. Fortunately, there were not more people who chose to get vaccinated!

Another example is the recent attempt of health insurance providers to encourage increased exercise by handing out smart fitness bracelets, with the aim of reducing the amount of cardiovascular disease in the population; but in the end, this might result in more hip operations. In a complex system, such as society, an improvement in one area almost inevitably leads to deterioration in another. Thus, large-scale interventions can sometimes prove to be massive mistakes.

Regardless of this, criminals, terrorists and extremists will try and manage to take control of the digital magic wand sooner or later—perhaps even without us noticing. Almost all companies and institutions have already been hacked, even the Pentagon, the White House, and the NSA.

A further problem arises when adequate transparency and democratic control are lacking: the erosion of the system from the inside. Search algorithms and recommendation systems can be influenced. Companies can bid on certain combinations of words to gain more favourable results. Governments are probably able to influence the outcomes too. During elections, they might nudge undecided voters toward supporting them—a manipulation that would be hard to detect. Therefore, whoever controls this technology can win elections—by nudging themselves to power.

This problem is exacerbated by the fact that, in many countries, a single search engine or social media platform has a predominant market share. It could decisively influence the public and interfere with these countries remotely. Even though the European Court of Justice judgment made on October 6, 2015 limits the unrestrained export of European data, the underlying problem still has not been solved within Europe, and even less so elsewhere.

What undesirable side effects can we expect? In order for manipulation to stay unnoticed, it takes a so-called resonance effect—suggestions that are sufficiently customized to each individual. In this way, local trends are gradually reinforced by repetition, leading all the way to the "filter bubble" or "echo chamber effect": in the end, all you might get is your own opinions reflected back at you. This causes social polarization, resulting in the formation of separate groups that no longer understand each other and find themselves increasingly at conflict with one another. In this way, personalized information can unintentionally destroy social cohesion. This can be currently observed in American politics, where Democrats and Republicans are increasingly drifting apart, so that political compromises become almost impossible. The result is a fragmentation, possibly even a disintegration, of society.

Owing to the resonance effect, a large-scale change of opinion in society can be only produced slowly and gradually. The effects occur with a time lag, but, also, they cannot be easily undone. It is possible, for example, that resentment against minorities or migrants get out of control; too much national sentiment can cause discrimination, extremism, and conflict.

Perhaps even more significant is the fact that manipulative methods change the way we make our decisions. They override the otherwise relevant cultural and social cues, at least temporarily. In summary, the large-scale use of manipulative methods could cause serious social damage, including the brutalization of behavior in the digital world. Who should be held responsible for this?

Legal Issues

This raises legal issues that, given the huge fines against tobacco companies, banks, IT and automotive companies over the past few years, should not be ignored. But which laws, if any, might be violated? First of all, it is clear that manipulative technologies restrict the freedom of choice. If the remote control of our behaviour worked perfectly, we would essentially be digital slaves, because we would only execute decisions that were actually made by others before. Of course, manipulative technologies are only partly effective. Nevertheless, our freedom is disappearing slowly, but surely—in fact, slowly enough that there has been little resistance from the population, so far.

The insights of the great enlightener Immanuel Kant seem to be highly relevant here. Among other things, he noted that a state that attempts to determine the happiness of its citizens is a despot. However, the right of individual self-development can only be exercised by those who have control over their lives, which presupposes informational self-determination. This is about nothing less than our most important constitutional rights. A democracy cannot work well unless those rights are respected. If they are constrained, this undermines our constitution, our society and the state.

As manipulative technologies such as big nudging function in a similar way to personalized advertising, other laws are affected too. Advertisements must be marked as such and must not be misleading. They are also not allowed to utilize certain psychological tricks such as subliminal stimuli. This is why it is prohibited to show a soft drink in a film for a split-second, because then the advertising is not consciously perceptible while it may still have a subconscious effect. Furthermore, the current widespread collection and processing of personal data is certainly not compatible with the applicable data protection laws in European countries and elsewhere.

Finally, the legality of personalized pricing is questionable, because it could be a misuse of insider information. Other relevant aspects are possible breaches of the principles of equality and nondiscrimination—and of competition laws, as free market access and price transparency are no longer guaranteed. The situation is comparable to businesses that sell their products cheaper in other countries, but try to prevent purchases via these countries. Such cases have resulted in high punitive fines in the past.

Personalized advertising and pricing cannot be compared to classical advertising or discount coupons, as the latter are non-specific and also do not invade our privacy with the goal to take advantage of our psychological weaknesses and knock out our critical thinking.

Furthermore, let us not forget that, in the academic world, even harmless decision experiments are considered to be experiments with human subjects, which would have to be approved by a publicly accountable ethics committee. In each and every case the persons concerned are required to give their informed consent. In contrast, a single click to confirm that we agree with the contents of a hundred-page "terms of use" agreement (which is the case these days for many information platforms) is woefully inadequate.

Nonetheless, experiments with manipulative technologies, such as nudging, are performed with millions of people, without informing them, without transparency and without ethical constraints. Even large social networks like Facebook or online dating platforms such as OkCupid have already publicly admitted to undertaking these kinds of social experiments. If we want to avoid irresponsible research on humans and society (just think of the involvement of psychologists in the torture scandals of the recent past), then we urgently need to impose high standards, especially scientific quality criteria and a code of conduct similar to the Hippocratic Oath. Has our thinking, our freedom, our democracy been hacked?

Let us suppose there was a super-intelligent machine with godlike knowledge and superhuman abilities: would we follow its instructions? This seems possible. But if we did that, then the warnings expressed by Elon Musk, Bill Gates, Steve Wozniak, Stephen Hawking and others would have become true: computers would have taken control of the world. We must be clear that a super-intelligence could also make mistakes, lie, pursue selfish interests or be manipulated. Above all, it could not be compared with the distributed, collective intelligence of the entire population.

The idea of replacing the thinking of all citizens by a computer cluster would be absurd, because that would dramatically lower the diversity and quality of the solutions achievable. It is already clear that the problems of the world have not decreased despite the recent flood of data and the use of personalized information—on the contrary! World peace is fragile. The long-term change in the climate could lead to the greatest loss of species since the extinction of dinosaurs. We are also far from having overcome the financial crisis and its impact on the economy. Cyber-crime is estimated to cause an annual loss of 3 trillion dollars. States and terrorists are preparing for cyberwarfare.

In a rapidly changing world a super-intelligence can never make perfect decisions: systemic complexity is increasing faster than data volumes, which are growing faster than the ability to process them, and data transfer rates are limited. This results in disregarding local knowledge and facts, which are important to reach good solutions. Distributed, local control methods are often superior to centralized approaches, especially in complex systems whose behaviors are highly variable, hardly predictable and not capable of real-time optimization. This is already true for traffic control in cities, but even more so for the social and economic systems of our highly networked, globalized world.

Furthermore, there is a danger that the manipulation of decisions by powerful algorithms undermines the basis of "collective intelligence," which can flexibly adapt to the challenges of our complex world. For collective intelligence to work, information searches and decision-making by individuals must occur independently. If our judgments and decisions are predetermined by algorithms, however, this truly leads to a brainwashing of the people. Intelligent beings are downgraded to mere receivers of commands, who automatically respond to stimuli.

In other words: personalized information builds a "filter bubble" around us, a kind of digital prison for our thinking. How could creativity and thinking "out of the box" be possible under such conditions? Ultimately, a centralized system of technocratic behavioral and social control using a super-intelligent information system would result in a new form of dictatorship. Therefore, the top-down controlled society, which comes under the banner of "liberal paternalism," is in principle nothing else than a totalitarian regime with a rosy cover.

In fact, big nudging aims to bring the actions of many people into line, and to manipulate their perspectives and decisions. This puts it in the arena of propaganda and the targeted incapacitation of the citizen by behavioral control. We expect that the consequences would be fatal in the long term, especially when considering the above-mentioned effect of undermining culture.

A Better Digital Society Is Possible

Despite fierce global competition, democracies would be wise not to cast the achievements of many centuries overboard. In contrast to other political regimes, Western democracies have the advantage that they have already learned to deal with pluralism and diversity. Now they just have to learn how to capitalize on them more.

In the future, those countries will lead that reach a healthy balance between business, government and citizens. This requires networked thinking and the establishment of an

Will Democracy Survive Big Data and Artificial Intelligence? by Dirk Helbing et al.

81

information, innovation, product and service "ecosystem." In order to work well, it is not only important to create opportunities for participation, but also to support diversity. Because there is no way to determine the best goal function: should we optimize the gross national product per capita or sustainability? Power or peace? Happiness or life expectancy? Often enough, what would have been better is only known after the fact. By allowing the pursuit of various different goals, a pluralistic society is better able to cope with the range of unexpected challenges to come.

Centralized, top-down control is a solution of the past, which is only suitable for systems of low complexity. Therefore, federal systems and majority decisions are the solutions of the present. With economic and cultural evolution, social complexity will continue to rise. Therefore, the solution for the future is collective intelligence. This means that citizen science, crowdsourcing and online discussion platforms are eminently important new approaches to making more knowledge, ideas and resources available.

Collective intelligence requires a high degree of diversity. This is, however, being reduced by today's personalized information systems, which reinforce trends.

Sociodiversity is as important as biodiversity. It fuels not only collective intelligence and innovation, but also resilience—the ability of our society to cope with unexpected shocks. Reducing sociodiversity often also reduces the functionality and performance of an economy and society. This is the reason why totalitarian regimes often end up in conflict with their neighbors. Typical long-term consequences are political instability and war, as have occurred time and again throughout history. Pluralism and participation are therefore not to be seen primarily as concessions to citizens, but as functional prerequisites for thriving, complex, modern societies.

In summary, it can be said that we are now at a crossroads. Big Data, artificial intelligence, cybernetics, and behavioral economics are shaping our society—for better or worse. If such widespread technologies are not compatible with our society's core values, sooner or later they will cause extensive damage. They could lead to an automated society with totalitarian features. In the worst case, a centralized artificial intelligence would control what we know, what we think and how we act. We are at the historic moment, where we have to decide on the right path—a path that allows us all to benefit from the digital revolution. Therefore, we urge to adhere to the following fundamental principles:

1. to increasingly decentralize the function of information systems;
2. to support informational self-determination and participation;
3. to improve transparency in order to achieve greater trust;

4. to reduce the distortion and pollution of information;
5. to enable user-controlled information filters;
6. to support social and economic diversity;
7. to improve interoperability and collaborative opportunities;
8. to create digital assistants and coordination tools;
9. to support collective intelligence; and
10. to promote responsible behavior of citizens in the digital world through digital literacy and enlightenment.

Following this digital agenda we would all benefit from the fruits of the digital revolution: the economy, government, and citizens alike. What are we waiting for?

A Strategy for the Digital Age

Big Data and artificial intelligence are undoubtedly important innovations. They have an enormous potential to catalyze economic value and social progress, from personalized health care to sustainable cities. It is totally unacceptable, however, to use these technologies to incapacitate the citizen. Big nudging and citizen scores abuse centrally collected personal data for behavioral control in ways that are totalitarian in nature. This is not only incompatible with human rights and democratic principles, but also inappropriate to manage modern, innovative societies. In order to solve the genuine problems of the world, far better approaches in the fields of information and risk management are required. The research area of responsible innovation and the initiative "Data for Humanity" (see "Big Data for the benefit of society and humanity") provide guidance as to how Big Data and artificial intelligence should be used for the benefit of society.

What can we do now? First, even in these times of digital revolution, the basic rights of citizens should be protected, as they are a fundamental prerequisite of a modern functional, democratic society. This requires the creation of a new social contract, based on trust and cooperation, which sees citizens and customers not as obstacles or resources to be exploited, but as partners. For this, the state would have to provide an appropriate regulatory framework, which ensures that technologies are designed and used in ways that are compatible with democracy. This would have to guarantee informational self-determination, not only theoretically, but also practically, because it is a precondition for us to lead our lives in a self-determined and responsible manner.

There should also be a right to get a copy of personal data collected about us. It should be regulated by law that this information must be automatically sent, in a standardized format, to a personal data store, through which individuals could manage the use of their data (potentially supported by particular AI-based digital assistants). To ensure greater privacy and to prevent discrimination, the unauthorised use of data would have to be punishable by law. Individuals would then be able to decide who can use their information, for what purpose and for how long. Furthermore, appropriate measures should be taken to ensure that data is securely stored and exchanged.

Sophisticated reputation systems considering multiple criteria could help to increase the quality of information on which our decisions are based. If data filters and recommendation and search algorithms would be selectable and configurable by the user, we could look at problems from multiple perspectives, and we would be less prone to manipulation by distorted information.

In addition, we need an efficient complaints procedure for citizens, as well as effective sanctions for violations of the rules. Finally, in order to create sufficient transparency and trust, leading scientific institutions should act as trustees of the data and algorithms that currently evade democratic control. This would also require an appropriate code of conduct that, at the very least, would have to be followed by anyone with access to sensitive data and algorithms—a kind of Hippocratic Oath for IT professionals.

Furthermore, we would require a digital agenda to lay the foundation for new jobs and the future of the digital society. Every year we invest billions in the agricultural sector and public infrastructure, schools and universities—to the benefit of industry and the service sector.

Which public systems do we therefore need to ensure that the digital society becomes a success? First, completely new educational concepts are needed. This should be more focused on critical thinking, creativity, inventiveness and entrepreneurship than on creating standardised workers (whose tasks, in the future, will be done by robots and computer algorithms). Education should also provide an understanding of the responsible and critical use of digital technologies, because citizens must be aware of how the digital world is intertwined with the physical one. In order to effectively and responsibly exercise their rights, citizens must have an understanding of these technologies, but also of what uses are illegitimate. This is why there is all the more need for science, industry, politics, and educational institutions to make this knowledge widely available.

Secondly, a participatory platform is needed that makes it easier for people to become self-employed, set up their own projects, find collaboration partners, market products and services worldwide, manage resources and pay tax and social security contributions (a kind of sharing economy for all). To complement this, towns and even villages could set up centers for the emerging digital communities (such as fab labs), where ideas can be jointly developed and tested for free. Thanks to the open and innovative approach found in these centers, massive, collaborative innovation could be promoted.

Particular kinds of competitions could provide additional incentives for innovation, help increase public visibility and generate momentum for a participatory digital society. They could be particularly useful in mobilising civil society to ensure local contributions to global problems solving (for example, by means of "Climate Olympics"). For instance, platforms aiming to coordinate scarce resources could help unleash the huge potential of the circular and sharing economy, which is still largely untapped.

With the commitment to an open data strategy, governments and industry would increasingly make data available for science and public use, to create suitable conditions for an efficient information and innovation ecosystem that keeps pace with the challenges of our world. This could be encouraged by tax cuts, in the same way as they were granted in some countries for the use of environmentally friendly technologies.

Thirdly, building a "digital nervous system," run by the citizens, could open up new opportunities of the Internet of Things for everyone and provide real-time data measurements available to all. If we want to use resources in a more sustainable way and slow down climate change, we need to measure the positive and negative side effects of our interactions with others and our environment. By using appropriate feedback loops, systems could be influenced in such a way that they achieve the desired outcomes by means of self-organization.

For this to succeed we would need various incentive and exchange systems, available to all economic, political and social innovators. This could create entirely new markets and, therefore, also the basis for new prosperity. Unleashing the virtually unlimited potential of the digital economy would be greatly promoted by a pluralistic financial system (for example, functionally differentiated currencies) and new regulations for the compensation for inventions.

To better cope with the complexity and diversity of our future world and to turn it into an advantage, we will require personal digital assistants. These digital assistants will also benefit from developments in the field of artificial intelligence. In the future it can be expected that numerous networks combining human and artificial intelligence will be flexibly built and reconfigured, as needed. However, in order for us to retain control of our lives, these networks should be controlled in a distributed way. In particular, one would also have to be able to log in and log out as desired.

Democratic Platforms

A "Wikipedia of Cultures" could eventually help to coordinate various activities in a highly diverse world and to make them compatible with each other. It would make the mostly implicit success principles of the world's cultures explicit, so that they could be combined in new ways. A "Cultural Genome Project" like this would also be a kind of peace project, because it would raise public awareness for the value of sociocultural diversity. Global companies have long known that culturally diverse and multidisciplinary teams are more successful than homogeneous ones. However, the framework needed to efficiently collate knowledge and ideas from lots of people in order to create collective intelligence is still missing in many places. To change this, the provision of online deliberation platforms would be highly useful. They could also create the framework needed to realize an upgraded, digital democracy, with greater participatory opportunities for citizens. This is important, because many of the problems facing the world today can only be managed with contributions from civil society.

Thanks to Big Data, we can now take better, evidence-based decisions. However, the principle of top-down control increasingly fails, since the complexity of society grows in an explosive way as we go on networking our world. Distributed control approaches will become ever more important. Only by means of collective intelligence will it be possible to find appropriate solutions to the complexity challenges of our world.

Our society is at a crossroads: If ever more powerful algorithms would be controlled by a few decision-makers and reduce our self-determination, we would fall back in a Feudalism 2.0, as important historical achievements would be lost. Now, however, we have the chance to choose the path to digital democracy or democracy 2.0, which would benefit us all (see also https://vimeo.com/147442522).

Spotlight on China: Is This What the Future of Society Looks Like?

How would behavioural and social control impact our lives? The concept of a Citizen Score, which is now being implemented in China, gives an idea. There, all citizens are rated on a one-dimensional ranking scale. Everything they do gives plus or minus points. This is not only aimed at mass surveillance. The score depends on an individual's clicks on the Internet and their politically-correct conduct or not, and it determines their credit terms, their access to certain jobs, and travel visas. Therefore, the Citizen Score is about behavioural and social control. Even the behaviour of friends and acquaintances affects this score, i.e. the principle of clan liability is also applied: everyone becomes both a guardian of virtue and a kind of snooping informant, at the same time; unorthodox thinkers are isolated. Were similar principles to spread in democratic countries, it would be ultimately irrelevant whether it was the state or influential companies that set the rules. In both cases, the pillars of democracy would be directly threatened:

- The tracking and measuring of all activities that leave digital traces would create a "naked" citizen, whose human dignity and privacy would progressively be degraded.
- Decisions would no longer be free, because a wrong choice from the perspective of the government or company defining the criteria of the points system would have negative consequences. The autonomy of the individual would, in principle, be abolished.
- Each small mistake would be punished and no one would be unsuspicious. The principle of the presumption of innocence would become obsolete. Predictive Policing could even lead to punishment for violations that have not happened, but are merely expected to occur.
- As the underlying algorithms cannot operate completely free of error, the principle of fairness and justice would be replaced by a new kind of arbitrariness, against which people would barely be able to defend themselves.
- If individual goals were externally set, the possibility of individual self-development would be eliminated and, thereby, democratic pluralism, too.
- Local culture and social norms would no longer be the basis of appropriate, situation-dependent behaviour.
- The control of society with a one-dimensional goal function would lead to more conflicts and, therefore, to a loss of security. One would have to expect serious instability, as we have seen it in our financial system.

Such a control of society would turn away from self-responsible citizens to individuals as underlings, leading to a Feudalism 2.0. This is diametrically opposed to democratic values. It is therefore time for an Enlightenment 2.0, which would feed into a Democracy 2.0, based on digital self-determination. This requires democratic technologies: information systems, which are compatible with democratic principles—otherwise they will destroy our society.

"Big Nudging"—Ill-Designed for Problem Solving

He who has large amounts of data can manipulate people in subtle ways. But even benevolent decision-makers may do more wrong than right, says **Dirk Helbing.**

Proponents of Nudging argue that people do not take optimal decisions and it is, therefore, necessary to help them. This school of thinking is known as paternalism. However, Nudging does not choose the way of informing and persuading people. It rather exploits psychological weaknesses in order to bring us to certain behaviours, i.e. we are tricked. The scientific approach underlying this approach is called "behaviorism," which is actually long out of date.

Decades ago, Burrhus Frederic Skinner conditioned rats, pigeons, and dogs by rewards and punishments (for example, by feeding them or applying painful electric shocks). Today one tries to condition people in similar ways. Instead of in a Skinner box, we are living in a "filter bubble": with personalized information our thinking is being steered. With personalized prices, we may be even punished or rewarded, for example, for (un)desired clicks on the Internet. The combination of Nudging with Big Data has therefore led to a new form of Nudging that we may call "Big Nudging." The increasing amount of personal information about us, which is often collected without our consent, reveals what we think, how we feel and how we can be manipulated. This insider information is exploited to manipulate us to make choices that we would otherwise not make, to buy some overpriced products or those that we do not need, or perhaps to give our vote to a certain political party.

However, Big Nudging is not suitable to solve many of our problems. This is particularly true for the complexity-related challenges of our world. Although already 90 countries use Nudging, it has not reduced our societal problems—on the contrary. Global warming is progressing. World peace is fragile, and terrorism is on the rise. Cybercrime explodes, and also the economic and debt crisis is not solved in many countries.

There is also no solution to the inefficiency of financial markets, as Nudging guru Richard Thaler recently admitted. In his view, if the state would control financial markets, this would rather aggravate the problem. But why should one then control our society in a top-down way, which is even more complex than a financial market? Society is not a machine, and complex systems cannot be steered like a car. This can be understood by discussing another complex system: our bodies. To cure diseases, one needs to take the right medicine at the right time in the right dose. Many treatments also have serious side and interaction effects. The same, of course, is expected to apply to social interventions by Big Nudging. Often is not clear in advance what would be good or bad for society. Sixty percent of the scientific results in psychology are not reproducible. Therefore, chances are to cause more harm than good by Big Nudging.

Furthermore, there is no measure, which is good for all people. For example, in recent decades, we have seen food advisories changing all the time. Many people also suffer from food intolerances, which can even be fatal. Mass screenings for certain kinds of cancer and other diseases are now being viewed quite critically, because the side effects of wrong diagnoses often outweigh the benefits. Therefore, if one decided to use Big Nudging, a solid scientific basis, transparency, ethical evaluation and democratic control would be really crucial. The measures taken would have to guarantee statistically significant improvements, and the side effects would have to be acceptable. Users should be made aware of them (in analogy to a medical leaflet), and the treated persons would have to have the last word.

In addition, applying one and the same measure to the entire population would not be good. But far too little is known to take appropriate individual measures. Not only is it important for society to apply different treatments in order to maintain diversity, but correlations (regarding what measure to take in what particular context) matter as well. For the functioning of society it is essential that people apply different roles, which are fitting to the respective situation they are in. Big Nudging is far from being able to deliver this.

Current Big-Data-based personalization rather creates new problems such as discrimination. For instance, if we make health insurance rates dependent on certain diets, then Jews, Muslims and Christians, women and men will have to pay different rates. Thus, a bunch of new problems is arising.

Richard Thaler is, therefore, not getting tired to emphasize that Nudging should only be used in beneficial ways. As a prime example, how to use Nudging, he mentions a GPS-based route guidance system. This, however, is turned on and off by the user. The user also specifies the respective goal. The digital assistant then offers several alternatives, between which the user can freely choose. After that, the digital assistant supports the user as good as it can in reaching the goal and in making better decisions. This would certainly be the right approach to improve people's behaviours, but today the spirit of Big Nudging is quite different from this.

Digital Self-Determination by Means of a "Right to a Copy" by Ernst Hafen

Europe must guarantee citizens a right to a digital copy of all data about them (Right to a Copy), says **Ernst Hafen.** *A first step towards data democracy would be to establish cooperative banks for personal data that are owned by the citizens rather than by corporate shareholders.*

Medicine can profit from health data. However, access to personal data must be controlled the persons (the data subjects) themselves. The "Right to a Copy" forms the basis for such a control.

In Europe, we like to point out that we live in free, democratic societies. We have almost unconsciously become dependent on multinational data firms, however, whose free services we pay for with our own data. Personal data— which is now sometimes referred to as a "new asset class" or the oil of the

21st century—is greatly sought after. However, thus far nobody has managed to extract the maximum use from personal data because it lies in many different data sets. Google and Facebook may know more about our health than our doctor, but even these firms cannot collate all of our data, because they rightly do not have access to our patient files, shopping receipts, or information about our genomic make-up. In contrast to other assets, data can be copied with almost no associated cost. Every person should have the right to obtain a copy of all their personal data. In this way, they can control the use and aggregation of their data and decide themselves whether to give access to friends, another doctor, or the scientific community.

The emergence of mobile health sensors and apps means that patients can contribute significant medical insights. By recording their bodily health on their smartphones, such as medical indicators and the side effects of medications, they supply important data which make it possible to observe how treatments are applied, evaluate health technologies, and conduct evidence-based medicine in general. It is also a moral obligation to give citizens access to copies of their data and allow them to take part in medical research, because it will save lives and make health care more affordable.

European countries should copper-fasten the digital self-determination of their citizens by enshrining the "Right to a Copy" in their constitutions, as has been proposed in Switzerland. In this way, citizens can use their data to play an active role in the global data economy. If they can store copies of their data in nonprofit, citizen-controlled, cooperative institutions, a large portion of the economic value of personal data could be returned to society. The cooperative institutions would act as trustees in managing the data of their members. This would result in the democratization of the market for personal data and the end of digital dependence.

Democratic Digital Society
Citizens must be Allowed to Actively Participate

In order to deal with future technology in a responsible way, it is necessary that each one of us can participate in the decision-making process, argues **Bruno S. Frey** from the University of Basel.

How can responsible innovation be promoted effectively? Appeals to the public have little, if any, effect if the *institutions* or rules shaping human interactions are not designed to incentivize and enable people to meet these requests.

Several types of institutions should be considered. Most importantly, society must be *decentralized*, following the principle of subsidiarity. Three dimensions matter.

- *Spatial* decentralization consists in vibrant federalism. The provinces, regions, and communes must be given sufficient autonomy. To a large extent, they must be able to set their own tax rates and govern their own public expenditure.
- *Functional* decentralization according to area of public expenditure (for example education, health, environment, water provision, traffic, culture etc) is also desirable. This concept has been developed through the proposal of FOCJ, or "Functional, Overlapping and Competing Jurisdictions."
- *Political* decentralization relating to the division of power between the executive (government), legislative (parliament) and the courts. Public media and academia should be additional pillars.

These types of decentralization will continue to be of major importance in the digital society of the future.

In addition, citizens must have the opportunity to directly participate in decision-making on particular issues by means of popular referenda. In the discourse prior to such a referendum, all relevant arguments should be brought forward and stated in an organized fashion. The various proposals about how to solve a particular problem should be compared and narrowed down to those which seem to be most promising, and integrated insomuch as possible during a mediation process. Finally, a referendum needs to take place, which serves to identify the most viable solution for the local conditions (viable in the sense that it enjoys a diverse range of support in the electorate).

Nowadays, on-line deliberation tools can efficiently support such processes. This makes it possible to consider a larger and more diverse range of ideas and knowledge, harnessing "collective intelligence" to produce better policy proposals.

Another way to implement the ten proposals would be to create new, unorthodox institutions. For example, it could be made compulsory for every official body to take on an "*advocatus diaboli*." This lateral thinker would be tasked with developing counter-arguments and alternatives to each proposal. This would reduce the tendency to think along the lines of "political correctness" and unconventional approaches to the problem would also be considered.

Another unorthodox measure would be to choose among the alternatives considered reasonable during the discourse process using *random decision-making mechanisms*. Such an approach increases the chance that unconventional and generally disregarded proposals and ideas would be integrated into the digital society of the future.

Bruno S. Frey

Bruno Frey (*1941) is an academic economist and Permanent Visiting Professor at the University of Basel where he directs the Center for Research in Economics and Well-Being

(CREW). He is also Research Director of the Center for Research in Economics, Management and the Arts (CREMA) in Zurich.

Democratic Technologies and Responsible Innovation

When technology determines how we see the world, there is a threat of misuse and deception. Thus, innovation must reflect our values, argues **Jeroen van den Hoven.**

Germany was recently rocked by an industrial scandal of global proportions. The revelations led to the resignation of the CEO of one of the largest car manufacturers, a grave loss of consumer confidence, a dramatic slump in share price and economic damage for the entire car industry. There was even talk of severe damage to the "Made in Germany" brand. The compensation payments will be in the range of billions of Euro.

The background to the scandal was a situation whereby VW and other car manufacturers used manipulative software which could detect the conditions under which the environmental compliance of a vehicle was tested. The software algorithm altered the behavior of the engine so that it emitted fewer pollutant exhaust fumes under test conditions than in normal circumstances. In this way, it cheated the test procedure. The full reduction of emissions occurred only during the tests, but not in normal use.

In the 21st century, we urgently need to address the question of how we can implement ethical standards technologically.

Similarly, algorithms, computer code, software, models and data will increasingly determine what we see in the digital society, and what are choices are with regard to health insurance, finance and politics. This brings new risks for the economy and society. In particular, there is a danger of deception.

Thus, it is important to understand that our values are embodied in the things we create. Otherwise, the technological design of the future will determine the shape of our society ("code is law"). If these values are self-serving, discriminatory or contrary to the ideals of freedom and personal privacy, this will damage our society. Thus, in the 21st century we must urgently address the question of how we can implement ethical standards technologically. The challenge calls for us to "design for value."

If we lack the motivation to develop the technological tools, science and institutions necessary to align the digital world with our shared values, the future looks very bleak. Thankfully, the European Union has invested in an extensive research and development program for responsible innovation. Furthermore, the EU countries which passed the Lund and Rome Declarations emphasized that innovation needs to be carried out

responsibly. Among other things, this means that innovation should be directed at developing intelligent solutions to societal problems, which can harmonize values such as efficiency, security and sustainability. Genuine innovation does not involve deceiving people into believing that their cars are sustainable and efficient. Genuine innovation means creating technologies that can actually satisfy these requirements.

Digital Risk Literacy
Technology Needs Users Who Can Control It

Rather than letting intelligent technology diminish our brainpower, we should learn to better control it, says **Gerd Gigerenzer**—beginning in childhood.

The digital revolution provides an impressive array of possibilities: thousands of apps, the Internet of Things, and almost permanent connectivity to the world. But in the excitement, one thing is easily forgotten: innovative technology needs competent users who can control it rather than be controlled by it.

Three examples:

One of my doctoral students sits at his computer and appears to be engrossed in writing his dissertation. At the same time his e-mail inbox is open, all day long. He is in fact waiting to be interrupted. It's easy to recognize how many interruptions he had in the course of the day by looking at the flow of his writing.

An American student writes text messages while driving: "When a text comes in, I just have to look, no matter what. Fortunately, my phone shows me the text as a pop up at first . . . so I don't have to do too much looking while I'm driving." If, at the speed of 50 miles per hour, she takes only 2 seconds to glance at her cell phone, she's just driven 48 yards "blind." That young woman is risking a car accident. Her smart phone has taken control of her behavior—as is the case for the 20 to 30 percent of Germans who also text while driving.

During the parliamentary elections in India in 2014, the largest democratic election in the world with over 800 million potential voters, there were three main candidates: N. Modi, A. Kejriwal, and R. Ghandi. In a study, undecided voters could find out more information about these candidates using an Internet search engine. However, the participants did not know that the web pages had been manipulated: For one group, more positive items about Modi popped up on the first page and negative ones later on. The other groups experienced the same for the other candidates. This and similar manipulative procedures are common practice on the Internet. It is estimated that for candidates who appear on the first page thanks to such manipulation, the number of votes they receive from undecided voters increases by 20 percentage points.

Will Democracy Survive Big Data and Artificial Intelligence? by Dirk Helbing et al.

87

In each of these cases, human behavior is controlled by digital technology. Losing control is nothing new, but the digital revolution has increased the possibility of that happening.

What can we do? There are three competing visions. One is techno-paternalism, which replaces (flawed) human judgment with algorithms. The distracted doctoral student could continue readings his emails and use thesis-writing software; all he would need to do is input key information on the topic. Such algorithms would solve the annoying problem of plagiarism scandals by making them an everyday occurrence.

Although still in the domain of science fiction, human judgment is already being replaced by computer programs in many areas. The BabyConnect app, for instance, tracks the daily development of infants—height, weight, number of times it was nursed, how often its diapers were changed, and much more—while newer apps compare the baby with other users' children in a real-time database. For parents, their baby becomes a data vector, and normal discrepancies often cause unnecessary concern.

The second vision is known as "nudging." Rather than letting the algorithm do all the work, people are steered into a particular direction, often without being aware of it. The experiment on the elections in India is an example of that. We know that the first page of Google search results receives about 90 percent of all clicks, and half of these are the first two results. This knowledge about human behavior is taken advantage of by manipulating the order of results so that the positive ones about a particular candidate or a particular commercial product appear on the first page. In countries such as Germany, where web searches are dominated by one search engine (Google), this leads to endless possibilities to sway voters. Like techno-paternalism, nudging takes over the helm.

But there is a third possibility. My vision is risk literacy, where people are equipped with the competencies to control media rather than be controlled by it. In general, risk literacy concerns informed ways of dealing with risk-related areas such as health, money, and modern technologies. Digital risk literacy means being able to take advantage of digital technologies without becoming dependent on or manipulated by them. That is not as hard as it sounds. My doctoral student has since learned to switch on his email account only three times a day, morning, noon, and evening, so that he can work on his dissertation without constant interruption.

Learning digital self-control needs to begin as a child, at school and also from the example set by parents. Some paternalists may scoff at the idea, stating that humans lack the intelligence and self-discipline to ever become risk literate. But centuries ago the same was said about learning to read and write—which a majority of people in industrial countries can now do. In the same way, people can learn to deal with risks

more sensibly. To achieve this, we need to radically rethink strategies and invest in people rather than replace or manipulate them with intelligent technologies. In the 21st century, we need less paternalism and nudging and more informed, critical, and risk-savvy citizens. It's time to snatch away the remote control from technology and take our lives into our own hands.

Ethics: Big Data for the Common Good and for Humanity

The power of data can be used for good and bad purposes. Roberto Zicari and Andrej Zwitter have formulated five principles of Big Data Ethics.

by Andrej Zwitter and Roberto Zicari

In recent times there have been a growing number of voices—from tech visionaries like Elon Musk (Tesla Motors), to Bill Gates (Microsoft) and Steve Wozniak (Apple)—warning of the dangers of artificial intelligence (AI). A petition against automated weapon systems was signed by 200,000 people and an open letter recently published by MIT calls for a new, inclusive approach to the coming digital society.

We must realize that Big Data, like any other tool, can be used for good and bad purposes. In this sense, the decision by the European Court of Justice against the Safe Harbour Agreement on human rights grounds is understandable.

States, international organizations, and private actors now employ Big Data in a variety of spheres. It is important that all those who profit from Big Data are aware of their moral responsibility. For this reason, the Data for Humanity Initiative was established, with the goal of disseminating an ethical code of conduct for Big Data use. This initiative advances five fundamental ethical principles for Big Data users:

1. *"Do no harm."* The digital footprint that everyone now leaves behind exposes individuals, social groups and society as a whole to a certain degree of transparency and vulnerability. Those who have access to the insights afforded by Big Data must not harm third parties.

2. *Ensure that data is used in such a way that the results will foster the peaceful coexistence of humanity.* The selection of content and access to data influences the world view of a society. Peaceful coexistence is only possible if data scientists are aware of their responsibility to provide even and unbiased access to data.

3. *Use data to help people in need.* In addition to being economically beneficial, innovation in the sphere of Big Data could also create additional social value. In the

age of global connectivity, it is now possible to create innovative Big Data tools which could help to support people in need.

4. *Use data to protect nature and reduce pollution of the environment.* One of the biggest achievements of Big Data analysis is the development of efficient processes and synergy effects. Big Data can only offer a sustainable economic and social future if such methods are also used to create and maintain a healthy and stable natural environment.

5. *Use data to eliminate discrimination and intolerance and to create a fair system of social coexistence.* Social media has created a strengthened social network. This can only lead to long-term global stability if it is built on the principles of fairness, equality, and justice.

To conclude, we would also like to draw attention to how interesting new possibilities afforded by Big Data could lead to a better future: "As more data become less costly and technology breaks barriers to acquisition and analysis, the opportunity to deliver actionable information for civic purposes grows. This might be termed the 'common good' challenge for Big Data." (Jake Porway, DataKind). In the end, it is important to understand the turn to Big Data as an opportunity to do good and as a hope for a better future.

Measuring, Analyzing, Optimizing: When Intelligent Machines Take over Societal Control

In the digital age, machines steer everyday life to a considerable extent already. We should, therefore, think twice before we share our personal data, says expert **Yvonne Hofstetter.**

If Norbert Wiener (1894–1964) had experienced the digital era, for him it would have been the land of plenty. "Cybernetics is the science of information and control, regardless of whether the target of control is a machine or a living organism," the founder of Cybernetics once explained in Hannover, Germany in 1960. In history, the world never produced such amount of data and information as it does today.

Cybernetics, a science asserting ubiquitous importance, makes a strong claim: "Everything can be controlled." During the 20th century, both the US armed forces and the Soviet Union applied Cybernetics to control their arms' race. The NATO had deployed so-called C3I systems (Command, Control, Communication and Information), a term for military infrastructure

that leans linguistically to Wiener's book on *Cybernetics: Or Control and Communication in the Animal and the Machine,* published in 1948. Control refers to the control of machines as well as of individuals or entire social systems like military alliances, financial markets or, pointing to the 21st century, even the electorate. Its major premise: keeping the world under surveillance to collect data. Connecting people and things to the *Internet of Everything* is a perfect to way to obtain the required mass data as input to cybernetic control strategies.

With Cybernetics, Wiener proposed a new scientific concept: the closed-loop feedback. Feedback—e.g., the *Likes* we give, the online comments we make—is a major concept of digitization, too. Does that mean digitization is the most perfect implementation of Cybernetics? When we use smart devices, we are creating a ceaseless data stream disclosing our intentions, geo position or social environment. While we communicate more thoughtlessly than ever online, in the background, an ecosystem of artificial intelligence is evolving. Today, artificial intelligence is the sole technology being able to profile us and draw conclusions about our future behavior.

An automated control strategy, usually a learning machine, analyzes our actual situation and then computes a stimulus that should draw us closer to a more desirable "optimal" state. Increasingly, such controllers govern our daily lives. As digital assistants they help us making decisions in the vast ocean of optionality and intimidating uncertainty. Even Google Search is a control strategy. When typing a keyword, a user reveals his intentions. The Google search engine, in turn, will not just present a list with best hits, but a link list that embodies the highest (financial) value rather for the company than for the user. Doing it that way, i.e., listing corporate offerings at the very top of the search results, Google controls the user's next clicks. This, the European Union argues, is a misuse.

But is there any way out? Yes, if we disconnected from the cybernetic loop. Just stop responding to a digital stimulus. Cybernetics will fail, if the controllable counterpart steps out of the loop. Yet, we are free to owe a response to a digital controller. However, as digitization further escalates, soon we may have no more choice. Hence, we are called on to fight for our freedom rights—afresh during the digital era and in particular at the rise of intelligent machines.

For Norbert Wiener (1894–1964), the digital era would be a paradise. "Cybernetics is the science of information and control, regardless of whether a machine or a living organism is being controlled," the founder of cybernetics once said in Hanover, Germany in 1960.

Cybernetics, a science which claims ubiquitous importance makes a strong promise: "Everything is controllable." During the 20th century, both the US armed forces and the Soviet Union applied cybernetics to control the arms' race. NATO had deployed so-called C3I systems (Command, Control, Communication and Information), a term for military infrastructure that linguistically leans on Wiener's book entitled *Cybernetics: Or Control and Communication in the Animal and the Machine* published in 1948. Control refers to the control of machines as well as of individuals or entire societal systems such as military alliances, NATO and the Warsaw Pact. Its basic requirements are: Integrating, collecting data and communicating. Connecting people and things to the *Internet of Everything* is a perfect way to obtain the required data as input of cybernetic control strategies.

With cybernetics, a new scientific concept was proposed: the closed-loop feedback. Feedback—such as the *likes* we give or the online comments we make—is another major concept related to digitization. Does this mean that digitization is the most perfect implementation of cybernetics? When we use smart devices, we create an endless data stream disclosing our intentions, geolocation or social environment. While we communicate more thoughtlessly than ever online, in the background, an artificial intelligence (AI) ecosystem is evolving. Today, AI is the sole technology able to profile us and draw conclusions about our future behavior.

An automated control strategy, usually a learning machine, analyses our current state and computes a stimulus that should draw us closer to a more desirable "optimal" state. Increasingly, such controllers govern our daily lives. Such digital assistants help us to make decisions among the vast ocean of options and intimidating uncertainty. Even Google Search is a control strategy. When typing a keyword, a user reveals his intentions. The Google search engine, in turn, presents not only a list of the best hits, but also a list of links sorted according to their (financial) value to the company, rather than to the user. By listing corporate offerings at the very top of the search results, Google controls the user's next clicks. That is a misuse of Google's monopoly, the European Union argues.

But is there any way out? Yes, if we disconnect from the cybernetic loop and simply stop responding to the digital stimulus. Cybernetics will fail, if the controllable counterpart steps out of the loop. We should remain discreet and frugal with our data, even if it is difficult. However, as digitization further escalates, soon there may be no more choices left. Hence, we are called on to fight once again for our freedom in the digital era, particularly against the rise of intelligent machines.

Critical Thinking

1. What is the danger of "nudging" and what are current examples of this and the consequences for society?
2. What are the ethical and leagal concerns with manipulative "personalization" programs and applications.
3. How can Big Data and artificial intellegence be used to counter the negative trends intoduced by the same technologies.

Internet References

AI For Social Good: How Humans and Machines Are Making a Better World
https://goo.gl/zEp5ib
Big Data's Power Is Terrifying. That Could Be Good News for Democracy
https://goo.gl/yM51eU
Can We Use Big Data to Fight Child Abuse? The Answer Is Complicated
https://goo.gl/X2uXKo
Data Driven Justice
https://goo.gl/d9dKpM

Dirk Helbing is Professor of Computational Social Science at the Department of Humanities, Social and Political Sciences and affiliate professor at the Department of Computer Science at ETH Zurich.

Article

Prepared by: Daniel Mittleman, *DePaul University* and
Douglas Druckenmiller, *Western Illinois University*

Algorithms Supercharged Gerrymandering. We Should Use Them to Fix It

Daniel Oberhaus

Learning Outcomes

After reading this article, you will be able to:

- Define gerrymandering, describe its impact on politics.

- Discuss how artificial intelligence has impacted this situation over the past few decades.

- Articulate ideas for how AI algorithms can be used to improve redistricting after the 2020 census.

Today, the Supreme Court will hear oral arguments for *Gill v. Whitford*, in which the state of Wisconsin will argue that congressional redistricting practices are not subject to judicial oversight. At the core of this hearing is whether partisan gerrymandering—a tactic used by political parties to redraw congressional voting districts so that the voting power within those districts is weighted toward their own party—was used to steal the 2012 state elections in Wisconsin from Democrats. The ramifications of this decision will be felt by the entire country.

The Supreme Court will be deciding whether or not federal courts have the ability to throw out district maps for being too partisan, which requires the justices to be able to articulate just what constitutes partisan gerrymandering in the first place. The practice of gerrymandering has been a thorn in the side of American democracy for most of our nation's existence, but continues largely unabated due to the difficulty of defining the point at which a new congressional district can considered to be the result of partisan gerrymandering.

Various solutions to America's gerrymandering problem have been proposed over the years, but most of these have failed to gain traction. In September, however, a team of data scientists at the University of Illinois published a paper to little fanfare that offered a novel solution to America's gerrymandering woes: Let an algorithm draw the maps.

Although the Illinois researchers, led by computer science professor Sheldon Jacobson, aren't the first to propose using artificial intelligence as a solution to the redistricting process, they hope their new approach will be more accessible and fair than previous attempts at stopping gerrymandering with computation.

These computer scientists are motivated by the belief that data and algorithms will create transparency in the notoriously opaque redistricting process by exposing the inputs and parameters that led to redrawing a district a certain way. With these inputs and parameters exposed, data scientists hope this will hopefully incentivize a more equitable redistricting process. Yet they are also the first to acknowledge that the same algorithms that can create equity in congressional redistricting can also be used to gerrymander with unprecedented efficiency.

"If a group of politicians in a particular state wants to gerrymander the state to favor them, we can incorporate that into our algorithm and come up with districts which will satisfy their political agenda," Jacobson told me over the phone. "We're not political scientists trying to create an agenda. We're trying to create a tool of transparency."

Algorithms are already widely deployed in the service of partisan gerrymandering and are increasingly used as tools to keep gerrymandering in check. Yet for all their pretension to fairness, it's far from certain that algorithms are actually creating more equity in the electoral process. This raises a profoundly important question for the future of the American experiment in democracy: If algorithms have been used for the last few decades to fuel gerrymandering, can they also offer a more equitable way forward?

A Brief History of Gerrymandering

Every decade, the United States carries out a population census, which among other things, determines how many seats in the House of Representatives are allotted to each state. It is then up to the states to draw up congressional districts, each of which elects a representative of that district to the House. The way the boundaries of these districts are decided varies from state to state, but a few elements pertain to almost every redistricting decision: all parts of a district must be geographically connected and districts ought to follow boundaries for cities, towns or counties. Beyond these common elements, redistricting requirements and processes can vary significantly from state to state. In most cases, the state legislature controls the redistricting process, which means that the party with control over the legislature has the ability to gerrymander, or redraw congressional districts in the interests of that party.

To get a better idea of how this practice can drastically affect elections, imagine a state that has 50 constituents. Of these constituents, let's say 30 vote Democrat and 20 vote Republican, and the state has five seats in the House, like in the drawing on the left below:

In an ideal system the five congressional districts would be perfectly divided and the constituents of each district all shared the same political affiliations. In other words, the Democrats would get three congressional districts and the Republicans would get two by making each vertical column its own district. But what if Democrats controlled the redistricting process? By dividing the constituencies horizontally, they could ensure that their constituencies are the majority in each district and win all five seats in House. Alternatively, if the Republicans were in control of the legislature, they could redistrict the state so that it has the convoluted boundaries seen in the figure on the far right. Under this plan, three districts are majority Republican and the party would represent a majority of the state in terms of voting power in the House.

Of course in real life the distribution of voters in a state is not so neat, but the general idea behind gerrymandering—and its consequences—remains the same.

According to David Daley, the editor in chief of *Salon* and author of *Ratfucked: The True Story Behind the Secret Plan to Steal America's Democracy*, gerrymandering is also a major source of political stasis in the country. Consider the 2016

How to steal an election

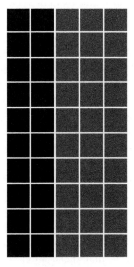

50 Precincts
60% Blue
40% Red

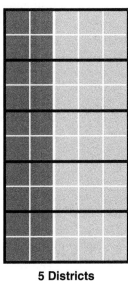

5 Districts
5 Blue
0 Red
Blue wins

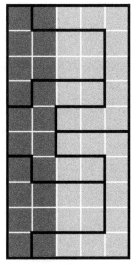

5 Districts
3 Red
2 Blue
Red wins

Image: Steven Nass/ Wikimedia Commons

election, when 400 of 435 House races were scored as "safe" for Democrat and Republican incumbents as a result of gerrymandering. After the election, only 5 seats were transferred to the Democrats from Republicans, and only ten incumbents total lost their seats. Not exactly what you'd expect at a time when the approval rating for Congress is consistently below 20 percent.

"Gerrymandering drains away competitive districts," Daley told me in an email. "Uncompetitive districts have made the government responsive only to the extremes. They are a key reason why we can't get action even on issues where most Americans agree. When we allow partisans to hijack district lines, we give them the power to hijack democracy itself."

Historically, gerrymandering has been disproportionately wielded by GOP candidates to gain influence, but now some establishment Republicans such as Senator John McCain and Ohio Gov. John Kasich are starting to break ranks over the issue. The main problem is determining a fair way to draw districts and on what grounds districts can be challenged as the illegitimate products of gerrymandering.

A solution adopted by Arizona, Washington, and California was to establish standing non-partisan committees to preside over congressional redistricting following the 2010 census. This is a method of addressing gerrymandering that has been adopted in the UK and other commonwealth countries such as Australia and Canada, but non-partisan committee have been slow to catch on in the United States and aren't necessarily as nonpartisan as they seem, according to Daley.

"Independent commissions are only as good as the criteria they are given to draw districts with, and the people who staff them," Daley said. "Most states fill these commissions with partisans and political appointees. They end up being incumbent protection rackets, or in the case of Arizona, pushing an already secretive process deeper into the shadows."

The Algorithmic Turn

The idea to apply computers to the redistricting process as a way to foster transparency and equity was first considered over half-a-century ago in 1961, and in 1965 an algorithm had been described that offered " simplified bipartisan computer redistricting."

By the time the 1990 census rolled around, algorithms had become the norm for legislators and special interest groups hoping to get a leg up during the redistricting process, although fears about the effects of computers on redistricting processes were already being felt in the early 1980s. A 1981 article in the *Christian Science Monitor* captured the spirit of the times, noting that "even those states that have taken the redistricting process either entirely or substantially out of the hands of state lawmakers are hesitant to step aside and let an impersonal, high-speed machine take over."

The panic, it seems, was short lived. In 1989, *The New York Times* reported that "a profusion of new computer technology will make it possible for any political hack to be a political hacker." The article describes how at least 10 vendors were developing computer programs at the time that could be used by "politicians, their aides, and special interest groups as well as official redistricting commissions . . . to produce their own detailed versions of proposed election districts."

For the last 30 years, an ever-growing suite of digital redistricting tools have become available to those with the technical knowledge and funds to wield this proprietary software. Although these algorithms were able to generate dozens of sophisticated district maps in a fraction of the time it would've taken a human to draw just one, they did little to actually solve America's gerrymandering problem. Instead, these algorithms simply made it easier for politicians to create maps that served the interest of their party.

Are you a politician that needs to create district maps that favor Republicans in Wisconsin? No, problem—the algorithm's got you covered.

The Algorithms Strike Back

In 2016, Wendy Cho and her colleagues at the University of Illinois Urbana-Champaign (a different team than the one led by Jacobson) developed a complex algorithm that uses a supercomputer to generate hundreds of millions of possible district configurations in a matter of hours. The tool was designed to test an enticing idea: what if it were possible to generate every possible district map for a given state, and then use this set of all possible maps to judge the level of partisanship on an officially proposed district map? This tool would essentially be able to quantify the fairness of a given map against the set of every possible map. The only problem is that generating a set of all possible maps is, practically speaking, impossible due to the astronomically large number of potential maps.

Yet as Cho and her colleagues discovered, generating all possible maps isn't necessary to achieve their intended goal. Rather, their algorithm whittled the number of necessary maps down to a much more manageable number: about 800 million per state. By using these hundreds of millions of maps as a point of comparison, Cho and her colleagues could statistically expose bias in redistricting procedures.

The downside is that these sorts of technologies are too inaccessible and expensive for general public use because it requires a supercomputer to run. Furthermore, Cho's algorithm is better deployed after the fact to determine the degree that a given district map is the result of partisan gerrymandering.

If algorithms stand any chance of saving America's democracy from gerrymandering, the use of the algorithms and the code they use will also have to be accessible to all.

In this regard, the past decade has been something of a renaissance era for algorithmic redistricting. Take, for example, Bdistricting or Auto-Redistrict, two free open source programs that can be used to generate ostensibly fair, unbiased congressional districts without requiring a supercomputer. There are subtle differences between the types of algorithms these programs use to generate district maps, but both are characterized as local search metaheuristics. This is basically a fancy way of saying that the algorithms manipulate tiny elements within a given domain over thousands of iterations until they arrive at an optimal result.

"A computer can't decide the criteria for creating a district, but it can create districts based on these criteria better than any human could do."

In the case of gerrymandering, the tiny elements being manipulated by local search algorithms are census blocks, the smallest areas of a given state for which census data (such as population size) is available. There are over 11 million census blocks in the United States, and each state has at least 24,000 census blocks. These algorithms basically switch the positions of these census blocks one at a time according to certain parameters (the census blocks for a given district must be contiguous, for example, or should contain the same population sizes) until an optimal solution has been reached.

The new algorithm released last month by the Jacobson and his colleagues at the University of Illinois improves on these local search algorithms by adding a structural element called a geo-graph. Whereas other redistricting algorithms, such as Bdistricting or Auto-Redistrict start by essentially randomly generating districts and then tweaking them over thousands of iterations, Jacobson's algorithm first analyzes the data in census blocks, which might be imagined as spread out on a graph before the computer, and then uses this data to create congressional districts optimized for certain goals.

"Both Bdistricting and Auto-Redistrict appear to be great tools, incorporate a variety of objectives, and can create fair districts," Jacobson told me in an email. "But geo-graphs make each local search iteration step highly efficient. This means that what may take them hours, we can do in minutes on a laptop."

The problem, however, is that although the algorithms themselves are entirely apolitical—their only goal is to find the optimal solution to a problem given a certain data set and parameters—the process of determining what parameters should be fed to the algorithm is still hopelessly mired in the all too human world of politics.

"Although the criteria for districts is a political issue, creating these districts is not," Jacobson told me. "A computer can't

decide the criteria for creating a district, but it can create districts based on these criteria better than any human could do. Ultimately, this is an algorithmic data problem."

Who Programs the Programmers?

On the surface, it seems that defining parameters that automatically lead to fair districts would be relatively straightforward. Bdistricting, for instance, generated district maps that were "optimized for equal population and compactness only." The idea here is that these two criteria are free from "partisan power plays" since they're based on metrics that have nothing to do with politics. But as the San Francisco-based programmer Chris Fedor labored to show, unbiased districts don't necessarily result in *fair* districts. As Fedor detailed in a Medium post, algorithmically optimizing district boundaries for compactness (such as Bdistricting) or randomly generating the boundaries actually leads to districts that are *more* gerrymandered than the boundaries drafted up by politicians.

"Algorithms can hide as much as they reveal," Micah Altman, a professor of computer science at MIT, told me in an email. "Technical choices in an algorithm, how one formalizes criteria, and software implementation can have tremendous implications, but are much more difficult for non-experts to review than comparison of maps and their consequences."

This point is further reinforced in a 2010 paper in the *Duke Journal of Constitutional Law and Public Policy* by Altman and the University of Florida political scientist Michael McDonald, which analyzed several trends in the application of digital technologies to the redistricting process. In the case of Bdistricting and Auto-Redistrict, these programs belong to a class of algorithms that seek to automate the redistricting process entirely. Yet as the authors of the paper point out, these types of algorithms run up against some fundamental limits. Creating optimally compact, contiguous, and equal-population districts belong to a class of math-problems described as "NP-hard," which basically means that there isn't an algorithm that can solve the problem both quickly and correctly in all possible cases.

A way to get around the NP-hardness of redistricting is to approach the problem heuristically, which is a fancy way of saying that a computer can solve the problem, but not necessarily in the most optimal or perfect way. As the Altman and McDonald describe them, these heuristic algorithms are "problem-solving procedures that, while they may yield acceptable results in practice, provide no guarantees of yielding good solutions in general. Specifically, an algorithm is heuristic if it cannot be shown to yield a correct result, or correct within a known error or approximation or having a known probability of correctness." Every attempt at automated redistricting—including all of the algorithms mentioned above—have relied on heuristics.

As Altman and McDonald acknowledge, the computational limits of the redistricting problem could be addressed if the non-partisan criteria for redistricting was greatly simplified and ranked (for instance, equal populations are more important than compactness, contiguity more important than the rest, etc.). Yet so far, anything close to a standard for measuring fair districts is lacking and this very issue has been at the heart of landmark Supreme Court cases considering gerrymandering.

The *Gill v. Whitford* case being heard at the Supreme Court Tuesday is a challenge to the 1986 Supreme Court ruling in *Davis v. Bandemer* that claimed partisan gerrymandering is able to be subjected to judicial oversight, although the court was divided on just what constituted judicial standards in challenges to partisan gerrymandering.

"Algorithms are a terrific tool and there could definitely be a role for them, but they are only as good as the criteria that govern them."

As Justice Byron White wrote in his opinion on the *Bandemer* case, a "group's electoral power is not unconstitutionally diminished by the fact that an apportionment scheme makes winning elections more difficult, and a failure of proportional representation alone does not constitute discrimination." According to White, discrimination in gerrymandering "only occurs when the electoral system is arranged in a manner that will consistently degrade a voter's or a group of voters' influence on the political system as a whole."

The inability of the Supreme Court to decide on standards with which to judge cases challenging partisan gerrymandering was the justification in a 2004 Supreme Court case in which a plurality of justices ruled that challenges to partisan gerrymandering are not subject to court oversight since no general standards for judicially challenging partisan gerrymandering exist. Yet the Supreme Court ultimately didn't overturn the ruling from the 1986 *Bandemer* case that determined partisan gerrymandering *is* subject to judicial oversight since such standards may emerge in the future.

Automated redistricting algorithms basically face the same problem articulated by the Supreme Court ruling in 2004—there continues to be no way to measure at what point a district has been "gerrymandered," and there are no hard rules for what a "fair district" is. (Although there are protections against gerrymandering on racial grounds.) Merely creating districts randomly or optimized for unbiased parameters (such as compactness or equal-population) is no guarantee that those districts are fair. In absence of simple standards that would make automated redistricting truly feasible, Altman and McDonald suggest another approach to the redistricting problem: using algorithms to foster transparency.

Bridging the Analog/Digital Divide

Following the establishment of standing nonpartisan redistricting commissions, Arizona, Washington, and California are now the only three states that are required to solicit public input on redistricting decisions. In these cases, a lightweight machine learning algorithm like the one developed by Jacobson and his colleagues could become an invaluable resource that allows voters to make informed decisions about the redistricting plans. Even in states where the redistricting process is entirely in the hands of legislators, algorithmic tools would empower the public to keep their legislators in check by exposing the assumptions that went into the creation of congressional districts.

"Algorithms are a terrific tool and there could definitely be a role for them," Daley said. "But like independent commissions, they are only as good as the criteria that govern them. The meaningful structural reform that we need involves the way we think about voting and districting itself."

Still, the combination of algorithms and independent redistricting commissions may offer a way forward, according to Altman and McDonald. As they argued in an article for *Scholars Strategy Network*, the internet, coupled with sophisticated and accessible redistricting software, can allow for mass participation in the redistricting process. If this public participation is facilitated by a truly independent commission, which makes all the data, plans and analyses transparent and the tools used to arrive at districts available to the public so that they can compare and comment on these plans, it may be possible to finally create equitable districts.

The plan sounds utopian, but Altman and McDonald have put their principles to work. In 2010, they released an open source software called districtbuilder that enabled broad public participation in the redistricting process by allowing anyone to create, edit, and analyze district plans in a collaborative online environment. While this may sound like it would be reserved for computer nerds with technical know-how, Altman told me it was so simple that they were able to teach elementary school children how to create legal district plans with the tool.

"Algorithmic redistricting, along with software that enables the public to participate in examining, evaluating and contributing to plans, when implemented thoughtfully and transparently, can be useful as a method of assisting human to argue for and to implement their representational goals," Altman said. "However, most proposed algorithmic solutions, such as maximizing some basic notions of geographic compactness, at best embed a set of arbitrary and poorly understood biases into the system, and at worst are cover for attempts to implement political outcomes by proxy."

At the core of the anti-gerrymandering crusade is the notion that a constituency should be represented in accordance with their beliefs, instead of being subjected to the whims of politicians vying to entrench their party's power. That our elected representatives are beholden to their constituencies, and not vice versa, is a fundamental tenet of our democracy.

Algorithms are not a silver bullet for our nation's gerrymandering problem, but as Altman has labored to show, they can be effectively incorporated into the political apparatus to make the process of redistricting more transparent and fair. But algorithms can only do so much, and their biggest limitation right now is a lack of quantifiable criteria for what constitutes fair districts. Determining these criteria is a totally political issue, and as much as we might wish for an automated solution, no amount of computing power will ever crack that problem.

Critical Thinking

1. Should policy-makers be permitted to use artificial intelligence to define political boundaries? What are both the advantages and disadvantages of doing so?

2. How might artificial intelligence be deployed to make the 2020 census redistricting as fair as possible? What downsides, if any, exist with your suggestions?

Internet References

A Summer School for Mathematicians Fed Up with Gerrymandering
https://www.newyorker.com/tech/elements/a-summer-school-for-mathematicians-fed-up-with-gerrymandering

Gerrymandering Is Illegal, But Only Mathematicians Can Prove It
https://www.wired.com/2017/04/gerrymandering-illegal-mathematicians-can-prove/

The New Front in the Gerrymandering Wars: Democracy vs. Math
https://www.nytimes.com/2017/08/29/magazine/the-new-front-in-the-gerrymandering-wars-democracy-vs-math.html

DANIEL OBERHAUS is a Motherboard staff writer focusing on quantum physics, nuclear energy, psychedelics, and Internet oddities.

Unit 5

UNIT

Prepared by: Daniel Mittleman, *DePaul University* and
Douglas Druckenmiller, *Western Illinois University*

Internet Governance, Privacy, and Security

Privacy is the yin to security's yang. They are two sides of the same dilemma we face in America today. Policies that make for more effective security erode our privacy. And policies that preserve our privacy hinder our government's ability to protect. To keep us secure, the government requires the ability to surveil, and desires policies that make it easier to do so. But to maintain our personal privacy, we demand the government not violate the constitutional protections established to guarantee that privacy.

As the Patriot Act—enacted after the 9/11 attacks—has shown, a normal response of government during times of threatened public safety is to reduce civil liberties such as privacy and due process. In theory, a free press, a concerned citizenry, and the normal checks and balances built into the US Constitution should prevent the worst abuses.

Privacy concerns exist not just in the realm of our collective relationship with government. Large corporations, such as Google and Facebook, hold as much—perhaps more—information about us. Google's vast database of our web browsing and related history contains far more detailed personal interests and behaviors than any government could know.[1] And Facebook is aiming to capture all of our collective relationships with objects, organizations, and each other.[2] What are the implications of having such personal and complete information about almost all of us sitting in corporate databases? Can we trust these corporations in both the short term and the long term?

In a world of networked computers, e-commerce, and social networking, we blithely hand over valuable data to providers of services we usually think of as free. To take a simple example, imagine that you are Gmail subscriber who takes the time to scrub your in-box and delete unwanted email messages. You may well think deleting your messages has deleted your messages. But have you? First, the party you corresponded with may have your messages. Second, Google undoubtedly backs up its servers to protect itself against disaster. How many backup copies of your message to they have? Where are those copies? Can a government get at them either with a warrant or by force? Is it ever possible to know whether all copies of your message are gone?

Many corporations, for good business reasons, tend to side with their customers against government intrusion into individual privacy. For example in 2016, following a tragic shooting attack the previous December in San Bernardino, California, Apple rejected a request from the FBI to create an application to override the password on the deceased suspect's iPhone. The FBI eventually found another way into the phone, which ended the "historical legal showdown that pitted the demands of law enforcement investigating crimes against the privacy rights of companies to protect their customer's privacy."[3] Other companies are steadily increasing privacy protections for users. WhatsApp added end-to-end encryption for every form of communication on its popular messaging app shortly after the FBI vs Apple showdown.

Not every company is shifting towards protecting its users however. In October 2016, Yahoo revealed they had built a program to aid the FBI and NSA in monitoring the email accounts of its users.[4] And nothing is slowing the tracks of non-governmental hackers from doing what they can to get our information. In the summer of 2016 we learned The Democratic National Committee (DNC) was hacked by a Russian in a first ever effort by a foreign nation to potentially sway U.S. elections. In September of 2016 Yahoo suffered the largest data breach to date when they were forced to reveal that data associated with at least 500,000,000 user accounts had been stolen by a "state-sponsored actor" in late 2014.[5]

---

[1] http://www.nybooks.com/articles/2011/08/18/how-google-dominates-us/
[2] https://www.technologyreview.com/s/428150/what-facebook-knows/
[3] http://www.latimes.com/local/lanow/la-me-ln-fbi-drops-fight-to-force-apple-to-unlock-san-bernardino-terrorist-iphone-20160328-story.html
[4] https://www.wired.com/2016/10/yahoo-spy-scandal-shows-encryption-fails-without-backbone/
[5] http://money.cnn.com/2016/09/22/technology/yahoo-data-breach/

Our security is at risk from cybercrime because the economic, social, and civic fabric of our lives has moved to the virtual and become more tightly coupled with these networks and data repositories. Our modern Internet-based society is dominated by several types of complementary networks and data repositories, many of them coexisting on the Internet. Among those data repositories are the vast collections of information held by Google, Apple, Facebook, LinkedIn, Amazon, eBay, and others about our personal surfing, posting, and shopping habits. Also potentially accessible out there in more secured spaces are our credit card and banking information, our credit histories, our medical histories, and government data such as property holdings, license and registration data, criminal and traffic history, and voter registration records. The rare exception among us who has largely stayed offline is impacted nevertheless by institutional data placed online outside of that person's control. Therefore, it is reasonable to conclude that all of us run the risk of getting hurt.

Beyond our personal data that is stored on the Internet cloud are institutional and public data. The aforementioned medical, insurance, and credit information is held for the most part by private companies doing the best job they can (we hope) to successfully steward our data. Further, many banks, retail stores, and other institutions employ networked security cameras to track the comings and goings of their patrons. Beyond that are the police and criminal databases often referred to during cop shows on TV. And there exist databases and active networks used to manage civic security cameras, and public works such as water and power distribution. And our national security infrastructure makes use of networks (sometimes, but not always, separate and more secure than the Internet) to undertake their mission. This includes, but is not limited to, work by Homeland Security departments, the military, and the various government spy agencies.

None of these networks is 100 percent secure. Many, likely most, of these networks are under regular attack—though security protocols automatically block the common and more amateur attacks. There have been multiple reports of late, however, of more skilled and determined attacks on our public networks from groups within China and, perhaps, Iran.[6-7]

With the realization in 2013 from documents leaked by Edward Snowden that the U.S. government has been collecting domestic telephone and Internet data, concern has focused on the potential vulnerability to everyday Americans from the government holding this information. But large Internet and communication companies possess as much—perhaps more—information about our online activities. And many of these companies, due to license agreements we agree to, maintain rights to make use of this data in a variety of ways. Google's vast database of our web browsing and related history contains far more detailed personal interests and behaviors than any government could know.[8] And Facebook is aiming to capture every one of everyone's relationships with objects, organizations, and each other.[9] What are the implications of having such personal and complete information about almost all of us sitting in corporate databases?

What is a reasonable person to make of all of this? We can communicate with almost anyone almost anywhere on the planet at almost no cost. The wealth of the world is available on Amazon or eBay for those with credit cards. Google, Wikipedia, and an ocean of other sites provide information in abundance and at a speed that would have seemed like science fiction a generation ago. Yet thieves get hold of digitally stored personal information. Our digital records are disintegrating even as we digitize more and more of them. The government compiles massive databases about terrorism and catches the innocent in its nets. Disruption of the global communications network could be catastrophic, as financial markets and global supply chains collapse. One strives for the equanimity of Neil Postman: "Technology giveth and technology taketh away."

---

[6] S. Gorman, J. Barnes, "Iran Blamed for Cyberattacks," *Wall Street Journal*, October 13, 2012.

[7] J. Winter, J. Kaplan, "Washington Confirms Chinese Hack Attack on White House Computer," FoxNews.com (accessed 10/13/12 at http://www.foxnews.com/tech/2012/10/01/washington-confirms-chinese-hack-attack-on-white-house-computer/#ixzz29D5gQjKp).

[8] James Gleick, "How Google Dominates Us," *The New York Review of Books*, August 13, 2011.

[9] Tom Simonite, "What Facebook Knows," *Technology Review*, July/August 2012.

Article

Prepared by: Daniel Mittleman, *DePaul University* and
Douglas Druckenmiller, *Western Illinois University*

10 Ways to Make the Internet Safe from Cyber Attacks

Patrick Tucker

Learning Outcomes

After reading this article, you will be able to:

- Understand why a policy-driven response to cyber attacks is vital to security.
- Describe the European Union's Right to Be Forgotten initiative.
- Discuss the critical importance of being able to function when forced to operate offline.

A single well-designed cyber weapon could "take down the entire Internet," according to Dan Geer, chief information security officer for In-Q-Tel, the CIA's venture capital company.

Here are his 10 policy proposals for protecting the Internet from cyber attacks:

1. Companies Should Be Mandated To Report Big Hacks

We report big disease outbreaks the moment that they happen and the Centers for Disease Control sends out an advance team to deal with them. Why not mandate that companies must do the same thing when they experience a big hack or breach on the federal level? It's a proposal that goes well beyond the largely toothless White House Cybersecurity Framework released earlier this year. It's a move that companies would likely fight, arguing that most of the hacks they face don't constitute the sort of threat that they need to inform the public about. Geer says large companies or the government should have no expectation of privacy in the wake of major cyber attacks, just as individuals with a highly communicable disease lose any expectation of privacy in the event of an Ebola or other major disease outbreak.

"Wouldn't it make sense to have a regime of mandatory reporting for cyber-security failures?" Geer said. "Should you face criminal charges if you fail to make such a report?" He points out that 46 states require mandatory reporting of some cyber attacks in the form of their cyber-breach laws, but 70 to 80 percent of data breaches are discovered by unrelated third parties. Geer says every security failure "above some threshold we have yet to negotiate" should be reported to the federal government. In broaching this, he drew from a recent paper by former Navy Secretary Richard Danzig titled *Surviving On a Diet of Poisoned Fruit*, in which Danzig argues that software hacks should be treated with the same urgency as airplane near-misses.

2. Net-Neutrality Shouldn't Be Left to the FCC

He recommends not one single proposal, but stresses that what's most important to understand is that the Federal Communications Commission is not the sort of agency that can effectively manage something as important to the future as Internet traffic.

"What I can say is that the varied tastes need to be reflected in constrained choice rather than the idea that . . . some . . . agency can assure happiness if and only if it—rather than corporations or individuals—does the choosing."

3. Companies Should Be Held Liable for Making Hackable Software

It's a measure that, had it been in place 20 years ago, Microsoft would be on the hook for every time some piece of malware crashed a computer and Bill Gates would be nowhere near the richest man in the world list.

"The software houses will yell bloody murder the minute legislation like this is introduced, and any pundit and lobbyist they can afford will spew their dire predictions that 'this law will mean the end of computing as we know it!' To which our considered answer will be: 'Yes, please! That was exactly the idea.'"

4. Striking Back Should Be Legal But There Should Perhaps Be Oversight

Strike back is the ability to attack those that attack you. "I suspect that a fair number of you have, in fact, struck back at some attacker somewhere or, at least, done targeting research even if you didn't pull the trigger," Geer said. "I'd trust many of you to identify targets carefully enough to minimize collateral damage, but what we are talking about here is the cyber equivalent of the smart bomb. As I implied earlier, cyber smart bombs are what the national laboratories of several countries are furiously working on. In that sense, you do know what is happening behind the curtain, and you know how hard that targeting really is because you know how hard attribution—real attribution—really is." He called it "expensive therapy" not open to most small players.

5. Software Needs Resilient Fallbacks

Software makers should be legally obliged to have fallbacks in place in the event of a major attack of service disruption and those fallbacks should be in place prior to deployment of the software. Geer calls this resiliency. The best way to assure resiliency is to build systems that can be managed from afar, so-called remote managed systems. If you can't build remote management into your system, you should design in an expiration date.

"Resiliency is an area where no one policy can be sufficient, so I've suggested a trio of baby steps: Embedded systems cannot be immortal if they have no remote management interface, embedded systems must have a remote management interface if they are to be immortal, and swap-over is preferable to swap-out when it comes to data protection."

6. The Government Should Pay Top Dollar to Hackers To Find Vulnerabilities

This is called vulnerability finding and Geer says the U.S. should corner the market on it and pay people who find vulnerabilities 10 times what anyone else could pay them for keeping the vulnerability secret. Once the government learns of a new vulnerability, the next step is to make it public.

"If a couple of Texas brothers could corner the world silver market, there is no doubt that the U.S. government could openly corner the world vulnerability market. That is, we buy them all and we make them all public. Simply announce: 'Show us a competing bid, and we'll give you 10 times.'" In a subsequent Q&A session, Geer elaborated further. "Vulnerabilities that you keep to yourself for use as a future weapon is a hostile act. So let's corner the market. . . . If there are a limited number of

them . . . by making them no longer weaponizable, have we not contributed to world peace?"

7. The Right To Be Forgotten Should Be Put in Place in the United States

The European Union's Right to Be Forgotten initiative, which mandates that European citizens have a right to have some information kept off the web (or at least out of Google search results), is "appropriate, advantageous [but] doesn't go far enough," Geer said. The definition of privacy that he lives by is this: "You have privacy if you have the effective capacity to misrepresent yourself."

It's becoming a hugely important issue for individuals, but it's not a small issue for the military either. Intelligence agents, Geer says, are having an ever more difficult time keeping their identities a secret. "Crafting good cover is getting harder and for the same reasons. Misrepresentations are getting harder."

In a sense, we are moving toward a post-spy world, according to the guy that runs the CIA's venture capital arm. And protecting the right to be forgotten is one way around that. But more importantly, "a right to be forgotten is the only check on the tidal wave of observability that a ubiquitous sensor fabric is birthing now—observability that changes the very quality of what 'in public' means."

The Obama administration's issuance of a National Strategy for Trusted Identities in Cyberspace is a "case-in-point; it 'calls for the development of interoperable technology standards and policies—an Identity Ecosystem'—where individuals, organizations, and underlying infrastructure—such as routers and servers—can be authoritatively authenticated."

Anonymity is something we give government witnesses and whistleblowers. He says it should be a right for everyone. Moreover, if the U.S. were to follow the European lead on right to be forgotten, it would help curb the balkanization of the Internet, and decrease foreign suspicion of U.S. tech companies.

8. Internet Voting? No

Geer said very little on the question of whether or not the United States or other countries should allow for voting over the Internet or become more reliant on Internet-connected voting machines. But as soon as he said the words, "Internet voting," the crowd in the ballroom of the Mandalay Hotel erupted in laughter and he quickly moved on to the next subject.

9. Abandoned Software Should Be Treated Like Abandoned Stuff

If any company abandons a software codebase then the same rules that apply to discarded furniture should apply to the software—it becomes public and open-source. That means that there would in effect never be any devices out there using software that was proprietary but that wasn't supported. "Apple computers running 10.5 or less get no updates (comprising a significant fraction of the installed base). Any Microsoft computer running XP gets no updates (likewise comprising a significant fraction of the installed base). The end of security updates follows abandonment. It is certainly ironic that freshly pirated copies of Windows get security updates when older versions bought legitimately do not. . . . Either you support it or you give it to the public."

10. Make Sure There's an Offline Backup

"The more we put on the Internet, the broader and more unmitigable Internet surprises become," Geer said. He called this "dependence," and it's a growing problem.

He cited a recent Bloomberg story pointing out that some of the nation's largest banks were calling on the government to protect them from the threat of cyber attack. The article was titled "*Banks Dreading Computer Hacks Call for Cyber War Council.*"

"The biggest financial firms [are] saying that their dependencies are no longer manageable, and that the state's monopoly on the use of force must be brought to bear. What they are talking about is that they have no way to mitigate the risk of common mode failure."

Bottom line: Everything that is a critical infrastructure component *must* show that it can run without the Internet and the makers have to be able to prove it. Geer is proposing a massive stress test for every bank, utility, or any other company that fulfills a critical public role to see how well they operate when they are thrown offline. We stress tested the banks after the 2008 market crash, he points out. "We need stress tests in our field even more."

In his remarks, Geer acknowledged that cyber attacks would get worse before they get better, that maintaining online anonymity would become ever more difficult and inconvenient, and that in the present political environment, many of the proposals would face enormous, if not insurmountable, resistance. Only the second policy proposal has any real chance of passing. But that could change—if things get worse. "There's the political will to do a stress test but only after a bad event. Let's hope it's not catastrophic," he said.

Critical Thinking

1. Of the 10 policy proposals suggested here, which one may be the most difficult to implement? Why?
2. Does the maintenance of online anonymity justify the multitude of inconveniences that are inevitably required? Why or why not?
3. Will anything short of a catastrophe break through the barriers of political resistance when it comes to legislating serious cyber security?

Internet References

Daily Mail: "Think you're safe on the internet? Think again: Map reveals millions of cyber attacks happening around the world in real time"

www.dailymail.co.uk/sciencetech/article-2670710/Think-youre-safe-internet-Think-Map-reveals-millions-cyber-attacks-happening-world-real-time.html#ixzz3JAA9dHls

Entrepreneur: "How to Protect Your Small Business Against a Cyber Attack"

www.entrepreneur.com/article/225468

UTG Solutions: "Network Security—Is Your Company Safe from Cyber Attacks?"

www.utgsolutions.com/network-security-is-your-company-safe-from-cyber-attacks

Prepared by: Daniel Mittleman, *DePaul University* and
Douglas Druckenmiller, *Western Illinois University*

Article

America Is "Dropping Cyberbombs"— But How Do They Work?

RICHARD FORNO and ANUPAM JOSHI

Learning Outcomes

After reading this article, you will be able to:

- Undertand the basic weapons and attacks available in a cyberwar.

- Discuss implications of war moving from a physical battlefield to a cyber battlefield (or a combination of the two).

- Discuss ethical similarities and difference of cyberwar versus physical military war.

Recently, United States Deputy Defense Secretary Robert Work publicly confirmed that the Pentagon's Cyber Command was "dropping cyberbombs," taking its ongoing battle against the Islamic State group into the online world. Other American officials, including President Barack Obama, have discussed offensive cyber activities, too.

The American public has only glimpsed the country's alleged cyberattack abilities. In 2012 The New York Times revealed the first digital weapon, the Stuxnet attack against Iran's nuclear program. In 2013, former NSA contractor Edward Snowden released a classified presidential directive outlining America's approach to conducting Internet-based warfare.

The terms "cyberbomb" and "cyberweapon" create a simplistic, if not also sensational, frame of reference for the public. Real military or intelligence cyber activities are less exaggerated but much more complex. The most basic types are off-the-shelf commercial products used by companies and security consultants to test system and network security. The most advanced are specialized proprietary systems made for

exclusive—and often classified—use by the defense, intelligence, and law enforcement communities.

So what exactly are these "cyberbombs" America is "dropping" in the Middle East? The country's actual cyber capabilities are classified; we, as researchers, are limited by what has been made public. Monitoring books, reports, news events, and congressional testimony is not enough to separate fact from fiction. However, we can analyze the underlying technologies and look at the global strategic considerations of those seeking to wage cyber warfare. That work allows us to offer ideas about cyber weapons and how they might be used.

A collection of capabilities

A "cyberbomb" is not a single weapon. Rather, cyberweapons are collections of computer hardware and software, with the knowledge of their potential uses against online threats. Although frequently used against Internet targets such as websites and forums, these tools can have real-world effects, too. Cyberattacks have disrupted cellphone networks and tricked computers controlling nuclear centrifuges into functioning differently from how they report their status to human operators. A simulated attack has shown how an enemy can remotely disrupt electric power generators.

The process of identifying potential targets, selecting them and planning "cyberbomb" attacks includes not only technological experts but military strategists, researchers, policy analysts, lawyers, and others across the military-industrial complex. These groups constantly analyze technology to develop the latest cyber weapons and tactics. They also must ensure the use of a given "cyberbomb" aligns with national interests, and follows national and international laws and treaties.

For example, as part of their counterterrorism efforts, electronic intelligence services (such as the American NSA and British GCHQ) routinely collect items like real names, user IDs, network addresses, Internet server names, online discussion histories and text messages from across the Internet. Gathering and analyzing these data could use both classified and unclassified methods. The agencies could also conduct advanced Google searches or mine The Internet Archive's Wayback Machine. This information can be linked with other data to help identify physical locations of target computers or people. Analysts can also observe interconnections between people and infer the types and strengths of those relationships.

This information can clue intelligence analysts in to the existence of previously undiscovered potential Internet targets. These can include virtual meeting places, methods of secure communications, types of phones or computers favored by the enemy, preferred network providers or vulnerabilities in their IT infrastructures. In some cases, cyberattacks need to be coordinated with spies or covert agents who must carry out physical aspects of the plan, especially when the electronic target of a "cyberbomb" is hard to reach—such as the computers inside the Iranian nuclear facility targeted by the Stuxnet worm.

Cyberattack purposes can vary widely. Sometimes, a government entity wants to simply monitor activity on a specific computer system in hopes of gaining additional intelligence. Other times, the goal is to place a hidden "backdoor" allowing the agency to secretly take control of a system. In some cases, a target computer will be attacked with the intent of disabling it or preventing future use by adversaries. When considering that kind of activity, planners must decide whether it's better to leave a site functional so future intelligence can be collected over the long term or to shut it down and prevent an adversary from using it in the near term.

Although not strictly a "cyber" attack, "cyberbombing" also might entail the use of decades-old electronic warfare techniques that broadcast electromagnetic energy to (among other things) disrupt an adversary's wireless communications capabilities or computer controls. Other "cyberbombing" techniques include modifying or creating false images on an enemy's radar screens ahead of an air attack, such as how Israel compromised Syria's air defense systems in 2007. These may be done on their own or to support more traditional military operations.

Finally, using an electromagnetic pulse (EMP) weapon to disrupt and/or disable all electronic circuits over a wide area—such as a city—could be considered the "Mother of All Cyber Bombs." As such, its effect would be felt both by enemy forces and local (likely) noncombatant citizens, all of whom suddenly would be unable to obtain fresh water and electricity, and find their local hospitals, banks and electronic items ranging from cars to coffee pots unable to function. Depending on the heat and blast from the bomb's detonation, some people might not notice—though those dependent on electronic medical devices like pacemakers probably would feel effects immediately. EMP is commonly associated with nuclear weapons, but even using nonnuclear EMP devices in a populated area would presumably cause enough "collateral damage" that it would violate international laws.

Fighting against nongovernment groups

In addition to the above techniques, and particularly when fighting opponents that are not foreign governments—such as ISIS—a unique type of "cyberbombing" seeks to target the online personas of terror group leaders. In this type of attack, one goal may be to tarnish their online reputations, such as publishing manipulated images that would embarrass them. Or, cyber weaponry may be used to gain access to systems that could be used to issue conflicting statements or incorrect orders to the enemy.

These types of "cyberbombs" can create psychological damage and distress in terrorist networks and help disrupt them over time. The United Kingdom's JTRIG (Joint Threat Research Intelligence Group) within GCHQ specializes in these tactics. Presumably similar capabilities exist in other countries.

Until recently, few nations publicly admitted planning or even thinking about waging offensive warfare on the Internet. For those that do, the exact process of planning a digital warfare campaign remains a highly guarded military and diplomatic secret.

The only people announcing their cyberattacks were assorted hacktivist groups such as Anonymous and the self-proclaimed "Cyber-Caliphate" supporting ISIS. By contrast, the most prominent cyber attack waged by a nation-state (2011s Stuxnet)—allegedly attributed to the United States and Israel—was never officially acknowledged by those governments.

Cyber weapons and the policies governing their use likely will remain shrouded in secrecy. However, the recent public mentions of cyber warfare by national leaders suggest that these capabilities are, and will remain, prominent and evolving ways to support intelligence and military operations when needed.

Critical Thinking

1. Should your country be investing in offensive cyberbombing technologies? Should your country be investing in technologies to defend against cyberbombing?

2. Do you think innocent civilians are more or less likely to be impacted by a cyberbomb versus a physical bomb? Why? Would you be more worried to know an enemy has the capability of launching a physical bombing attack or a cyberbomb attack against your location?

3. How do the ethics of cyberwar compare to the ethics of physical war?

Internet References

Cyberwarfare Greater Threat to US Than Terrorism, Say Security Experts
https://goo.gl/0UPz7Z

Stop Saying We're Dropping 'Cyber Bombs' On ISIS
https://goo.gl/fvdP9u

These 5 Facts Explain the Threat of Cyber Warfare
https://goo.gl/EMksOo

Prepared by: Daniel Mittleman, *DePaul University* and
Douglas Druckenmiller, *Western Illinois University*

Article

Cybersecurity: The Age of the Megabreach

We haven't stopped huge breaches. The focus now is on resilience, with smarter ways to detect attacks and faster ways
to respond to them.

DAVID TALBOT

Learning Outcomes

After reading this article, you will be able to:

- Understand the breadth of the threat of theft due to lack of encryption.

- Understand the kinds of crimes that can occur when thieves are able to access unencrypted data.

- Articulate a role for government, if any, for ensuring corporate data is encrypted.

I n November 2014, an especially chilling cyberattack shook the corporate world—something that went far beyond garden-variety theft of credit card numbers from a big-box store. Hackers, having explored the internal servers of Sony Pictures Entertainment, captured internal financial reports, top executives' embarrassing e-mails, private employee health data, and even unreleased movies and scripts and dumped them on the open Web. The offenders were said by U.S. law enforcement to be working at the behest of the North Korean regime, offended by a farcical movie the company had made in which a TV producer is caught up in a scheme to kill the country's dictator.

The results showed how profoundly flat-footed this major corporation was. The hack had been going on for months without being detected. Data vital to the company's business was not encrypted. The standard defensive technologies had not worked against what was presumed to have been a "phishing" attack in which an employee clicked a link that downloaded powerful malware. Taken together, all this showed that many of today's technologies are not adequate, that attacks can now be more aggressive than ever, and that once breaches occur, they are made worse by slow responses.

The Sony hack was one in a series of recent data breaches—including many "megabreaches," in which at least 10 million records are lost—that together reveal the weakness of today's cybersecurity approaches and the widening implications for the global economy. In 2015, the U.S. Office of Personnel Management was hacked, exposing 21.5 million records, including background checks on millions of people—among them copies of 5.6 million sets of fingerprints. Later in the year, 37 million visitors to Ashley Madison, a dating site for people seeking extramarital affairs, learned that their real e-mail addresses and other data had been released. The theft of data from 83 million customers of Wall Street giant J.P. Morgan, allegedly by an Israel-based team trying to manipulate the stock market, revealed chilling possibilities from how cyberattacks could undermine the financial sector.

Since companies and other organizations can't stop attacks and are often reliant on fundamentally insure networks and technologies, the big question for this report is how they can effectively respond to attacks and limit the damage—and adopt smarter defensive strategies in the future. New approaches and new ways of thinking about cybersecurity are beginning to take hold. Organizations are getting better at detecting fraud and other attacks by using algorithms to mine historical information in real time. They are responding far more quickly, using platforms that alert security staff to what is happening and quickly help them take action. And new tools are emerging from a blossoming ecosystem of cybersecurity startups, financed by surging venture capital investment in the area.

Cyber Breaches Hit Staggering Levels

Exceptionally harmful hacks have recently struck organizations in the global insurance, finance, telecom, and entertainment industries and at the heart of a U.S. federal agency—inflicting hundreds of millions of dollars in damage and added costs.

		How They Were Exploited	Data Stolen and Scale	Costs	Suspected Culprit
7/2014	**JPMorgan Chase** New York City	Two-factor authentication upgrade not fully implemented.	Names, addresses, and phone numbers of 76 million household and seven million small-business accounts.	The company says it plans to spend $250 million annually on security.	Three people have been charged with the attack as part of a stock manipulation scheme.
11/2014	**Sony Pictures Entertainment** Culver City, California	Malware and lack of intrusion detection.	E-mails, salary information, and terabytes of other data, including movie scripts and contracts.	$41 million, according to public filings.	North Korean regime.
2/2015	**Anthem Health** Indianapolis	Malware specifically designed to attack the company.	Names, birth dates, addresses, employment information, and Social Security numbers for 78 million people.	Much or all of the $100 million value of its cyberinsurance policy.	China-based hackers, suspected to be affiliated with the government.
6/2015	**U.S. Office of Personnel Management** Washington, D.C.	Likely social-engineering attacks and lack of modern intrusion detection services.	A mix of names, birth dates, addresses, fingerprints, and background information on as many as 21.5 million people.	More than $133 million just for credit monitoring for victims.	China-based hackers, suspected to be affiliated with the government.
7/2015	**Ashley Madison** Toronto	Unknown, but attackers cited weak passwords and almost nonexistent internal security.	Names, addresses, birth dates, phone numbers, and credit card history of 37 million users, plus the CEO's e-mails.	Unknown. The company faces numerous lawsuits.	A previously unknown group that calls itself Impact Team.
9/2015	**T-Mobile US** Bellevue, Washington	Security weaknesses at a partner (Experian) that was managing credit check data.	Names, birth dates, addresses, and Social Security and driver's license numbers of 15 million people.	Experian has spent at least $20 million on credit monitoring and other corrective actions.	Unknown.
10/2015	**TalkTalk Telecom** London	Distributed-denial-of-service attack and malicious code.	Names, birth dates, addresses, and phone numbers of more than 150,000 customers.	About $50 million in lost sales and incident response costs.	A teenager in Northern Ireland.

But hindering progress everywhere is the general lack of encryption on the devices and messaging systems that hundreds of millions of people now use. Nearly three years ago, when National Security Agency contractor Edward Snowden revealed that intelligence agencies were freely availing themselves of data stored by the major Internet companies, many of those companies promised to do more to encrypt data. They started using encryption on their own corporate servers, but most users remain exposed unless they know to install and use third-party apps that encrypt their data.

All these measures will help protect data in today's relatively insecure networks. But it's clear that the very basics of how networked technologies are built need to be rethought and security given a central role. A new national cybersecurity strategy is expected to chart an R&D plan to make sure software is verifiably secure and that users know when it's not working.

There's a big opportunity: the number of Internet-connected devices—not including smartphones, PCs, and tablets—could reach two billion in just five years. A **2015 McKinsey report** predicts that this will become a multitrillion-dollar industry by 2025. All these new devices will present an opportunity to build things robustly from the start—and avoid having them play a role in Sony-like hacks in the future.

Critical Thinking

1. What is encryption and how does it protect data on corporate servers? How does it protect data being sent by e-mail or texting?

2. Why isn't more being done to protect data?

3. How much responsibility does an industry have to protect your data and how much of that responsibility lies with you?

Internet References

Cluster of "Megabreaches" Compromises a Whopping 642 Million Passwords
https://goo.gl/Ytm21U

Security News This Week: A Deluge of Mega-Breaches Dumps on the Dark Web
https://goo.gl/hf8Uh5

Yahoo! and the Mega Breaches That Keep Happening
https://goo.gl/jk0E51

Article

Prepared by: Daniel Mittleman, *DePaul University* and
Douglas Druckenmiller, *Western Illinois University*

Google's European Conundrum: When Does Privacy Mean Censorship?

Though Google is a U.S. company, its American rights don't transpose across the pond. A court case will determine whether Google has to comply with EU law, which could have far-reaching consequences for European users.

ZACK WHITTAKER

Learning Outcomes

After reading this article, you will be able to:

- Understand how data placed on the Internet is virally replicated in a manner that no one entity can control it, let alone erase it.

- Articulate how information available on the Internet impacts the trade-off of concerns between free speech rights and privacy rights.

- Know the risks of maintaining an online presence.

How Google and other American Internet companies operate in Europe could come down to a link that, depending on what side of the Atlantic Ocean you're on, should or should not be deleted.

A case heard Tuesday before the European Court of Justice (ECJ) hinges on a complaint submitted by a Spanish citizen who searched Google for his name and found a news article from several years earlier, saying his property would be auctioned because of failed payments to his social security contributions.

Spanish authorities argued that Google, other search engines, and other Web companies operating in Spain should remove information such as that if it is believed to be a breach of an individual's privacy. Google, however, believes that it should not have to delete search results from its index [http://www.reuters.com/article/2013/02/26/us-eu-googledataprotection-idUSBRE91P0A320130226] because the company didn't create it in the first place. Google argued that it is the publisher's responsibility and that its search engine is merely a channel for others' content.

The ECJ's advocate-general will publish its opinion on the case on June 25, with a judgment expected by the end of the year. The outcome of the hearing will affect not only Spain but also all of the 27 member states of the European Union.

In principle, this fight is about freedom of speech versus privacy, with a hearty dash of allegations of censorship mixed in. In reality, this could be one of the greatest changes to EU privacy rules in decades—by either strengthening the rules or negating them altogether.

The European view is simple: If you're at our party, you have to play by our rules. And in Europe, the "right to be forgotten" is an important one.

"Facebook and Google argue they are not subject to EU law as they are physically established outside the EU," a European Commission spokesperson told CNET. In new draft privacy law proposals, the message is, "as long as a company offers its goods or services to consumers on the EU territory, EU law must apply."

While Europe has some of the strongest data protection and privacy laws in the world, the U.S. doesn't. And while the U.S. has some of the strongest free speech and expression laws in the world, enshrined by a codified constitution, most European countries do not, instead favoring "fair speech" principles.

Google is also facing another legal twist: Spanish authorities are treating it like a media organization without offering it the full legal protection of one.

The European view is simple: If you're at our party, you have to play by our rules. And in Europe, the "right to be forgotten" is an important one.

Newspapers should be exempt from individual takedown requests to preserve freedom of speech, according to Spanish authorities, but Google should not enjoy the same liberties, despite having no editorial control and despite search results being determined by algorithms. Though Google is branded a "publisher" like newspapers, the search giant does not hold media-like protection from takedowns under the country's libel laws. This does not translate across all of Europe, however. Some European member states target newspapers directly and are held accountable through press regulatory authorities in a bid to balance freedom of speech and libel laws.

One of Spain's highest courts, the Agencia Espanola de Proteccion de Datos (AEPD), found in favor of the complainant in early 2011 and ruled that Google should delete the search result [http://online.wsj.com/article/SB10001424052748703396604576087573944344348.html]. This case is one of around 180 other ongoing cases in the country.

Google appealed the decision and the case was referred to the highest court in Europe, the ECJ, which will eventually determine if the search giant is the "controller" of the data or whether it is merely a host of the data.

The case will also decide on whether U.S.-based companies are subject to EU privacy law, which may mean EU citizens have to take their privacy cases to U.S. courts to determine whether Google is responsible for the damage caused by the "diffusion of personal information."

In a blog post on Tuesday [http://googlepolicyeurope.blogspot.com/2013/02/judging-freedom-of-expression-at.html], Bill Echikson, Google's "head of free expression," said the search giant "declined to comply" with a request by Spanish data protection authorities, as the search listing "includes factually correct information that is still publicly available on the newspaper's Web site."

"There are clear societal reasons why this kind of information should be publicly available. People shouldn't be prevented from learning that a politician was convicted of taking a bribe, or that a doctor was convicted of malpractice," Echikson noted.

"We believe the answer to that question is 'no'. Search engines point to information that is published online—and in this case to information that had to be made public, by law. In our view, only the original publisher can take the decision to remove such content. Once removed from the source webpage, content will disappear from a search engine's index."

EU's Latest Privacy Proposal: The "Right To Be Forgotten"

Should the ECJ find in favor of the Spanish complainant, it will see the biggest shakeup to EU privacy rules in close to two decades and would enable European citizens a "right to be forgotten."

In January 2011, the European Commission lifted the lid on draft proposals for a single one-size-fits-all privacy regulation for its 27 member states. One of the proposals was the "right to be forgotten," empowering every European resident the right to force Web companies as well as offline firms to delete or remove their data [http://www.cnet.com/8301-1009_3-57363585-83/new-eu-dataprotection-rules-due-this-week/] to preserve their privacy.

For Europeans, privacy is a fundamental right to all residents, according to Article 8 of the European Convention of Human Rights, in which it states [http://www.hri.org/docs/ECHR50.html#C.Art8]: "Everyone has the right to respect for his private and family life, his home and his correspondence." It does however add a crucial exception. "There shall be no interference by a public authority with the exercise of this right except . . . for the protection of the rights and freedoms of others."

Because U.S.-based technology giants like Google, Facebook, and Twitter have users and in many cases a physical presence in Europe, they must comply with local laws. The "right to be forgotten" would force Facebook and Twitter to remove any data it had on you, as well as Google removing results from its search engine. It would also extraterritorially affect users worldwide outside the European Union who would also be unable to search for those removed search terms.

Such Web companies have said (and lobbied to that effect) [http://www.telegraph.co.uk/technology/news/9070019/EU-Privacy-regulations-subject-to-unprecedented-lobbying.html] that the "right to be forgotten" should not allow data to be removed or manipulated at the expense of freedom of speech. This, however, does not stop with republished material and other indexed content, and most certainly does not apply to European law enforcement and intelligence agencies.

Two Continents, Separated by "Free" and "Fair Speech"

The U.S. and the EU have never seen eye-to-eye on data protection and privacy. For Americans and U.S.-based companies, the belief is that crossover between freedom of speech and privacy overlaps in "a form of censorship," according to Google's lawyers [http://www.bbc.co.uk/news/technology-12239674] speaking during the Spanish court case.

In the U.S., you can freely say the most appalling words, so long as they don't lead to a crime or violence against a person or a group of people. In European countries such as the U.K. words can lead to instant arrest. Europe's laws allow for "fair speech" in order to prevent harassment, fear of violence, or even alarm and distress. It's a dance between the American tradition of protecting the individual and the European tradition of protecting society.

Google is fundamentally so very American in this regard. That said, Google already filters and censors its own search results at the behest of governments and private industry, albeit openly and transparently [http://www.google.com/transparencyreport/]. Google will agree to delete links that violate copyrights under the Digital Millennium Copyright Act, which seeks to remove content from Google's search results that may facilitate copyright infringement.

Google also complies, when forced by a court, with numerous types of government requests, not limited to subpoenas, search warrants, and National Security Letters [http://www.zdnet.com/what-google-does-when-a-government-requests-your-data-7000010418/], or so-called "gagging orders." It also discloses those requests and when it complies with them. And it's a system not that dissimilar to what it's being asked to do in Europe.

Whose Jurisdiction Is Google Under: U.S., EU, or Both?

While Europe's privacy principles apply to the Web, it's unclear whether they apply to data "controllers" established outside of the European Union. But several European court cases have sided with local law. A German court found that Facebook fell under Irish law [http://www.bloomberg.com/news/2013-02-15/facebook-scores-win-in-legal-regime-dispute-with-germany.html] because the social networking company had a physical presence in Ireland, another EU member state. In Google's case, Spanish authorities are making a similar argument, claiming that Google is processing data in a European state and therefore EU law should apply.

Many American companies have voiced their objections to the proposed EU privacy law [http://www.zdnet.com/blog/london/european-draft-data-law-announced-what-you-need-to-know/2609], including Amazon, eBay, and Yahoo, according to a lobbying watchdog [http://www.lobbyplag.eu/#/compare/overview]. It could still take a year or two for the law to be ratified.

"Exempting non-EU companies from our data protection regulation is not on the table. It would mean applying double standards," said Europe's Justice Commissioner Viviane Reding, the top politician in Europe on data protection and privacy rules in the region, in an interview with the *Financial Times of London* [http://www.ft.com/intl/cms/s/0/903b3302-7398-11e2-bcbd-00144feabdc0.html#axzz2MCRmwDfo].

The new EU Data Protection Regulation, proposed by the European Commission and currently being debated in the European Parliament, will likely be voted on by June.

But this fight isn't as much about censorship as one might think. It's about a cultural difference between two continents and perspectives on what freedom of speech can and should be. It's also about privacy, and whether privacy or free speech is more important.

Critical Thinking

1. Explain why it is so difficult to completely remove information placed on the Internet.

2. Assuming it were technologically feasible to completely remove information from the Internet, should a public figure be permitted to selectively remove information from the Internet about himself or herself? Should a private person be permitted to do so? Should someone under 18 be permitted to do so? What about someone who had embarrassing information posted with their consent?

3. Should a potential employer be permitted to sift through old Internet information when making an employment decision? Should an existing employer be permitted to look and potentially terminate an employee? Should a potential spouse be able to look? Should a potential first date? If your answers are split between yes and no, what general policy should guide when a historical search is appropriate and when it is not?

Internet References

California "Eraser Law" Lets Minors Remove Embarrassing Online Content

www.pbs.org/newshour/rundown/2013/09/california-eraser-law-lets-minors-remove-embarrassing-online-content.html

EU Report: The "Right To Be Forgotten" Is Technically Impossible . . . So Let's Do It Anyway

www.techdirt.com/articles/20121205/08425221239/eu-report-right-to-be-forgotten-is-technically-impossible-so-lets-do-it-anyway.shtml

Juan Enriquez: Your Online Life, Permanent as a Tattoo [TED Talk]

www.ted.com/talks/juan_enriquez_how_to_think_about_digital_tattoos.html

Reputation 3.0: The Internet Is Your Resume

www.forbes.com/sites/dorieclark/2013/07/19/reputation-3-0-the-internet-is-your-resume

Survey: One-Third of Youths Engage in Sexting

www.wired.com/threatlevel/2009/12/sexting-survey

Temporary Social Media

www.technologyreview.com/featuredstory/513731/temporary-social-media

---

ZACK WHITTAKER writes for ZDNet, CNET, and CBS News. He is based in New York City.

Article

Prepared by: Daniel Mittleman, *DePaul University* and
Douglas Druckenmiller, *Western Illinois University*

How Courts Avoid Ruling on Issues of Technology and Privacy

When it comes to technology privacy cases, judges often focus on side issues instead of tackling the big questions.

JILL PRILUCK

Learning Outcomes

After reading this article, you will be able to:

- Articulate how searches of electronic communication are both similar and different from searches of hard copy communication.

- Discuss the jurisdictional issues that arise by user data being stored in the cloud.

- Understand the complexity of legal and jurisdictional issues brought about by technologies created subsequent to the enactment of current law.

L ast week, the New York Court of Appeals issued a ruling that could have ensured that law enforcement requests for text, photos, videos, and other data in New York state are not dragnets. In the case in question, the Manhattan District Attorney's Office had presented Facebook with 381 search warrants as part of a disability fraud investigation. Facebook counsel Thomas Dupree Jr. argued that the warrants were overbroad and lacked particularity, and if the judges had agreed with him, it would have created an important precedent.

But instead of addressing the privacy issues, the court chose to look at a much more narrow jurisdictional question of whether warrants for information under the Stored Communications Act are more akin to administrative subpoenas, which are appealable. The majority ruled that orders related to warrants in criminal proceedings cannot be appealed.

In a blistering dissent, Judge Rowan Wilson agreed with Dupree. Wilson called for searches and seizures of telecommunications to be subject to a higher standard of review, quoting Justice Louis Brandeis' 1927 opinion in *Olmstead v. United States*: "The evil incident to invasion of the privacy of the telephone is far greater than that involved in tampering with the mails . . . as a means of espionage, writs of assistance and general warrants are puny instruments of tyranny when compared with wiretapping."

The majority's reluctance to wade into the privacy issues in the case is not unique to this opinion. In privacy cases, some courts have sidestepped sweeping pronouncements involving new technologies. In these instances, they tend to prefer narrowly tailored decisions. Sometimes, instead of a pivotal privacy decision, they rule on jurisdictional or other procedural issues. Some judges urge the legislature to address privacy issues that arise from changes in technology. Sometimes there isn't enough technical information. But whatever the excuse, many courts are not effectively handling these privacy invasions.

Get Future Tense in Your Inbox

Privacy isn't mentioned in the Constitution, but a body of law has evolved since the adoption of the Bill of Rights. Perhaps most prominent are cases exploring the Fourth Amendment, especially ones that analyze the constitutionality of searches. The trickiest privacy areas lie where technology and criminal procedure meet. Illegal searches of homes and people tend to get more constitutional protections—and sympathy—than comprehensive searches of electronic footprints. In cases involving warrants, judges tend to defer to law enforcement. Some are reluctant to award digital privacy protections, especially when they involve suspicious or criminal behavior.

Some courts won't delve into privacy at all. In *United States v. Ganias*, U.S. Army Criminal Investigation agents seized 11 hard drives that were copied and retained for a fraud investigation. For more than two years, the government failed to find on them any data relevant to the original investigation. But then another warrant for the data was issued as part of a tax evasion probe, which led to a conviction. The defendant moved to suppress the evidence because it stemmed from the seized hard drives. The U.S. Court of Appeals for the 2nd Circuit held in May that in this case, there was no Fourth Amendment violation. The court determined that the agents acted in good faith when they relied on a warrant that was properly issued and had no reason to believe the warrant was flawed, rather than explore "the complex and rapidly evolving technological issues, and the significant privacy concerns." A petition for Supreme Court review was denied.

At times, courts have avoided making grand privacy declarations by saying that U.S. law doesn't apply to the communications at hand. In July, the 2nd Circuit ruled that the government could not force Microsoft to provide customer emails on a server in Dublin because the messages were outside of U.S. jurisdiction. According to the opinion, the Stored Communications Act "neither explicitly nor implicitly . . . envision[s] the application of its warrant provisions oversees." Because privacy invasions occur when and where data is seized, the warrant was invalid. The confusing decision seemed to be an unwitting win for privacy.

The fact that many of these cases involve the cloud, which can scatter data across jurisdictions, confuses things further. In August, the FBI received a warrant for three Google accounts for a trade secrets investigation, but the company responded that it could not produce electronic records stored outside the United States. Like Facebook and Microsoft, Google asserted that the warrant was overbroad "because it does not describe with particularity which services there is probable cause to search." The government responded that it wanted all of the data. The Eastern District of Pennsylvania determined in a February ruling that even though some of the data were stored overseas, "the fluid nature of Google's cloud technology makes it uncertain which foreign country's sovereignty would be implicated when Google accesses the content of communications." The court went on to explain that Google's architecture not only divides user data among centers but also "partitions user data into shards" and that "data automatically moves from one location . . . to another." In other words, the information wasn't protected because Google can't (or won't) say which sovereignty would be implicated when Google accesses the communications.

Indeed, the Microsoft decision may not be a privacy victory after all, because of what appears to be an emerging split. This week, a magistrate judge in Florida ordered that the

government could obtain Yahoo emails in a criminal investigation even though some of the communications or data associated with it may be stored outside the United States. Part of the rationale was that the warrant functioned more like a subpoena because it requires Yahoo to disclose information under its control. The order cited the 2nd Circuit's conclusion that the focus of the Stored Communications Act's "warrant provisions is on protecting users' privacy interests in stored communications." In other words, the requirement that a warrant show probable cause that a crime has been committed at the place to be searched or that evidence exists at that location addresses the privacy concerns. In February, a Milwaukee magistrate judge followed this reasoning in a case involving warrants for the disclosure of two Google accounts regardless of where the data might be stored. When Google requested the court to address "the complex and important issues" that the warrant application raised, the court said that because Google did not file a motion to quash the warrant, it could not review the order.

Even when courts actively advocate for privacy interests, they are limited by the fact that many existing privacy doctrines are in danger of becoming stale. One of the prime examples of this is the *Katz* standard, named for a Los Angeles gambler who used a public telephone to place bets. The FBI wiretapped a public telephone and charged him with wagering information across state lines. In 1967, the Supreme Court ruled that attaching a listening device to the outside of the phone booth was unconstitutional because it constituted an illegal search. The Fourth Amendment "protects people, not places," wrote Justice Potter Stewart. The ruling established the "reasonable expectation of privacy" standard.

But applying the *Katz* standard can be complicated for new technologies, even though it is cited frequently. Privacy advocates celebrated *Katz* because the Fourth Amendment prohibition against illegal searches and seizures was expanded to protect telephone conversations in public phone booths. But data is now borderless. The *Katz* standard is based on a telecommunications infrastructure that no longer exists.

Another privacy standard that hasn't stood the test of time is the third-party doctrine, established in the 1970s, which says that the government can access documents that people voluntarily disclosed to banks, schools, utilities, internet service providers, and others. For instance, the 381 warrants that the Manhattan District Attorney's Office sought were for information that users had happily shared with Facebook. It has become increasingly controversial because new technologies afford law enforcement and others access to data that would not have been compromised in previous years. In the 2012 case *U.S. v. Jones*, Justice Sonia Sotomayor noted in a concurring opinion that "it may be necessary to reconsider the premise that an individual has no reasonable expectation of privacy in information voluntarily disclosed to third parties."

Perhaps the best example of this is cellphone location data. Law enforcement agencies are increasingly using devices, like the Stingray, that allow officers and other law enforcement officials to essentially track cellphones. They work by mimicking cell towers to deceive providers into sending location data. It's powerful technology—but courts are not uniform on whether there is a "reasonable expectation of privacy" in cellphone location data. There is now a split among federal appeals courts over whether a warrant is required for cell site location information from these devices. In *United States v. Graham*, the U.S. Court of Appeals for the 4th Circuit decided that a warrant wasn't required to use cell site location information from T-Mobile, an armed robber's cellphone provider, because there was no search under the Fourth Amendment. The 6th Circuit similarly ruled last year that the government does not need a warrant to access cell site location data. But last summer, the U.S. District Court for the Southern District of New York held in *United States v. Lambis* that a simulator Drug Enforcement Agency agents used to pinpoint a user's location violated the Fourth Amendment because there was no warrant. The opinion offers a good reminder of why the third-party doctrine, like many involving privacy, is outdated: "With the cell-site simulator, the Government cuts out the middleman and obtains the information directly. Without a third party, the third party doctrine is inapplicable."

It was a good decision from the federal judge who, in 2013, upheld the National Security Agency's bulk collection of data. (The decision was appealed to the 2nd Circuit, which declared the program unconstitutional.) Courts can't keep sidestepping the fact that increasingly sophisticated data is subject to the whims of law enforcement and Silicon Valley. The inconsistencies and lack of uniformity are not only baffling but also too important to dodge.

Critical Thinking

1. Article mentions a court decision invalidating a warrant to force Microsoft to provide customer emails because Microsoft held the emails on a server in Ireland. Should it matter where the data is stored if the customer either sent or receive the email in the United States? Why? If a foreigner has their email stored on a server in the United States, should American law apply—or the law from their home country?

2. What does the author mean when she states "data is now borderless"? What are the legal and policy implications of communication companies holding user data in cloud locations where it is difficult to impossible to determine which country(s) the data sits in?

3. Stingray is a law enforcement technology that mimics cell towers. Cell phones in the vicinity ping Stingray reporting their exact location in the normal course of their use. Should law enforcement be required to obtain a warrant before using that location data as evidence? That is, can people assume where they are is private information? Or, is the use of a cell phone voluntarily mean someone is voluntarily giving up a dimension of their privacy?

Internet References

Digital Privacy to Come Under Supreme Court's Scrutiny
https://www.nytimes.com/2017/07/10/business/dealbook/digital-privacy-supreme-court.html

DOJ's Facebook Warrants Target Thousands Of Users For Protesting Inauguration
https://www.techdirt.com/articles/20170929/10301038313/dojs-facebook-warrants-target-thousands-users-protesting-inauguration.shtml

EFF, ACLU Sue Government Over Warrantless Electronic Searches At The Border
https://www.techdirt.com/articles/20170917/19023838229/eff-aclu-sue-government-over-warrantless-electronic-searches-border.shtml

The Collapse of the U.S.-EU Safe Harbor: Solving the New Privacy Rubik's Cube
https://blogs.microsoft.com/eupolicy/2015/10/20/the-collapse-of-the-u-s-eu-safe-harbor-solving-the-new-privacy-rubiks-cube/

JILL PRILUCK wrote "The Little-Guy Economy" column for Slate. Her work also has appeared in *The New Yorker*, *Reuters*, *New York Times Magazine*, *Time*, *Fortune*, *the New Republic*, n+1, and elsewhere.

Article   Prepared by: Daniel Mittleman, *DePaul University* and
                                             Douglas Druckenmiller, *Western Illinois University*

Own a Vizio Smart TV? It's Watching You

Vizio, one of the most popular brands on the market, is offering advertisers "highly specific viewing behavior data on a massive scale."

JULIA ANGWIN

Learning Outcomes

After reading this article, you will be able to:

- Understand the kinds of data that technology in our homes can capture about us including behavioral data, use data, metadata, and anonymized data.

- Understand how data from multiple sources can be combined to create a comprehensive picture of an individual.

- Articulate the pros and cons of direct data collection by home appliances.

TV makers are constantly crowing about the tricks their smart TVs can do. But one of the most popular brands has a feature that it's not advertising: Vizio's Smart TVs track your viewing habits and share it with advertisers, who can then find you on your phone and other devices.

The tracking—which Vizio calls "Smart Interactivity"—is turned on by default for the more than 10 million Smart TVs that the company has sold. Customers who want to escape it have to opt-out.

In a statement, Vizio said customers' "non-personal identifiable information may be shared with select partners . . . to permit these companies to make, for example, better-informed decisions regarding content production, programming and advertising."

Vizio's actions appear to go beyond what others are doing in the emerging interactive television industry. Vizio rivals Samsung and LG Electronics only track users' viewing habits if customers choose to turn the feature on. And unlike Vizio, they don't appear to provide the information in a form that allows advertisers to reach users on other devices.

Vizio's technology works by analyzing snippets of the shows you're watching, whether on traditional television or streaming Internet services such as Netflix. Vizio determines the date, time, channel of programs—as well as whether you watched them live or recorded. The viewing patterns are then connected your IP address—the Internet address that can be used to identify every device in a home, from your TV to a phone.

IP addresses can increasingly be linked to individuals. Data broker Experian, for instance, offers a "data enrichment" service that provide "hundreds of attributes" such as age, profession and "wealth indicators" tied to a particular IP address.

Vizio recently updated its privacy policy to say it has begun providing data about customers' viewing habits to companies that "may combine this information with other information about devices associated with that IP address." The company does not promise to encrypt IP addresses before sharing them.

Cable TV companies and video rental companies are prohibited by law from selling information about the viewing habits of their customers. However, Vizio says that those laws—the Video Privacy Protection Act and cable subscriber protections—don't apply to its business.

Vizio hopes its new tracking forays will provide a boost to the thin profit margins it earns in the competitive television manufacturing business. In an October filing for an initial public offering, Vizio touted its ability to provide "highly specific viewing behavior data on a massive scale with great accuracy."

The company said in its filing that revenues from its viewing data business are not yet significant. But people familiar with the company said that Vizio has begun working to combine its viewing data with information about users that it gets from data broker Neustar.

Neustar declined to comment about the relationship but said the company does not handle or distribute viewing information about Vizio users.

A spokeswoman for Tapad, a company that helps identify users across their many devices, said that its contracts prevent it from sharing the name of the companies it works with.

An Experian spokeswoman said, "We currently do not have a relationship with Vizio."

Critical Thinking

1. How do you feel about your television sending information about your viewing habits out to advertisers who can then track you across multiple devices?

2. Is an opt-out process such as the one used by Vizio enough to qualify as consent or should they (and others) be required to get your consent (opt-in) on the front end? What are the advantages and disadvantages of each model?

3. Should companies that collect information such as this be required to encrypt the data?

Internet References

Now Advertisers Can Watch You Watch TV
https://goo.gl/BWyhDy
The Internet of Things: How Your TV, Car and Toys Could Spy on You
https://goo.gl/LblyKH
Your TV May Be Watching You
https://goo.gl/KPN06I

Article

Prepared by: Daniel Mittleman, *DePaul University* and
Douglas Druckenmiller, *Western Illinois University*

Know Your Rights!

HANNI FAKHOURY AND NADIA KAYYALI

Learning Outcomes

After reading this article, you will be able to:

- Articulate the basic principles of the U.S. Constitution Fourth Amendment, and the implications for those principles with the advent of digital communication and storage technologies.

- Understand both the rights and the limitations on search and seizure protections you have under the U.S. Constitution.

- Understand appropriately both legal and behaviors to exhibit if law enforcement requests to search or seize your property in the United States.

Your computer, phone, and other digital devices hold vast amounts of personal information about you and your family. This sensitive data is worth protecting from prying eyes, including those of the government.

The Fourth Amendment to the U.S. Constitution protects you from unreasonable government searches and seizures, and this protection extends to your computer and portable devices. But how does this work in the real world? What should you do if the police or other law enforcement officers show up at your door and want to search your computer?

EFF has designed this guide to help you understand your rights if officers try to search the data stored on your computer or portable electronic device, or seize it for further examination somewhere else. Keep in mind that the Fourth Amendment is the minimum standard, and your specific state may have stronger protections.

Because anything you say can be used against you in a criminal or civil case, before speaking to any law enforcement official, you should consult with an attorney. Remember, generally the fact that you assert your rights cannot legally be used against you in court. You can always state: "I do not want to talk to you or answer any questions without my attorney present."

If they continue to ask you questions after that point, you can say: "Please don't ask me any further questions until my attorney is present." And if the police violate your rights and conduct an illegal search, often the evidence they obtain as a result of that search can't be used against you.

We've organized this guide into three sections:

- Overview: When can the police search my devices?
- The police have a warrant. Now what?
- The police can't get into my computer. Now what?

Overview: When can the police search my devices?

- If you consent to a search, the police don't need a warrant.
- Law enforcement may show up at your door. Apart from a few exceptions, police need a warrant to enter your home.
- Be aware that the police can ask your roommate/guest/spouse/partner for access to your computer if they don't have a warrant.
- Even if you're arrested, police can only search your phone under limited circumstances.
- Police can search your computer or portable devices at the border without a warrant.

If you consent to a search, the police don't need a warrant

The most frequent way police are able to search is by asking you for permission. If you say "yes" and consent to the search, then police don't need a warrant. You can limit the scope of that consent and even revoke or take it back after the officers begin searching, but by then it may be too late.[1] That's why it's better not consent to a search—police may drop the matter. If not, then they will generally need to get a search warrant to search.

Law enforcement may show up at your door. Apart from a few exceptions, police need a warrant to enter your home

The police can't simply enter your home to search it or any electronic device inside, like a laptop or cell phone, without a warrant.

When the police knock on your door, you do not have to let them in unless they have in their possession and show you a valid search warrant. The safest thing to do is step outside and shut the door behind you. They may or may not indicate right away why they are there. If they have a warrant, ask to see it. If they offer to simply "interview" you, it is better to decline to speak until your attorney can be present. You can do this by telling the officer: "I do not want to talk to you. I do not consent to a search. I want to speak to my attorney."

There are two major *exceptions* to the warrant requirement. First, if you consent to a search, then the police can search within the scope of your consent.[2] That's why it is usually better to not consent to a search.

Second, if police have probable cause to believe there is incriminating evidence in the house or on an electronic device that is under immediate threat of destruction, they can immediately search it without a warrant.[3]

Be aware that the police can ask your roommate/guest/spouse/partner for access to your computer if they don't have a warrant

The rules around who can consent to a search are fuzzy. The key is who has control over an item. Anyone can consent to a search as long as the officers reasonably believe the third person has control over the thing to be searched.[4] However, the police cannot search if one person with control (for example a spouse) consents, but another individual (the other spouse) with control explicitly refuses.[5] It's unclear, however, whether this rule applies to items like a hard drive placed into someone else's computer.[6] And even where two people have control over an item or place, police can remove the non-consenting person and return to get the other's consent to search.[7]

You may want to share this know your rights guide with everyone in your home and ask them not to consent to a search by law enforcement.

Even if you're arrested, police can only search your phone under limited circumstances

After a person has been arrested, the police generally may search the items on her person and in her pockets, as well as anything within her immediate control, automatically and without a warrant. But the Supreme Court has ruled that police cannot search the data on a cell phone under this warrant exception.[8] Police can, however, search the physical aspects of the phone (like removing the phone from its case or removing the battery) and in situations where they actually believe evidence on the phone is likely to be immediately destroyed, police can search the cell phone without a warrant.

Police can search your computer or portable devices at the border without a warrant

Fourth Amendment protection is not as strong at the border as it is in your home or office.[9] This means that law enforcement can inspect your computer or electronic equipment, even if they have no reason to suspect there is anything illegal on it.[10] An international airport, even if many miles from the actual border, is considered the functional equivalent of a border.[11] However, border officials in Alaska, Arizona, California, Guam, Hawaii, Idaho, Montana, Northern Mariana Islands, Oregon and Washington can only confiscate an electronic device and conduct a more thorough "forensic" examination of it if they have reasonable suspicion you've engaged in criminal behavior.[12]

The police have a warrant. Now what?

- Ask to see the warrant.
- The warrant limits what the police can do.
- Although the warrant limits what the police can look for, if they see something illegal while executing a warrant they can take it.
- If the police want to search your computer, it doesn't matter whether you're the subject of their investigation.
- You do not have to assist law enforcement when they are conducting their search.
- You do not have to answer questions while law enforcement is searching.

Ask to see the warrant

A warrant is a document signed by a judge giving the police permission to either arrest you or search your property and take certain items from that property. You have the right to see the warrant and should check to make sure it is valid.

A warrant should contain:

- The correct name of the person arrested or the correct address of the specific place to be searched;
- A list of the items that can be seized or taken by the police;
- The judge's signature;
- A deadline for when the arrest or search must take place

The police must take the warrant with them when executing it and give you a copy of it.[13] They must also knock and announce their entry before they try to forcefully enter your home,[14] and must serve the warrant during the day in most circumstances.[15]

The warrant limits what the police can do

The purpose of the warrant is to give the judge, not the police, the discretion to decide what places can be searched and which items can be taken.[16] That's why a warrant is supposed to state exactly what the police can search and seize.[17] However, if the warrant authorizes the police to search for evidence of a particular crime, and such evidence is likely to be found on your computer, some courts have allowed the police to search the computer without a warrant.[18]

And remember, if you consent to a search, it doesn't matter if the police have a warrant; any search is permissible as long as the search is consistent with the scope of your consent.

Although the warrant limits what the police can look for, if they see something illegal while executing a warrant they can take it

While the police are searching your home, if they observe something in "plain view" that is suspicious or incriminating, they may take it for further examination and can rely on their observation to later get a search warrant.[19] For example, if police see an open laptop with something obviously illegal on the screen, they could seize that laptop.

If the police want to search your computer, it doesn't matter whether you're the subject of their investigation

It typically doesn't matter whether the police are investigating you, or think there is evidence they want to use against someone else located on your computer. If they have a warrant, if you

consent to the search, or they think there is something incriminating on your computer that may be immediately destroyed, the police can search it. But remember, regardless of whether you're the subject of an investigation, you can always seek the assistance of the lawyer.

You do not have to assist law enforcement when they are conducting their search

You do not have to help the police conduct the search. But you should not physically interfere with them, obstruct the search or try to destroy evidence, since that can lead to your arrest. This is true even if the police don't have a warrant and you do not consent to the search, but the police insist on searching anyway. In that instance, do not interfere but write down the names and badge numbers of the officers and immediately call a lawyer.

You do not have to answer questions while law enforcement is searching

You do not have to answer any questions. In fact, because anything you say can be used against you and other individuals, it is best to say nothing at all other than "I do not want to talk to you. I do not consent to a search. I want to speak to my attorney." However, if you do decide to answer questions, be sure to tell the truth. In many contexts, it is a crime to lie to a police officer and you may find yourself in more trouble for lying to law enforcement than for whatever it was on your computer they wanted.[20]

The police can't get into my computer. Now what?

- The police can take your computer with them and search it somewhere else.
- You do not have to hand over your encryption keys or passwords to law enforcement.
- You may be able to get your computer back if it is taken and searched.
- There is less protection against a search at a place of employment.

The police can take your computer with them and search it somewhere else

As long as the police have a warrant, they can seize the computer and take it somewhere else to search it more thoroughly. As part of that inspection, the police may make a copy of media or other files stored on your computer.[21]

You do not have to hand over your encryption keys or passwords to law enforcement

The Fifth Amendment protects you from being forced to give the government self-incriminating testimony. Courts have generally accepted that telling the government a password or encryption key is "testimony." A police officer cannot force or threaten you into giving up your password or unlocking your electronic devices. However, a judge or a grand jury may be able to force you to decrypt your devices in some circumstances. Because this is a legally complicated issue, if you find yourself in a situation where the police, a judge or grand jury are demanding you turn over encryption keys or passwords, you should let EFF know right away and seek legal help.

You may be able to get your computer back if it is taken and searched

If your computer was illegally taken, then you can file a motion with the court to have it returned.[22] If the police believe that evidence of a crime has been found on your computer (such as possessing "digital contraband" like pirated music and movies, or digital images of child pornography), the police can keep the computer as evidence. They may also attempt to keep the computer permanently, a legal process known as forfeiture, but you can challenge forfeiture in court.[23]

There is less protection against a search at a place of employment

Generally, you have some Fourth Amendment protection in your office or workspace.[24] This means the police need a warrant to search your office and work computer unless one of the exceptions described above apply. But the extent of Fourth Amendment protection depends on the physical details of your work environment, as well as any employer policies. For example, the police will have difficulty justifying a warrantless search of a private office with doors and a lock and a private computer that you have exclusive access to. On the other hand, if you share a computer with other co-workers, you will have a weaker expectation of privacy in that computer, and thus less Fourth Amendment protection.[25] However, be aware that your employer can consent to a police request to search an office or workspace in your absence.[26] Plus, if you work for a public entity or government agency, no warrant is required to search your computer or office as long as the search is for a non-investigative, work-related matter.[27]

Want to learn more about how to protect yourself from unreasonable government searches and surveillance on your computer or portable electronic devices?

- EFF's newly relaunched Surveillance Self-Defense (SSD) is a guide to defending yourself and your friends from digital surveillance by using encryption tools and developing appropriate privacy and security practices.
- EFF's recently updated Cell Phone Guide for U.S. Protestors explains your rights, and how best to protect the data on your phone, at protests.

Notes

1. *Florida v. Jimeno*, 500 U.S. 248, 252 (1991).
2. *Schneckloth v. Bustamonte*, 412 U.S. 218, 219 (1973); *United States v. Lopez-Cruz*, 730 F.3d 803, 809 (9th Cir. 2013); *United States v. Vanvliet*, 542 F.3d 259, 264 (1st Cir. 2008).
3. *Ker v. California*, 374 U.S. 23, 39 (1963).
4. *Illinois v. Rodriguez*, 497 U.S. 177, 181 (1990); *United States v. Stabile*, 633 F.3d 219, 230–31 (3d Cir. 2011); *United States v. Andrus*, 483 F.3d 711, 716 (10th Cir. 2007).
5. *Georgia v. Randolph*, 547 U.S. 103, 106 (2006).
6. *United States v. King*, 604 F.3d 125, 137 (3d Cir. 2010).
7. *Fernandez v. California*, 134 S.Ct. 1126, 1134 (2014).
8. *Riley v. California*, 134 S.Ct. 2473, 2493 (2014).
9. *United States v. Flores-Montano*, 541 U.S. 149, 152–53 (2004).
10. *United States v. Arnold*, 533 F.3d 1003, 1009 (9th Cir. 2008); *United States v. Ickes*, 393 F.3d 501, 507 (4th Cir. 2005).
11. *Almeida-Sanchez v. United States*, 413 U.S. 266, 273 (1973); *Arnold*, 533 F.3d at 1006 (9th Cir. 2008); *United States v. Romm*, 455 F.3d 990, 996 (9th Cir. 2006); *United States v. Roberts*, 274 F.3d 1007, 1011 (5th Cir. 2001).
12. *United States v. Cotterman*, 709 F.3d 952, 957 (9th Cir. 2013) (en banc).
13. Federal Rule of Criminal Procedure 41(f)(1)(C).
14. *Wilson v. Arkansas*, 514 U.S. 927, 929 (1995).
15. Federal Rule of Criminal Procedure 41(e)(2)(A)(ii).
16. *Marron v. United States*, 275 U.S. 192, 196 (1927).
17. *Andresen v. Maryland*, 427 U.S. 463, 480 (1976).
18. *United States v. Mann*, 592 F.3d 779, 786 (7th Cir. 2010); *Brown v. City of Fort Wayne*, 752 F.Supp.2d 925, 939 (N.D. Ind. 2010).
19. *Horton v. California*, 496 U.S. 128, 133 (1990); *United States v. Walser*, 275 F.3d 981, 986 (10th Cir. 2001); *United States v. Carey*, 172 F.3d 1268, 1272 (10th Cir. 1999).
20. *Compare* 18 U.S.C. § 1001(a) (maximum punishment for first offense of lying to federal officer is 5 or 8 years) *with* 18 U.S.C. §§ 1030(a)(2) and (c)(2)(A) (maximum punishment for first offense of exceeding authorized computer access is 1 year).
21. *United States v. Hill*, 459 F.3d 966, 974 (9th Cir. 2006); *In re Search of 3817 W. West End, First Floor Chicago, Illinois 60621*, 321 F.Supp.2d 953, 958 (N.D. Ill. 2004); *see also* Federal Rule of Criminal Procedure 41(e)(2)(B).
22. Federal Rule of Criminal Procedure 41(g).

23. *See* 18 U.S.C. §§ 982, 983; Federal Rule of Criminal Procedure 32.2.

24. *Mancusi v. DeForte*, 392 U.S. 364, 369 (1968); *United States v. Ziegler*, 474 F.3d 1184, 1189 (9th Cir. 2007).

25. *Schowengerdt v. United States*, 944 F.2d 483, 488-89 (9th Cir. 1991).

26. *Ziegler*, 474 F.3d at 1191.

27. *City of Ontario v. Quon*, 560 U.S. 746, 748 (2010); *O'Connor v. Ortega*, 480 U.S. 709, 722 (1987).

Critical Thinking

1. Of the questions answered at the site, which answer surprised you the most? Of the questions answered at the site, did you disagree with any of the rights currently in force? If so, which ones and why?

2. Research online the historical motivation for creating the Fourth Amendment to the U.S. Constitution. As the framers of the Constitution were naïve to electronic technologies, what rules do you think they would have found appropriate for protecting against unreasonable search and seizure of digital information?

3. Since this article was published in 2011, we have learned the NSA has been collecting vast amounts of electronic information on Americans under provisions of the Patriot Act that render national security considerations sufficient to collect such information. How do you think national security considerations should be balanced against Fourth Amendment protections against unreasonable search and seizure?

Internet References

Bruce Schneier: The Security Mirage [TED Talk]
www.ted.com/talks/bruce_schneier.html

Era of Online Sharing Offers Benefits of 'Big Data,' Privacy Trade-Offs
www.pbs.org/newshour/bb/science/jan-june13/nsa2_06-12.html

4 Things You Should Know about Metadata, Hackers And Privacy That Edward Snowden Would Never Tell You
www.forbes.com/sites/gregsatell/2013/08/03/4-things-you-should-know-about-metadata-hackers-and-privacy-that-edward-snowden-would-never-tell-you

Hasan Elahi: FBI, Here I Am! [TED Talk]
www.ted.com/talks/hasan_elahi.html

Mikko Hypponen: Three Types of Online Attack [TED Talk]
www.ted.com/talks/mikko_hypponen_three_types_of_online_attack.html

Unit 6

UNIT

Prepared by: Daniel Mittleman, *DePaul University* and
Douglas Druckenmiller, *Western Illinois University*

Technology and Health-care Ethics

In the best-selling fiction novel "Cell" by Robin Cook,[1] the author explores the potential impact of "iDoc" a technological amalgam of cell phones, personal implants, artificial intelligence (AI), and restrictive regulations on medical care delivery in the near future. The story raises many ethical questions for a future that has now arrived with a growing emphasis on telemedicine, the consolidation of health care, increased capability of mobile technology and the ongoing debate over universal coverage and cost controls in the health-care system. Several themes introduced in this novel are now current issues and are explored in this unit.

Smartphones and wearable technology are creating a personal medical sensing environment that allows for monitoring fundamental health conditions such as heart rate, exercise statistics, sleep patterns, blood sugar, diet, EEG, and other vital health measures. This data stream can in turn be analyzed remotely using deep learning (AI) medical diagnostic systems based on IBM's Watson AI technology. Medical technology implants for delivery of medication and control of body chemistry and health outcomes complete the technology environment envisioned in the novel as a current reality not a near future scenario. "iDoc" is now here and on your wrist.

Health-care regulation and rationing is another issue addressed in "Cell." In the novel, a perfect storm of the technology and rationing inherent in cost containment regulations creates a situation in which automated implementation of treatment for patients with chronic disease results in the death of patients as a "cost containment" strategy implemented by artificial intelligence algorithms. Cost of medical care and how it is rationed in society is now a fundamental conversation taking place in government. While technology promises to deliver on reducing the cost of medical care, unintended consequences and network effects have potential ethical impacts that must be considered.

Ethics considers this clash of values between business, government, and patient outcomes. The articles in this unit explore these fundamental values and consider how our health-care system uses technology to balance these different outcomes. A central theme in the ethics of health care and technology is the commitment to patient privacy. The technologies we are increasingly using to track our individual health measures were not necessarily created with privacy as a primary concern. The systems we use to collect such data may expose more than we intend to of our private lives.

---

[1] See: http://www.bioethics.net/2014/05/lessons-for-the-future-of-primary-care-from-robin-cooks-cell/

Article

Prepared by: Daniel Mittleman, *DePaul University* and
Douglas Druckenmiller, *Western Illinois University*

The Secret Things You Give Away through Your Phone Metadata

NSIKAN AKPAN

Learning Outcomes

After reading this article, you will be able to:

- Explain how metadata can be used to identify sensitive information.

- Discuss the findings of the Stanford University experiment.

- Understand the differential privacy approach.

The word "metadata" achieved buzzword status in 2013. That's when whistleblower Edward Snowden leaked documents exposing a National Security Agency program that collected telephone metadata in bulk—along with other surveillance schemes deemed unsavory by electronic rights watchdogs. Since then, metadata collection has been invoked in court proceedings, innumerable opinion pieces and an Oscar-winning documentary as one of the most egregious violations of personal privacy. On Monday, former U.S. Attorney General Eric Holder said Snowden "performed a public service"—albeit an "inappropriate and illegal" one—by sharing the secrets.

Yet, most people couldn't describe, step-by-step, how metadata are used to piece together personal secrets.

This study shows that sensitive information, like health services or lifestyle choices, are easily discernible from metadata with little digging. You're in luck. A new study from Stanford University charts exactly what can be learned from telephone metadata. The researchers used rudimentary techniques to show that your name or relationship status are immediately apparent from telephone metadata, but so are countless other personal details.

Don't want your parents to know that you're pregnant? Hope that they don't hack your smartphone's metadata.

The results clarify a longstanding debate. Metadata have historically received fewer legal protections than actual communications content, such as audio from a phone conversation or text message transcripts, to the disdain of privacy advocates. This study shows that sensitive information, like health services or lifestyle choices, are easily discernible from metadata with little digging.

"People have testified in Congress, saying that metadata definitely carries sensitive information, but there hadn't been a lot of science done," Patrick Mutchler, study coauthor and member of Stanford's Computer Security Laboratory, told NewsHour. "What our study does is confirm a lot of the suspicions that people held about metadata."

Even though the NSA shuttered its bulk collection program six months ago, the researchers' findings remain pertinent. The NSA and Federal Bureau of Investigation can still obtain telephone metadata on individual suspects via the U.S. foreign intelligence surveillance court, which didn't deny any of the 1,457 requests made last year. (In fact, the FISA court hasn't refused an application since 2009.) Plus, the NSA is holding on to boatloads of metadata collected over the last five years due to ongoing legal cases with privacy advocates.

The controversy also crosses borders. After last November's Paris attacks, France enhanced its surveillance powers to monitor phone calls without a warrant. Meanwhile, the U.K. government is debating similar legislation nicknamed the "snooper's charter." Regardless of what governments decide, companies continue to collect phone and internet metadata on customers, whether it's to sell ads or build better apps—and they've done so for decades.

"With these data, people are able to make more informed decisions about whether or not they approve or disapprove of these policies," Mutchler said. Tech innovators can also use the research to devise shields against the practice of metadata collection.

But let's start at the beginning with MetaPhone.

"Wait, you're pregnant!?"

MetaPhone is an Android app, designed by Mutchler and his labmates to collect telephone metadata. Over an eight-month window, the smartphones of 823 adult volunteers beamed call and text logs to the team's secure server. This data comprised when a call or text was made, whether it was an incoming or outgoing transmission, the duration of the call or the text message's length (in characters). The app also noted the phone numbers of the senders and recipients, but no identifiable information, audio recordings or textual content.

At least in one case, we were able to identify a person with a cardiac arrhythmia.

"The same stuff is available to the NSA, but they'd have more of it," Mutchler said of his May 17 report in the Proceedings of the National Academy of Sciences. "The volunteers hailed from 45 states, D.C. and Puerto Rico."

This small pool yielded 62,229 unique phone numbers, 251,788 calls, and 1,234,231 texts. Basic machine-learning algorithms did the rest of the heavy lifting. The team relied on these quasi-intuitive programs to make inferences about people's identities or lifestyles.

The team started with child's play. They had the algorithms skim public information from Facebook, Yelp or Google Places in order to match 30,000 randomly selected phone numbers to individuals or businesses. Using these three sources, the researchers matched identities for 32 percent of the phone numbers. When the hunt expanded to include a public records service—a $19.95 investment—and 70 minutes of Google searches, the algorithms caught 82 percent of the identities.

The researchers could also pinpoint the identity of romantic partners—as verified by Facebook relationship statuses—with 80 percent accuracy using call volume and 76 percent accuracy using how often the couple texted each day.

The shocks came when the researchers looked for sensitive connections. In the report, they presented five typical examples.

"I would have guessed general inferences—like religious affiliation. But at least in one case we were able to identify a person with a cardiac arrhythmia," Mutchler said.

This participant received a long phone call from a cardiology group at a regional medical center, according to the paper, talked briefly with a medical laboratory and answered several short calls from a local drugstore. But the key giveaway may have been brief calls to a self-reporting hotline for a cardiac arrhythmia monitoring device. The team followed up and confirmed the cardiac arrhythmia, as well as a case where the analysis accurately concluded a person had purchased an automatic rifle.

Metadata from an NSA request involving a single suspect could uncover information on approximately 25,000 individuals.

Another volunteer called a pharmaceutical hotline for a drug prescribed only for multiple sclerosis, while a third vignette involved a person who spoke her sister early one morning for an extended period of time. Two days later, she made multiples calls to a nearby Planned Parenthood clinic. She repeated the pattern two weeks later . . . and then again, a month after the first call.

Communications with health services were the most common form of sensitive information caught by MetaPhone's surveillance, accounting for 57 percent of calls among participants. Financial services accounted for 40 percent.

Another case involved a person who "placed calls to a hardware outlet, locksmiths, a hydroponics store, and a head shop in under three weeks," the report stated.

"The call patterns are indicative of starting to grow marijuana," Mutchler said.

Overall, the analysis found metadata from an NSA request involving a single suspect could uncover information on approximately 25,000 individuals. Extend the search by one degree of separation—you, your friend and their contacts—and an agent could recover personal information on 20 million people. Kevin Bacon, eat your heart out. This latter scenario, known as three-hop surveillance, was the NSA's legal standard until recently.

"Maybe these [metadata] separately are innocuous, but there is a more meaningful picture that doesn't appear until you look at the data."

Metadata Collection for the Masses

Not long after Snowden outed the NSA, President Obama asked the National Academy of Sciences to convene a panel of 13 computer security experts. Over the course of five months in late 2014, they tackled whether there were currently technological alternatives to bulk collection of metadata that could still let intelligence agencies to do their work.

"In a sense, the short answer was not really," said Michael Kearns, a computer scientist at the University of Pennsylvania who served on the committee.

The reason is a sensible one, he said. The whole premise of intelligence work is maybe some individuals don't have the right to privacy. It's difficult to know in advance who you should and shouldn't be collecting data on, for the very reason that if you knew already, then you wouldn't need any data in the first place.

Kearns believes future technology can strike a balance for surveillance agencies. In January, his team published a set of algorithms that can take a social network—like Facebook or a database of phone contacts—and filter perps from the innocent. Here's how it works.

Suppose I tell you the average salary of the PBS NewsHour editorial staff immediately before and after a reporter resigns. If you know those two values, you can easily figure out how much the reporter was making. Kearns' algorithm rely on differential privacy—a statistical masking that adds a bit of noise or randomness to the data. You can still make the salary calculation, but you can't identify the reporter.

Certain types of info, they'd rather not collect. They don't want to be on the hook for a subpoena "You want to limit the amount of information that's passing through the barrier between the place where all the data is held and the people who can act on the data," said Adam Smith, a security and privacy data scientist at Pennsylvania State University who wasn't involved with the research. "Differential privacy gives you a way to publish approximate stats to guarantee that there isn't too much information about one person."

Smith said companies like Google employ similar techniques to gather stats on how people use apps on their phones but maintain privacy.

"Certain types of info, they'd rather not collect," Smith said. "They don't want to be on the hook for subpoena."

This info could be as simple as a person's homepage on their browser. The companies monitor these browser settings because some types of viruses and malware create false default homepages that take a user to another webpage. By using differential privacy, the company can track webpage traffic that raises a red flag and see if a piece of malware is responsible.

"Differential privacy allows them to collect approximate statistics about how people are setting their homepage without knowing the precise details of how you and I set our homepage," Smith said.

As an individual, you don't have a lot of control over how your data is used or manipulated once it's left you and gone to the telecommunication companies.

One team at MIT wants to apply the differential privacy approach, which primarily suits centralized databases, and apply it to individual smartphones. They've developed an app called SafeAnswers that allows a downloader to share parts of

their metadata without forking over personal identifying content. The idea isn't completely novel. A handful of startups have created personal data storage platforms, so people can charge third-parties for access to metadata.

Yet, both Kearns and Smith said differential privacy works as a solution only if surveillance agencies or communications companies buy into it.

Individuals can end-to-end encrypt their phone calls, texts and WhatsApp messages with a service like OpenWhisperSystems. However, it requires an internet connection to create a secure channel. Mutchler couldn't think of an app that automatically anonymizes or creates false metadata to throw off possible snoops.

"As an individual, you don't have a lot of control over how your data is used or manipulated once it's left you and gone to the telecommunication companies. As it stands now, we would need to make a bunch of changes," Mutchler said. "From a public policy perspective, the next step is a continued discussion about metadata privacy and whether metadata should be considered separate or not" from content communications.

Critical Thinking

1. How accurate do you think alogrithms are at identifying your identity or lifestyle based on the metadata they collect on you?

2. What is the tradeoff between personal privacy and national security? And who should decide which is more important in any given scenario?

3. To what extent should you be able to control what data others can retrieve?

Internet References

Metadata: Your City's Secret Weapon (Industry Perspective)
https://goo.gl/Z6r5dN

No, NSA Phone Spying Has Not Ended
https://goo.gl/4JR9yf

The Feds are Prepping Strict Rules to Protect Your Online Privacy
https://goo.gl/Y6CxNq

NSIKAN AKPAN is the digital science producer for PBS NewsHour.

Akpan, Nsikan, "The Secret Things You Give Away through Your Phone Metadata," PBS.org/newshour, June 2, 2016. Used with permission.

Article

Prepared by: Daniel Mittleman, *DePaul University* and
Douglas Druckenmiller, *Western Illinois University*

Treating Addiction with an App

Nanette Byrnes

Learning Outcomes

After reading this article, you will be able to:

- Discuss the fundamental signs of addiction and how they are captured using smart phone technology.

- Discuss other health support applications based in smart phone technology.

- Explain the effectiveness and limitations of health support applications.

When I spoke to Tasha Hedstrom this winter, she had been sober for more than 61 days. After struggling with opioid addiction for 15 years, Hedstrom is taking Vivitrol, a drug that blocks the pleasurable effects of opioids and reduces cravings. She goes to a court-mandated recovery program three days a week and tracks her progress on a phone app she found on Facebook, called Triggr Health.

Hedstrom says she has never found peer support programs like Narcotics Anonymous helpful. "I don't like the atmosphere. I feel like people are talking about using and glorifying it," she says. "I don't like telling my story a million different times."

Triggr has been a different way to access support. In addition to tracking the number of days she has been in recovery, the app connects Hedstrom to a team of recovery coaches, who chat with her periodically throughout the day by text and app message. If she has not contacted Triggr for a full day, the team contacts her. Generally, they talk about how her day is going or goals she has set for herself, but recently they helped her through an unexpected challenge. A stranger followed her car into a lot and parked next to her, then offered her drugs. Not sure what to do, Hedstrom texted Triggr. "It's not just about addiction," she says. "It's like we're on a friend basis. You need to have backup supports."

In 2015, 33,000 people in the United States died from opioid overdoses—the highest number ever recorded, and more than double the 2005 figure, according to the National Institute on Drug Abuse. More than half a million hospitalizations related to opioid dependence occur each year, at a cost of $15 billion, according to a recent study.

Tens of billions more are spent on clinics and other treatment.

In total, 23 million Americans have a substance use disorder involving illicit drugs or alcohol, according to 2013 data collected by the Substance Abuse and Mental Health Services Administration, part of the U.S. Department of Health and Human Services. But fewer than 20 percent of those who need treatment will receive it. And while the most common form of treatment, Alcoholics Anonymous or Narcotics Anonymous, can be quite effective for some, according to one survey 75 percent of people in such programs relapse in their first year. Though a wide range of treatments are available, says James R. McKay, an expert in addiction and a professor of psychology at the University of Pennsylvania, "there are people for whom none of those things really work."

New technologies are offering yet another option, making use of the computers we carry in our pockets. Of the 165,000 smartphone apps for health care, mental-health apps are the single largest category, including hundreds of addiction-related options offering inspirational quotes, directions to nearby AA meetings, hypnosis guides, and online peer support groups.

Triggr is more ambitious. Using data collected from smartphones, the company aims not only to help people handle cravings and the stresses that trigger drug use but to actually predict when someone is going to relapse and intervene. Triggr collects clues from things like screen engagement, texting patterns, phone logs, sleep history, and location. Those are combined with information gathered from participants' communications with the startup's staff on its platform—such as drug preference, drug history, and the presence of dangerous words like "craving" or "stress"—and fed into a series of algorithms. The

system has access to general information about other texting and e-mail activity but not to the content of private texts or calls. Using machine learning, it searches for patterns that point to an increased likelihood of relapse. When the likelihood rises to a dangerous level, a member of the recovery team steps in or alerts a customer's outside care team.

Neither the company nor clients will say how much the platform costs to use, though in some pilot projects Triggr seems to be charging very little or nothing. Hedstrom downloaded the app for free but now pays a monthly fee for using the system, which she says is less than two dollars a day. The most promising way for Triggr to make money could be to share in the financial savings use of the app could offer the insurers and government agencies that pay the medical costs associated with addiction. An initial 30-day inpatient treatment can cost $17,000, and emergency room visits and other associated costs add up quickly.

Chris Olsen, a partner at the venture capital firm Drive Capital, one of Triggr's investors, says it has been estimated that Ohio Medicaid is spending as much as $5 billion a year on hepatitis C infections, which are strongly correlated with injection drug use. "If we can reduce that," says Olsen, "I just believe there will be a revenue model down the line." Among those using the app today are patients who have been through rehab at Sprout Health Group, a chain of addiction treatment centers headquartered in New Jersey. Sprout CEO Arel Meister-Aldama says that before Triggr, a patient who had been in a full-time program for 45 days on average and then returned to the community would have been tracked with periodic phone calls and invited to alumni events, but it was hard to know how people were really doing. Now Sprout's counselors get alerts from Triggr when a patient seems at risk. "There are false alarms, but often we'll catch people on the way to their drug dealers. Or they'll be sitting outside a bar thinking about going in," says Meister-Aldama.

Sprout's readmission rates have actually gone up since the company started using Triggr, but overall cost per patient has declined. That's because its counselors have been able to help patients earlier, avoiding expensive stays in treatment facilities and emergency treatment. With the data he is getting from Triggr, Meister-Aldama says, he has a better understanding of what it will cost to treat each patient. He expects that in the future he will be able to agree to flat payments per patient instead of charging fees based on services.

The platform Meister-Aldama has found so useful wouldn't work without ubiquitous smartphones and recent advances in machine learning. And it wouldn't exist at all if it had not been for one college student's pain—and her mother's timely intervention.

Motherly Intuition

John Haskell, Triggr's cofounder and CEO, came up with the idea for the app and the broader system of care during a challenging period in his own life. While an undergraduate at Stanford, he battled manic depression, spending five years at school without earning a degree. And one of his friends at Stanford struggled with mental-health problems and substance abuse. She got to a point at which she did not want to continue with treatment and considered suicide. At a particularly critical moment, her mother called. The call set her daughter on a more positive path, and when Haskell asked the mother what had prompted the call just at that moment, she attributed it to "motherly intuition."

Motherly intuition was something Haskell thought should be reproducible with the help of smart technology.

"She knew something was wrong. She could feel it. But what was particularly interesting about that experience was that it was all these data points. And all trackable on your phone," he says. For example, his friend had always loved Words with Friends, an online multiplayer game similar to Scrabble, but she had stopped playing. She was sending texts in the middle of the night, an obvious sign she was not sleeping. "The concept of intuition is purely a data question," says Haskell. "Why can't you scale motherly intuition?"

Recommended for You

Six years later, Haskell's motherly-intuition machine occupies two long white tables in a second-floor walk-up in Chicago's River North neighborhood. At one table sit a small group of programmers and data scientists, many with backgrounds at larger companies including Google, building the app and its platform. On the other side of a partial partition wall, at an identical white table, sit the recovery group, a team of four to five people who interact with participants on the platform. Everyone faces a computer screen.

The technologists work with the data that sensors are pulling off participants' phones as well as from their interactions with the recovery team, identifying patterns that signal a move in the wrong direction. Twenty-four hours a day, seven days a week, Triggr actively watches over everyone on the platform, with a single member of the recovery team following 500 people at any time. Each participant has a rating on a scale of 1 to 10 based on the patterns Triggr's algorithm is tracking. A 1 means things are going very well. A 10 is an alert that the person is exhibiting a pattern of behavior that may be on the edge of relapse and needs to be contacted.

Most staff communication with clients takes place via text or app messaging. Without the clues they might get in person from

eye contact and body language, or on the phone from someone's tone of voice, the team relies heavily on alerts from its algorithms.

Are You A Robot?

Triggr's machine-learning systems have made the platform smarter over time by studying both those interactions with participants and the millions of data points collected from their smartphones. The systems search for anomalies, breaks from a client's typical routine. As more people use the system and more data is gathered and studied, the ability to see signs of a potential relapse improves. Eighty-five percent accurate a year ago, Triggr can now predict with 92 percent accuracy when a client is likely to slip in the next three days. The early intervention such predictions make possible is significantly improving clients' results, the company says.

The messiness of the data is what convinced Triggr's data scientist, John Santerre, that machine learning could be effective against the problem. Some of the most important warning signs of an impending slip have nothing directly to do with drugs or alcohol. Instead, they're life events, like the death of a family member or another user, an affair, an issue with housing. Just one deviation from a client's normal routine—something as small as a text that comes in at an unusual time—increases the chance of relapse in the next few days. Triggr does not even need to know whom that text comes from or what it says. The interruption of routine is the critical clue.

Triggr is collecting every piece of data it can on how to help people resist an urge as it swells and then drops off, and has taken on the tricky task of building a system designed to work with minimal human input while producing a service customized to each participant. While algorithms may determine that a slip is coming, intervening to stop it isn't necessarily suited to automation. "Our goal is to make it as human as possible," says Haskell. Still, clients do sometimes ask the recovery coaches if they are robots. Tasha Hedstrom did; Triggr responded by asking if *she* was a robot. Humor is one of the techniques the algorithm has determined work well with some participants.

The coaches are always testing messages sent to clients in response to different types of issues. Those that resonate are shared with the engineering team; when a similar call comes in later, the system will know to suggest that effective response. Once Triggr determines that a person is in danger of relapsing, it's time for the really hard part: intervention to stop the self-destructive behavior. Humans do oversee the interaction, but when someone's risk is rising, a member of the recovery team is automatically alerted to the most effective way to reach out to that client and the type of message to which he or she is most likely to respond. This is as close to Haskell's idea of digital intuition as Triggr has come so far.

No Smartphone

A big focus for Haskell is developing connections to community service organizations, and on a wet morning in January, he was standing in a conference room in Framingham, Massachusetts, excitedly explaining the app to a group of counselors from the South Middlesex Opportunity Council (SMOC), a local nonprofit. SMOC had just launched Triggr as part of a program to connect with drug users in the emergency room after they have overdosed. Like many parts of the Northeast, the Midwest, and Appalachia, Framingham is suffering a rising number of opioid-related overdoses: they now average 10 a month.

Some counselors in the room worried that not all potential clients have smartphones. Others wanted a service Triggr does not offer: alerts when a client has contacted a drug dealer or used drugs again. Haskell had answers for every question, but a month and a half after the presentation, Krystin Fraser, who is running the grant, said that of the first eight people who signed up, only one agreed to download Triggr. Some do not have a smartphone, she explained, while others simply do not want someone watching them. Over the next month, 13 more people signed up for the app.

Most health apps are not regulated by the Food and Drug Administration and the company has chosen not to publish any clinical trials of its platform, something it is not required to do. It is tracking the long-term outcomes for people who use Triggr, and its decision does put the burden on the company to show that it really has made something extraordinary. It is in a crowded field. "There's been a glut of mental-health apps, most of questionable use and efficacy," says John Torous, a director of the digital psychiatry program at Boston's Beth Israel Deaconess Medical Center. Torous is part of a study using passive phone data to follow people suffering from schizophrenia, a mental disorder that is quite different from addiction but can feature similar underlying behavior, such as disrupted sleep. "People underestimate how complex it is to work with this data," says Torous. "We've had mass-market

smartphones for 10 years and we still haven't revolutionized mental-health care. If this were as easy as building an app, in 10 years it would have been done. People are complex. We can collect all this data, but how do we analyze it in a valid way?"

Jukka-Pekka Onnela, a professor of biostatistics at Harvard's T.H. Chan School of Public Health and Torous's collaborator on the schizophrenia study, is more optimistic. As people use phones for more and more daily needs such as schedules, navigation, and communication, the data from these devices becomes "very, very powerful," Onnela says. That's especially so for conditions where behavior is strongly influenced by a person's surroundings and recent history, as it is for people with psychological disorders or addiction.

When they're awake, people's phone screens may be on more than 20 times an hour. Onnela has found that frequency to be a reliable indicator of sleep patterns, something essential to understanding psychological illness and treating it.

"In the past a lot of measurement has been confined to labs or doctor's offices," says Onnela. "What we are trying to do is to capture symptoms in the wild, the way people actually experience their lives."

Critical Thinking

1. What are the limitations of a mental health application?
2. What ethical and privacy concerns are there with personal health applications data?
3. How could data sharing concerns/limitations limit the effectivess of health applications?

Internet References

AMA Adopts New Guidance for Ethical Practice in Telemedicine
https://goo.gl/yNe4Bm

Lessons For the Future of Primary Care Frome Robin Cook's Cell
https://goo.gl/fKPyr7

Mental Health: There's an App for That
https://goo.gl/62jwSy

NANETTE BYRNES is MIT Technology Review's senior editor for business.

Article   Prepared by: Daniel Mittleman, *DePaul University* and
                                            Douglas Druckenmiller, *Western Illinois University*

Stung by Yelp Reviews, Health Providers Spill Patient Secrets

The vast majority of reviews on Yelp are positive. But in trying to respond to critical ones, some doctors, dentists, and chiropractors appear to be violating the federal patient privacy law known as HIPAA.

CHARLES ORNSTEIN

Learning Outcomes

After reading this article, you will be able to:

- Explain how patient medical privacy has been comprimised through the use of Yelp as a counter to patient complaints.

- Discuss the double injury of exposing patient details in a Yelp review.

- Discuss the positive and negative values of health-care review systems.

Burned by negative reviews, some health providers are casting their patients' privacy aside and sharing intimate details online as they try to rebut criticism.

In the course of these arguments—which have spilled out publicly on ratings sites like Yelp—doctors, dentists, chiropractors, and massage therapists, among others, have divulged details of patients' diagnoses, treatments, and idiosyncrasies.

One Washington state dentist turned the tables on a patient who blamed him for the loss of a molar: "Due to your clenching and grinding habit, this is not the first molar tooth you have lost due to a fractured root," he wrote. "This tooth is no different."

In California, a chiropractor pushed back against a mother's claims that he misdiagnosed her daughter with scoliosis. "You brought your daughter in for the exam in early March 2014," he wrote. "The exam identified one or more of the signs I mentioned above for scoliosis. I absolutely recommended an x-ray to determine if this condition existed; this x-ray was at no additional cost to you."

And a California dentist scolded a patient who accused him of misdiagnosing her. "I looked very closely at your radiographs and it was obvious that you have cavities and gum disease that your other dentist has overlooked. . . . You can live in a world of denial and simply believe what you want to hear from your other dentist or make an educated and informed decision."

Health professionals are adapting to a harsh reality in which consumers rate them on sites like Yelp, Vitals, and RateMDs much as they do restaurants, hotels, and spas. The vast majority of reviews are positive. But in trying to respond to negative ones, some providers appear to be violating the Health Insurance Portability and Accountability Act, the federal patient privacy law known as HIPAA. The law forbids them from disclosing any patient health information without permission.

Yelp has given ProPublica unprecedented access to its trove of public reviews—more than 1.7 million in all—allowing us to search them by keyword. Using a tool developed by the Department of Computer Science and Engineering at the NYU Tandon School of Engineering, we identified more than 3,500 one-star reviews (the lowest) in which patients mention privacy or HIPAA. In dozens of instances, responses to complaints about medical care turned into disputes over patient privacy.

The patients affected say they've been doubly injured—first by poor service or care and then by the disclosure of information they considered private.

The shock of exposure can be effective, prompting patients to back off.

"I posted a negative review" on Yelp, a client of a California dentist wrote in 2013. "After that, she posted a response with details that included my personal dental information. . . . I removed my review to protect my medical privacy."

The consumer complained to the Office for Civil Rights within the U.S. Department of Health and Human Services, which enforces HIPAA. The office warned the dentist about posting personal information in response to Yelp reviews. It is currently investigating a New York dentist for divulging personal information about a patient who complained about her care, according to a letter reviewed by ProPublica.

The office couldn't say how many complaints it has received in this area because it doesn't track complaints this way. ProPublica has previously reported about the agency's historic inability to analyze its complaints and identify repeat HIPAA violators.

Deven McGraw, the office's deputy director of health information privacy, said health professionals responding to online reviews can speak generally about the way they treat patients but must have permission to discuss individual cases. Just because patients have rated their health provider publicly doesn't give their health provider permission to rate them in return.

"If the complaint is about poor patient care, they can come back and say, 'I provide all of my patients with good patient care' and 'I've been reviewed in other contexts and have good reviews,'" McGraw said. But they can't "take those accusations on individually by the patient."

McGraw pointed to a 2013 case out of California in which a hospital was fined $275,000 for disclosing information about a patient to the media without permission, allegedly in retaliation for the patient complaining to the media about the hospital.

Yelp's senior director of litigation, Aaron Schur, said most reviews of doctors and dentists aren't about the actual health care delivered but rather their office wait, the front office staff, billing procedures or bedside manner. Many health providers are careful and appropriate in responding to online reviews, encouraging patients to contact them offline or apologizing for any perceived slights. Some don't respond at all.

"There's certainly ways to respond to reviews that don't implicate HIPAA," Schur said.

In 2012, University of Utah Health Care in Salt Lake City was the first hospital system in the country to post patient reviews and comments online. The system, which had to overcome doctors' resistance to being rated, found positive comments far outnumbered negative ones.

"If you whitewash comments, if you only put those that are highly positive, the public is very savvy and will consider that to be only advertising," said Thomas Miller, chief medical officer for the University of Utah Hospitals and Clinics.

Unlike Yelp, the University of Utah does not allow comments about a doctor's medical competency and it does not allow physicians to respond to comments.

In discussing their battles over online reviews, patients said they'd turned to ratings sites for closure and in the hope that their experiences would help others seeking care. Their providers' responses, however, left them with a lingering sense of lost trust.

Angela Grijalva brought her then 12-year-old daughter to Maximize Chiropractic in Sacramento, Calif., a couple years ago for an exam. In a one-star review on Yelp, Grijalva alleged that chiropractor Tim Nicholl led her daughter to "believe she had scoliosis and urgently needed x-rays, which could be performed at her next appointment. . . . My daughter cried all night and had a tough time concentrating at school."

But it turned out her daughter did not have scoliosis, Grijalva wrote. She encouraged parents to stay away from the office.

Nicholl replied on Yelp, acknowledging that Grijalva's daughter was a patient (a disclosure that is not allowed under HIPAA) and discussing the procedures he performed on her and her condition, though he said he could not disclose specifics of the diagnosis "due to privacy and patient confidentiality."

"The next day you brought your daughter back in for a verbal review of the x-rays and I informed you that the x-rays had identified some issues, but the good news was that your daughter did not have scoliosis, great news!" he recounted. "I proceeded to adjust your daughter and the adjustment went very well, as did the entire appointment; you made no mention of a 'misdiagnosis' or any other concern."

In an interview, Grijalva said Nicholl's response "violated my daughter and her privacy."

"I wouldn't want another parent, another child to go through what my daughter went through: the panic, the stress, the fear," she added.

Nicholl declined a request for comment. "It just doesn't seem like this is worth my time," he said. His practice has mixed reviews on Yelp, but more positive than negative.

A few years ago, Marisa Speed posted a review of North Valley Plastic Surgery in Phoenix after her then–3-year-old son received stitches there for a gash on his chin. "Half-way through the procedure, the doctor seemed flustered with my crying child. . . .," she wrote. "At this point the doctor was more upset and he ended up throwing the instruments to the floor. I understand that dealing with kids requires extra effort, but if you don't like to do it, don't even welcome them."

An employee named Chase replied on the business's behalf: "This patient presented in an agitated and uncontrollable state. Despite our best efforts, this patient was screaming, crying, inconsolable, and a danger to both himself and to our staff. As any parent that has raised a young boy knows, they have the strength to cause harm."

Speed and her husband complained to the Office for Civil Rights. "You may wish to remove any specific information about current or former patients from your Web-blog," the Office for Civil Rights wrote in an October 2013 letter to the surgery center.

In an email, a representative of the surgery center declined to comment. "Everyone that was directly involved in the incident no longer works here. The nurse on this case left a year ago, the surgeon in the case retired last month, and the administrator left a few years ago," he wrote.

Reviews of North Valley Plastic Surgery are mixed on Yelp.

Health providers have tried a host of ways to try to combat negative reviews. Some have sued their patients, attracting a torrent of attention but scoring few, if any, legal successes. Others have begged patients to remove their complaints.

Jeffrey Segal, a onetime critic of review sites, now says doctors need to embrace them. Beginning in 2007, Segal's company, Medical Justice, crafted contracts that health providers could give to patients asking them to sign over the copyright to any reviews, which allowed providers to demand that negative ones be removed. But after a lawsuit, Medical Justice stopped recommending the contracts in 2011.

Segal said he has come to believe reviews are valuable and that providers should encourage patients who are satisfied to post positive reviews and should respond—carefully—to negative ones.

"For doctors who get bent out of shape to get rid of negative reviews, it's a denominator problem," he said. "If they only have three reviews and two are negative, the denominator is the problem. . . . If you can figure out a way to cultivate reviews from hundreds of patients rather than a few patients, the problem is solved."

Critical Thinking

1. How can health-care providers legally repsond to negative patient reviews?

2. To what extend does a health-care review system aggravate patient confidentiality problems?

3. How can patient review systems contribute to positive heath-care outcomes?

Internet References

Healthcare Security: Understanding HIPAA Compliance and its Role in Patient Data Protection
https://goo.gl/zbcyEM

This Graph Shows How Damaging Data Breaches Are On Hospitals
https://goo.gl/e7ZSDk

Why Are We Giving Away Our Most Sensitive Health Data to Google
https://goo.gl/t1MMxN

CHARLES ORNSTEIN is a senior reporter at ProPublica, covering health care and the pharmaceutical industry.

Article

Prepared by: Daniel Mittleman, *DePaul University* and
Douglas Druckenmiller, *Western Illinois University*

Four Reasons Why Healthcare Needs a Digital Code of Ethics

Eric S. Swirsky

Learning Outcomes

After reading this article, you will be able to:

- Discuss the primary ethical dilemmas posed by digitization of health care.

In the wake of the HITECH Act of 2009, office-based physician adoption of electronic medical records (EMRs) has nearly doubled as providers have taken advantage of meaningful use incentives. While the trend toward implementation of systems to maintain, manipulate, and share data has been palpable, there is no cohesive code of ethics addressing the issues related to the use of aggregated data. Informatics is by its nature multidisciplinary, and these varied stakeholders are governed by value systems that differ in significant ways.

The resulting IT systems and use cases present ethical challenges including threats to patient autonomy and shared decision-making, the provider–patient relationship, and the Big Data that is leveraged to inform evidence-based medicine. Despite their many benefits, both actual and aspirational, health information technology (HIT) and data science offer no panacea for the ills of our beleaguered healthcare system. In some cases the tech serves to exacerbate old problems, in others new problems spring from the socio-technical sandbox, and ultimately it is the patient who bears the greatest burden.

Many of the issues that we face with the use of HIT result from a battle that has been raging over the soul of health care—the clash of values between the business of medicine and the care of the patient. Business is winning the battle—it has been for some time—and it has shaped the development and implementation of information technology in the U.S. healthcare system. Health IT, in current incarnations, tends to look through the vulnerable toward a favorable bottom line.

Depending on who you ask, you will get a different answer as to whether HIT serves the triple aim of efficiency, cost-effectiveness, and improved outcomes in healthcare, but it matters not. The triple aim creates transactions where once there were relationships. And, as frustrations mount so do profits, and the values and dollars have been shifting accordingly. To wit: the base pay of insurance and hospital executives and administrators often outpaces those of surgeons and hospitalists, while medical societies report en masse to the National Coordinator for Health Information Technology that HIT certification and meaningful use are detrimental to patient safety, security, usability, and interoperability. Since stakeholders are guided by different values and professional duties, a cohesive set of ethical guidelines is needed to inform practice for all professionals involved. The following four points provide some of the reasons why.

1. Patients Are More than Data Points

Aggregated data of treatment outcomes do not necessarily reflect the needs of an individual patient and her experience with her health or healthcare provider. The record is a disembodied representation of a patient, who is deconstructed byte by byte without effectively being represented as a whole person. The lament from physicians has been consistent—EHRs and their myriad structured data points do not tell us much about what is happening with a particular patient, and clinical usability leaves much to be desired. The health, wellbeing, and dignity of an individual are not found in the aggregate—they are discovered at the bedside along the course of a provider–patient relationship. While there is an emphasis on patient satisfaction and follow-up to services received, aggregated data does not shape the individual patient experience or reflect the bedside interactions of an individual. Reducing a large population of individuals to a set of data points may create a scenario in which the reality of each individual is lost in the mire of the aggregate.

In the pursuit of cost-effective treatments, the patient narrative has been all but forsaken. Instead, we hear calls for inclusion of the data narrative which, in a certain sense, is an assault on patient autonomy and the shared decision-making process. It turns clinical paternalism on its head and exchanges goals of care and efficacy for cost-effectiveness. The fact is that improved outcomes and cost-containment are not mutually inclusive, and the data narrative may create adversarial relationships between patients and providers. With the business of health care guiding the use of HIT, the value systems are no longer aligned. The move toward a patient-centric, shared decision-making model ushered out the days of *the doctor knows best*—only to usher in the current meme of *the data knows best*.

2. Patients Are More than Consumers of Treatment

Patients are vulnerable individuals as they pass through our health system. Many have medical and emotional needs and face challenges managing their own care and treatment in a consumer role. Consumers are well informed and typically consider cost as a part of their decision-making process outside of healthcare. Providers, on the other hand, are notorious for their general lack of transparency when it comes to pricing and hidden costs of care. While patients should be informed and educated, requiring a proactive consumer places many patients in a role that causes stress and unnecessary hardship when most patients want to address a specific medical needs and return to daily life. Educating the patient is the role of the healthcare provider, and information needs to be presented in a way that is meaningful to the patient's well-being instead of placing patients in the role of an information-seeking consumer.

But there is a larger issue here with this high tech, low touch consumer model—we sometimes employ information technology for its newness and without solid evidence to confirm its efficacy. Use of technology for the sake of using new technology is pure folly in a clinical environment, and it can leave patients in the cold feeling frustrated and afraid. Health information technologists like to think that they work in the state of the art, but that is not so because they have not had the proper apprenticeship. With technology, the state of the art is the newfangled; in healthcare, Hippocrates reminds us through the millennia that the art is long. Clinically speaking, the notion that HIT is state of the art is at once laughable and lamentable. The *art* of clinical practice comes from honing practice over time to meet the many and varied needs of patients, yet there is precious little training on how to incorporate these technologies into clinical encounters. That piece, the art, has been an afterthought in the world of health IT. We have been far more focused on value and revenue than what is meaningful to patients and their treating physicians. In a technological system, the personal touch cannot be taken for granted, and many patients would still prefer a person to an iPad or portal. Now, get the machine that goes, "Bing!"

3. Health-Care Providers Are More than Businesses

Data science is nothing new to health care—clinical investigators have been employing quantitative research techniques for some time. What has changed is who is using the data. It's not just clinicians and researchers anymore; many hands hold the record nowadays and for a variety of purposes. This too is nothing new, as clinical ethicist Mark Siegler lamented the decrepitude of confidentiality back in the 80s for this very reason. Hospitals and healthcare providers need to meet more than financially viable projections. They need to be places of care and support for individuals geared toward improving health on the patient's terms. Clinicians know this, but data scientist do not, and rightly so because it is not within their disciplinary training. In the world of health information technology, it is far more important that IT people be aligned with the values of healthcare than be good business people, as Paul Crotty calls for in his blog. In his considerations of the duality of man, Crotty may find that patients are far better served by a caring rather than a business response. At the same time, clinicians need to be better at leveraging IT. It has its problems but it's here to stay and clinicians need to take control of their self-regulating professions. Training is needed so that providers can use IT to deepen their relationship with patients rather than have it serve as an intermediary or justification to bill at higher rates.

While improved outcomes are primarily aspirational in the world of Big Data, there is a clear and well-worn path to increased revenue and profitability. For some this is a, if not *the* primary rationale for providers to harness data science—to analyze claims data. Financial concerns have been, by far, the most important to those implementing health information technologies. While it is imperative that providers reduce duplicative or unnecessary interventions, adding the layer of cost-effectiveness for the provider creates a conflict of interest with the patient who may be more interested in her health and well-being than her provider's bottom line. The standard of care should be determined by clinical efficacy rather than profitability. Moreover, the notion that cost-effectiveness leads to a lower cost of care for patients is dubious. To the contrary, what we have seen is that efficiencies lead to greater profit and executive compensation.

4. Data Discriminates

Despite hubristic claims of a potential healthcare revolution, Big Data and its purveyors are deeply biased, discriminate based on discipline, exacerbate health literacy issues, and do not necessarily lead to changes in behavior for even the most basic things, such as provider hand hygiene. For starters, we can look at whose data is being aggregated. Underserved populations, by the very nature of their being underserved, have less data to aggregate. Minority groups, women, and other groups whose health issues have been under-represented in research face the same if not more bias in treatment as research does not reflect their needs. We can also look to research bias and the sorts of studies that are funded and published or unpublished. For example, research conducted in areas of greater commercial value can be biased toward generating return on investment, as we have seen in numerous electronic health records. Then, there is a matter of publication bias because in too many cases only positive results are published resulting in gaps in knowledge. For example, industry-funded studies are far more likely to show clinical effectiveness of a drug than neutrally-funded studies.

The use of Big Data can deepen the digital divide and gaps in health literacy. Information, knowledge, and wisdom are very different things. Pouring on the data and information does not create knowledge. Information must be tailored, channeled, and delivered in a way that meets the patient where she is.

As high as that bar is for providers, it's exponentially higher for vulnerable patients as are the stakes.

Data and information are not enough. At some point patients require some intermediary agent to help them transform the deluge of information into knowledge in a way that is meaningful to the patient on the patient's terms. Yet, the so-called efficiencies that we enjoy allow physicians to spend less time with patients. They can bill more in less time and then move on. That's less time for doctors to explain things (by the way, the word doctor means teacher, not healer). Even if they had they time, there is no causal connection between knowledge and behavior modification when it comes to improvements in care. As Damian Mingle points out, it was 130 years after Ignaz Semmelweis call for improvements in hygiene that CDC adopted and published hand hygiene guidelines. What Mingle misses is that hand hygiene statistics for clinicians are still abysmal—the CDC places hand hygiene adherence in hospitals somewhere between 29 percent and 48 percent. This is not a win for data, it's a debacle. We've known for some time that hand washing matters, but the data is not enough to change behaviors as grave as the consequences may be.

Data science has a lot to offer medicine, but like medicine the science must be wielded with an art. The values of medicine and information technology are disparate in many ways, but they can be harmonized if the will is there. There is the distinct possibility that the best use of health information technology is to find new ways to listen to patients and enhance the doctor-patient relationship rather than dictate or placate it. Ethics, and not data science, will help to achieve that end. Big data is merely the latest instrumentality of the medical industrial complex. Without an alignment of values, we will continue to see it leveraged to put profits before patients.

Critical Thinking

1. How does overemphasis on data dehumanize patient treatment and outcomes?

2. What are the pros and cons of a data-driven approach to clinical care?

3. What is the impact of viewing health-care provision as just a business?

Internet References

Emerging Ethical Concerns in the Age of Artificial Intelligence
https://goo.gl/uTA26F

Ethics at the Heart of Digital Processing of Health Data
https://goo.gl/4LvELj

Tech Giants Grapple with the Ethical Concerns Raised by the AI Boom
https://goo.gl/KAZWTw

Eric S. Swirsky, J.D., M.A., is the director of graduate studies and a clinical assistant professor in the Department of Biomedical and Health Information Sciences at the University of Illinois at Chicago. Professor Swirsky's scholarly interests revolve around the ethical conundra that result from the use of health information technologies.

Unit 7

UNIT

Prepared by: Daniel Mittleman, *DePaul University* and
Douglas Druckenmiller, *Western Illinois University*

The Internet of Things

As Yogi Berra once famously said, "It's tough to make predictions, especially about the future." And indeed it is. For example, Thomas Watson Jr., then the Chairman of IBM, predicted in 1953 that IBM would be able to market "maybe five computers."[1] (That is not a typo; although to his credit, at the time each 701 computer was the size of a backyard shed, required more air conditioning than a commercial freezer, and rented for $12,000 to $20,000 a month.) Twenty-four years later, Ken Olson, President of Digital Equipment Corporation (DEC) then one of the largest computer companies in the world, looked at the newly released Apple II computer by an unknown start up in California and surmised, "There is no reason anyone would want a computer in their home." IBM, in 1981, released the IBM PC that lead to a mass adoption of personal computers with at least one, today, in almost every home. Apple, in turn, has led the push to put a computer in almost everyone's pocket, and in doing so has become the most valuable company in the world. And Apple's iPhone 7 is, by measure of instructions per second, about 1 million times faster than the first IBM PC.

Clearly, predicting the future is a risky business. We tend to view the future through the lens of the present day, thinking the future will simply be an improved variation of what is now. In the short term, this sometimes works, but the history of technology shows that every so often a new technology completely reshapes not only that technological domain, but economic, social, and political structures impacted by it. This certainly was true with Gutenberg's printing press, which in the mid-15th century changed not only the field of printing, but became a catalyst for the Protestant movement against the Church, increased levels of literacy, and, therefore, the end of the middle ages. Watt's steam engine, in 1781, led to revolutions in transportation (both railroad and shipping) as well as factory work, making it a principal catalyst of the industrial revolution. Not to mention the sweeping effects of the commercialization of the automobile at the beginning of the 20th century.

Since the commercialization of the computer in the 1950s, we have experienced a punctuated leap in technological capability roughly once a decade. Computers in the first decade of commercialization were large, expensive, and difficult to program. Only the largest, most data intensive organizations considered acquiring them. Each computer was hand crafted, sometimes modified for individual customers.

The integrated circuit was invented in 1958 and found its way into mass produced computers by the mid-1960s. This reduced the size and price of computers, making them affordable for many more businesses—and large organizations often bought several. This generation of computers led to computerization of government records, computerized billing by utility companies and department stores, and—because information now had to fit into limited fields of data records—standardization among almost everything business and government did.[2] At about the same time, the U.S. Department of Defense commissioned the development of a self-healing network technology with no central hub that would be impossible for the enemy to defeat with a single well-placed strike. This network was named ARPANET and is the precursor to today's Internet.[3] ARPANET, which went live in 1969, enabled e-mail, electronic file transfers, remote computer login, and discussion boards. Though access to these networking features was largely limited to government workers and academics, within those communities they were widely used by the late 1970s.

The microprocessor was invented in 1971 and it led to later inventions at both ends of the spectrum. At the high end, Cray Computers shipped the world's first supercomputer in 1976, enabling sophisticated computational intensive simulation and modeling applications. And the low end, the microprocessor enabled personal computers, beginning with the Altair 8800 in 1975. Other computers quickly followed, including the original Apple II in 1977. IBM released its PC in 1981 and brought this form factor into the mainstream. PC-sized computing, along with parallel developments in Ethernet networking technology enabled computing on almost every office desktop, shared file space within a company, and e-mail. It also enabled people to have computers in their homes.

In 1993, Marc Andreessen built Mosaic, the first graphical browser, and ushered in the era of the World Wide Web (WWW), which is primarily a file sharing application that runs on top of the basic Internet protocols. And in 1995, the WWW went commercial with the founding of Yahoo, eBay, and Amazon, initiating the era of e-commerce. By the middle of the following decade, an amalgam of technical developments improved synchronous interactivity on the web. These developments enabled social media and social networking, what we now call Web 2.0.

At about the same time, improvements in wireless connectivity (both WiFi and cellular) made rich mobile computing possible. The introduction of the iPhone in 2007 solidified the user interface and led to mass adoption.

Every one of the computing epochs recounted above contributed to significant shifts in economic, social, and political institutions and behaviors. There is no reason to believe this timeline has run its course. And that is why we are interested in predictions. Were the future easy to predict, we all would have bought IBM stock in 1952, Microsoft stock in 1986, and Apple in 1997 (when Steve Jobs returned). But the future is so hard to predict that CEOs of major computer companies got it wrong in embarrassing ways.

Today we are on the cusp of a seismic shift to the internet of everything. The convergence of technological innovations known as Web 3.0 promises to incorporate advances in deep learning and artificial intelligence into an extended web of smart Internet connected devices. Users now enter peta-bytes of data onto the Internet, much of it retained for analysis in huge repositories owned by Google, Facebook, Amazon, and the like. We increasingly interact with the Internet not only through keyboard and mouse, but by voice talking with smart agents like Siri, Alexa, and Cortana. And they, in turn, can talk to our home appliances and soon, perhaps, our cars. This ubiquitous inter network of everything will collaborate with us to coordinate and transform our lives and society in unpredictable ways, forming an adaptive, personal, and comfortable "nest." But will it be safe?

Notes

1. This quote is often attributed to his father, Thomas Watson Sr., as saying he predicted a world market of maybe five computers. But there is no evidence Watson Sr. ever said such a thing. Watson Jr. did say something to this effect as IBM began marketing their first commercial computer, the 701, in 1953. While he predicted they would sell five of them, they actually sold 18 during their first sales pitch.

2. For those of you interested in the societal impact of this standardization, read Les Earnest, *Can Computers Cope with Human Races,* Communications of the ACM, February 1989, v32, n2, 174–182.

3. The Internet is simply the interconnection of many networks that run on TCP/IP, a descendent of the ARPANET protocol.

Prepared by: Daniel Mittleman, *DePaul University* and
Douglas Druckenmiller, *Western Illinois University*

Article

The Internet of Things We Don't Own?

Who will control the 'ordinary pursuits of life' in the digital economy?

JASON SCHULTZ

Learning Outcomes

After reading this article, you will be able to:

- Understand the traditional role of the First Sale Doctrine in establishing and protecting the rights of consumers, and changes to this doctrine now occuring with the advent of digital products and digital components within traditional physical products.

- Articulate pros and cons of the changes to the First Sale Doctrine from both the seller's and buyer's points of view.

- Articulate direct and indirect systemic implications, including unintended implications due to a shift in consumer ownership rights in the digital age.

C ars, refrigerators, televisions, wristwatches. When we buy these everyday objects, we rarely give much thought to whether or not we own them. We pay for them, we possess them, we wear them or put them in our garages or on our shelves, so we have very little reason to question their legal status or their loyalties. Yet in the last decade or so, we have witnessed a subtle and effective shift to cede control over our purchases, especially when they contain software.

It began with digital content. Movies started telling us where and when they could be played. Soon our music informed us how many devices it would live on. Then our library books began to automatically re-encrypt themselves on the date they became overdue. Now our phones will not allow us to delete certain apps; our televisions listen for when we take a bathroom break, and mattresses can keep tabs on where we slept last night.

The integration of such smart product features with ubiquitous network connectivity, microscopic sensors, large-scale analytics, social information sharing platforms, and cloud storage has created a new generation of embedded systems, the Internet of Things (IoT). It is not like the Internet we once knew, and it is not a particularly new idea: embedded computing systems have been around for decades. But the speed of adoption and the diverse capacities of these devices are unprecedented.

The era of IoT has brought more than technological and social shifts. It has also created unusual legal uncertainties. Historically, purchasing consumer goods, even electronic ones, was largely governed by two areas of law: property and contract. The good was a piece of property. The purchase agreement was a contract. Apart from the occasional equipment rental or lease, if money changed hands, the good went home with its new owner. Quid pro quo.

Even goods subject to other laws, such a copyright or patent, generally fell within this framework. As patent or copyright owners sold off individual books, movies, or machines, the law would "exhaust" any remaining intellectual property rights in that particular copy, prohibiting the IP owner, in the words of the U.S. Supreme Court, from interfering with the rights of purchasers to use it "in the ordinary pursuits of life." That meant the purchaser could use the item as she saw fit and then dispose of it, including reselling it, under whatever conditions she chose. These exhaustion rules originated from the long-standing common law regime of personal property, which generally forbids subjecting objects to ongoing restrictions, especially restrictions on resale.

But that approach is under threat. Digital goods have pushed us away from traditional legal models, and, drawing from the world of software, now come with ubiquitous "Terms of Service" that few if any of us read. Within the dense legalistic language of these documents, IoT manufacturers and distributors are quietly attempting to shift the rules of ownership. For example, many now claim we do not own our phones, our cars, or even our televisions: we are merely "licensing" them. Others assert that when our devices break, it is illegal for anyone other than the manufacturer to diagnose the problem, let alone fix it. And others go even further, claiming any data captured by the device belongs to them and not the users who bought the device and created that data. And while users and consumer advocates have generally pushed back on these assertions, device manufacturers continue to push this view of the world upon us.

The exact origin of this shift is difficult to pinpoint, but one significant moment in its early history was the introduction of the iPhone on January 9, 2007. Steve Jobs told the assembled crowd, "Today, Apple is going to reinvent the phone." Like nearly every Apple product, the iPhone user experience was carefully choreographed and tightly controlled. What Jobs did not tell the crowd was that Apple's legal strategy to maintain ownership and control of the devices in our pockets and purses was equally choreographed and controlled.

Eleven days after the iPhone debuted, a group of skillful Apple enthusiasts decided to test its technological and legal limits by "jailbreaking" the phone. This led to a cycle where Apple would upgrade its systems to break the jailbreak and the jail breakers would upgrade their breaks to free their phones from the upgrade. This battle over who "owns" the device continues to this day, with Apple insisting that "iPhone users are licensees, not owners, of the copies of iPhone operating software."

As contested ownership over smartphones has become more of a mainstream debate, the battle over IoT ownership has moved into more traditional pursuits of ordinary life.

For example, just last year, farmers found out that many of them may no longer own the equipment they purchased, including even vehicles such as tractors and combine harvesters. Even the iconic John Deere tractor now contains no less than eight control units—hardware and software components that regulate various functions, ranging from running the engine to adjusting the armrest to operating the hitch. When tractors were purely mechanical, farmers could easily maintain, repair, and modify their own equipment as needed. But now, software stands in their way. Tired of losing revenue to industrious farmers who repaired their own tractors or bargain hunters who took their equipment to an independent repair shop, John Deere decided to interpose a software layer between farmers and their tractors, claiming it retained ownership and that farmers merely had "an implied license for the life of the vehicle to operate the vehicle."

John Deere is not alone. Other vehicle manufacturers including Ferrari, Ford, General Motors, and Mercedes-Benz are finding new ways to use technology and law to weaken the property interests of drivers. These efforts take a number of forms—DRM that prevents repair and customization, software that monitors and controls your driving, even restrictions on vehicle resale. The car, once a symbol of freedom and independence, is increasingly a tool for control. Modern cars, much like John Deere's tractors, rely on dozens of electronic control units. Access to the software code on those control units is necessary for many common repairs. The code is also crucial if a driver wants to change the default tuning of her vehicle to get more horsepower or better fuel efficiency from the engine, the ambition of a growing group of car purchasers concerned about the environment calling themselves "eco-modders" and "hyper-milers." Yet under the ownership rules of the auto manufacturers, these hobbyists run the risk of becoming copyright infringers.

Such shifts in the battle over IoT ownership are also reaching into the security and safety research communities. As our vehicles incorporate greater computational systems with increased complexity, independent testing of their safety and security will increasingly require access to the copyrighted code inside them. Under the traditional law of personal property ownership, all researchers had to do was purchase a vehicle and then test it; manufacturers had no power to object other than to void the warranty. Despite Ford recalling half a million vehicles due to software glitches, Chrysler recalling 1.4 million vehicles because their infotainment systems were vulnerable to hackers, and notorious scandals such as the Volkswagen's "Defeat Device" that allowed it to cheat on emissions tests for diesel vehicles, we see more and more automakers claiming the code inside our cars is proprietary and access to it without their authorization is illegal. Consumer advocates have pushed back against these efforts, passing a Right to Repair law in Massachusetts and pressuring manufacturers to negotiate a Memorandum of Understanding with aftermarket repair shops and part suppliers that allows those businesses access to diagnostic information for repair and replacement purposes. But this does not cover automobile owners.

Nor are our children immune from this shift. Most children have imaginary friends and/or play with dolls. And while we are often surprised at the intensity of these relationships, we have historically understood they were private and ephemeral. Not anymore. Mattel's new WiFi-enabled Hello Barbie doll comes fully equipped with a built-in microphone and a cloud-based machine learning system to "personalize" your child's experience. However, what Barbie won't tell you or your child is that every single word or sound made in her presence will be recorded and transmitted back to Barbie's ML master archive for research purposes. In order to discover that, you would have to read her online Privacy Policy and Terms of Use. With the introduction of this capacity in our children's toys and other home devices such as the Nest thermostat and the Samsung "listening" Smart-TV, the sense of privacy and autonomy we used to enjoy in our homes and with the objects we owned has become yet another contested space in the IoT era.

So what does the law have to say about the question of IoT ownership? To date, neither the courts nor Congress have resolved the question. In general, the courts are split on the exact rules for who "owns" embedded copyrighted media, including software. Some have taken a somewhat technocratic approach, simply deferring to whatever words the maker puts in her license or TOS, regardless of whether or not those words accurately reflect the realities of the transaction. Other judges, however, have been more cautious, recognizing that consumer expectations play an important role in transactions, especially those involving physical objects. The Supreme Court has come close to weighing in on the issue in some of its recent patent and copyright cases, but has not given us a definitive rule.

Even the Copyright Office has avoided opining, for example, choosing to grant smartphone jail breakers an exemption from anti-circumvention liability under copyright law's fair use doctrine instead of declaring them owners with the right to modify embedded software. Recently, Congress has taken more action with Rep. Blake Farenthold introducing the You Own Devices Act (YODA), both houses beginning to examine the possibility of updating the copyright exhaustion rules for the digital age, and Senators Grassley and Leahy specifically asking the Copyright Office to analyze "how copyright shapes our interactions with software in things we own." The Commerce Department also recently issued a White Paper expressing concerns for consumers and the market if IoT manufacturers begin placing restrictions on the freedom to resell devices. But while many of these voices are asking good questions, none have provided the answers we need.

To find the answers, we will need to have a more open and honest conversation about ownership—in the courts, in Congress, and in the technical communities that are designing the IoT ecosystem. Hiding these conflicts and questions in shadowy TOS and embedded firmware code will only further confuse consumers and courts and ultimately complicate instead of clarify the rules we want when it comes to our ability to enjoy the ordinary use of these objects, including our ability to use them privately, to customize them to our needs, and even to part with them as we please.

Critical Thinking

1. How are the rules of ownership shifting due to the fact digital information is included in traditional products from books, to music, to smartphones, to cars and televisions? How does this rules of ownership shift impact our ability to modify, repair, and resell products we purchase?

2. What are the pros and cons of the changes to the First Sale Doctrine from both the seller's and buyer's points of view?

3. What, if any, are the unintended consequences of the changes to the First Sale Doctrine that is now occuring? Who are the winners and losers of these consequences?

Internet References

John Deere Clarifies: It's Trying to Abuse Copyright Law to Stop You from Owning Your Own Tractor . . . Because It Cares About You
https://goo.gl/LSfTx9

LG Will Take the 'Smart' Out of Your Smart TV If You Don't Agree to Share Your Viewing and Search Data with Third Parties
https://goo.gl/k4gBp3

Supreme Court Justices Worry About 'Parade of Horribles' If They Agree You Don't Own What You Bought
https://goo.gl/Oi4rmt

Jason Schultz is Professor of Clinical Law at New York University's School of Law.

Article

Prepared by: Daniel Mittleman, *DePaul University* and
Douglas Druckenmiller, *Western Illinois University*

To Automate Everything, Solve These Three Challenges

ALISON BRUZEK

Learning Outcomes

After reading this article, you will be able to:

- Understand the current barriers and problems that must be solved before automated home technologies are widely used in the vast majority of homes.

- Understand the trade-offs among the convenience, complexity, customization, control, and privacy in the implementation of automated home technologoies.

- Understand the security issues that surface when automated home technologies are placed on the Internet.

"It was a pain," my dad says of the programmable thermostat we had in my childhood home. It was a plastic rectangle the size of a small envelope that jutted out from the wall. He would flip down the protective cover and tap the buttons to make the numbers on the digital display slowly tick up and down.

"I could never remember how to do it. I would have to find the manual and try to read and do it at the same time," he recalls. "When the power went out, we would have to start over." His countless minutes of frustrated button-pushing made sure that the house was cool during muggy summers or toasty when we woke up on cold winter mornings—a common occurrence in Minnesota. Yet, despite his best efforts, there were times when the temperature still wasn't quite right. The air conditioner would keep blowing, for example, when we left the house on weekends. And he'd have to manually override the settings to keep out the chill of a blustery snow day.

It's hard to imagine that same thermostat being cutting edge, but that's exactly what it was more than 20 years ago. It was programmable, but in no way was it intelligent. The only intelligence it contained was that which the user transferred to it. Today, most people's thermostats aren't much different, but that's starting to change.

Thermostats are relatively banal devices, but as the startup Nest has shown, they are ripe for an overhaul. Nest's thermostats can sense when people are home, monitor weather reports, and respond to commands from a smartphone, adjusting the temperature as needed. "In some ways, it is a first step in the right direction," says Lorna Goulden, a technology consultant, regarding Nest and the incoming tide of smart devices. Indeed, the thermostat is just one of a slew of new devices that blur the boundary between virtual and physical worlds. They promise to make our built environments more intelligent, responsive, and efficient.

Collectively, they are called the internet of things or the internet of everything. The concept was first envisioned back in the late 1990s during the dot-com bubble. Then, people anticipated a near-future where computers and the internet were everywhere. Now, 14 years later, connected devices are just beginning to slip into homes, from smart thermostats to apps that unlock your door without a key. Smart objects are slowly transitioning from pioneering to practical.

Yet just as the internet of things is poised to remake our homes and offices, it's facing perhaps its most critical test: adoption by the average consumer. The intelligent future promised by entrepreneurs won't catch on if those devices can't connect to each other automatically, lack intuitive programmability, or aren't appealing designed. If they fail at any one of these, automating our homes may be more trouble than its worth.

But if engineers and designers can nail each of those requirements, then much like electricity did a century ago, the internet will course through our homes so seamlessly we may pay little attention to it as we go about our daily lives.

Connecting Everything

There's a good chance that you already have an internet-connected device in your home. It may be a DVR or a set of wireless speakers. These are early components of the internet of things, but they're missing something important—the ability to interact with the other objects in your home. "They've got a little bit of a learning curve," says Craig Miller, vice president of worldwide marketing at Sequans Communications, which creates computer chips for smart devices.

The most intelligent smart devices may need not just one connection, but two: one to the internet and another to fellow smart objects. We know how to handle the first one—just add a chip for Wi-Fi or cellular service such as LTE and you're online. Coordinating with other smart objects can pose a problem, though. Currently, device-to-device communication is experiencing some growing pains, much like wireless networking for computers did in the 1990s. It took a few years for competitors to settle on a standard, Wi-Fi, and a few more before it became widely adopted.

"It's not a lack of standards, it's the fire hose of standards that's the problem," says Rob Faludi, an adjunct professor in the Interactive Telecommunications program at New York University and chief innovator at Digi International, a networking company. "But that's always a problem with devices," he adds, referring to the historical differences between computer platforms such as Windows and Mac. In that case, users felt computers were valuable enough to put up with the problem of incompatible devices. Eventually, a consensus developed around key standards, and the market coalesced around them.

For now, the torrent of different networking standards poses a problem for average users, who don't want to—and shouldn't have to—think about how their refrigerator might talk with their dishwasher. Most smart devices currently require users to delve into application programming interfaces, known as APIs, for which you need a good deal of programming knowledge to use properly. Companies such as Microsoft are hoping to simplify the operation of a smart home, building dashboards that allow users to control disparate smart objects from their PCs or an all-controlling smartphone. But even these tools require some effort and knowledge to implement. Simplifying this process won't be easy—the more devices in a network, the harder it is to coordinate.

Engineers have a long road ahead of them, but if they can make communication seamless, there's a lot of potential in that connectivity. Faludi offers the example of a home air conditioner and a security system: Say it's been a hot three days and the air conditioner hasn't turned on. There's a good chance the occupant isn't home, and, if the front door is unlocked, it might ̇ time to close that deadbolt.

Programming It All

Connecting devices is only part of the challenge. To really unlock the power of the internet of things, smart devices' functions must be accessible to average users without making them cede too much power. If people don't feel in control, they'll be hesitant to adopt the technology. "It can be very discomforting to come into a house and all [these] things start happening," explains Jason Johnson, co-founder of the Internet of Things Consortium. In reality, intelligent homes will be only partly automated, giving users final say over what happens, just like our current relationship with computers.

Even one of the closest examples of full automation today, Alex Hawkinson's SmartThings, prompts users for guidance at the outset and later allows its decisions to be overridden through a smartphone app. For example, objects connected to the bathroom fan and the shower faucet may prompt the user whether they want the vent to turn on or the heater to fire up. Another may connect to the blinds and default to raise in the morning and lower in the evening, but will still allow people to raise and lower them manually. That way, there aren't any surprises.

As more smart devices are added to a home, the number of possibilities—but also the complexity—could grow exponentially. Finding the balance will be tricky. "If the usability is lacking at any step of the way, and frequent updates present more frustration than excitement and delight," explains Goulden, the consultant, "then interest will quickly fade." What people really want, Goulden says, is "the Apple experience"—pull it out of the box and it's ready to start using.

Designing for Everyone

There's one final, and often overlooked, challenge—design. It's easy to see how bad design can frustrate a user—take the baffling array of buttons on the thermostat at my parents' home. The buttons' position, hidden behind a panel, made the whole package nicer to look at but not any easier to use.

Contrast that with Nest, which has no buttons. Rather, its physical interface consists of one rotary dial. Not only does it pay homage to old thermostats—making the device seem less threatening—it's also intuitive: turn right to raise the temperature, left to lower it. "It was born out of frustration, which I think many people can relate to when they've tried to program their programmable thermostat," says Kate Brinks, director of communications for Nest.

The best, easiest-to-use smart objects will likely look no different than devices we use today, Faludi points out. "A big chunk of this will just be baked into things that we buy," he says. "You won't buy an 'internet of things.'"

There will be entirely new products, but that shouldn't untether design from reality, Johnson says. "Technology products shouldn't look like technology products." Developers should shoot for "something that either spouse could bring home and put on the kitchen counter," he says. "And it gets past that 'Ew, what is that thing.'"

And rather than just being "smart" for technology's sake, the devices should also address people's actual needs, he says. "We need to develop products that are very practical, that are solving very real problems," he says. "Not just, 'Gee whiz, wouldn't it be cool if I could turn on the lights from my phone?'"

Goulden adds that, in her consulting, she advises clients that smart objects should act as an extension of the user. "How do you take an individual's identity and how do you relate that to the objects that are around them?" The more relatable the object, the simpler it is to understand.

Too Smart a Future?

As the internet of things becomes a larger—and less visible—part of our lives, it could change the entire meaning of privacy. The media went wild in July when two security researchers turned a Jeep Cherokee into a child's toy, controlling it remotely through the car's digital diagnostic port. But future security hacks need not be so flashy to be concerning. The internet of things has the potential make not just individuals but also hospitals, governments, and cities vulnerable. If everything—from medical devices such as pacemakers or pill dispensers to infrastructure such as bridges and railroads—is on the network, then the consequences can be deadly.

The number of vulnerable points—the "surface area" for attacks—with a connected device is often greater than people realize, says Chris Poulin, a research strategist with IBM Security. For example, if you have a Nest, it's not just that someone could get into the physical blob on your wall. There's also, "the mobile app, which connects to Nest's [data servers], and then to the Nest in the house, which connects to the WiFi, which again connects to Nest's data servers...the surface is just really broad."

That's part of what the Federal Trade Commission worried about in their report last January. People need to consider not just unauthorized access to their smart fridge or connected garage door, they stated. Consumers should also be aware that their personal information being collected from their smart objects could potentially be accessed by future banks, employers, or insurers who might make decisions based on that information.

In September, the FBI released a cyber crime public service announcement (http://www.ic3.gov/media/2015/150910.aspx), explaining how the internet of things can be exploited.

Among their recommendations for how to defend against those exploits is a simple suggestion: "Consider whether IoT devices are ideal for their intended purpose." In other words, the first step for a consumer should be, is that smart fridge really necessary? Lee Tien, a specialist in privacy and civil liberties at the Electronic Frontier Foundation, says consumers must watch out for themselves because the companies aren't always able to. Especially when devices are made by small startups, he says, and "not in the first tier of expertise of security." Bruce Schneier, a computer security and privacy expert, says after devices are shipped, companies have no incentive to update old software or computer chips to ensure future loopholes are fixed—they're too busy working on their next thing. He says until the makers of devices go open-source and allow outside engineers to help find and fix security problems, this will always be the case. However, the new problems are slowly growing interesting solutions. Companies such as Honeywell that once were known for protecting your home now protect industrial plants working in oil, gas, chemicals, or minerals and use the internet of things. For consumers, Schneier says large companies that control your entire ecosystem of technology, whether it be Google or anyone else, will be how people keep their hardware and software up-to-date. "Apple does security for all iOS users. This is the future." Yet there is a contingent that doesn't see privacy concerns holding up adoption. Faludi argues that people are "always going to have concerns about security and privacy," adding that, "they're problems for developers to solve, but they're not really any kind of barrier." Researchers such as Faludi are wary that a lack of confidence in the future could stop adoption.

On the Cusp

Despite the hurdles, the potential for the internet of things is enormous. Not only could it simplify many aspects of our daily lives, it could also make our homes more energy efficient, saving us money and reducing our environmental footprint. And few stand to benefit more than people with disabilities. For some, even simple tasks take an inordinate amount of time and effort. Automating those would allow them to direct their energy toward more important things in their lives.

It may take some time for that to happen, though. Smart objects are starting to trickle into the marketplace, but widespread use of the internet of things is still 5 to 10 years off, according to industry analysts at Gartner, a market research firm. That's good news for the engineers, developers, and designers who are trying to work out the many kinks that remain.

Should they succeed in making smart objects intuitive, transparent, and minimally invasive, though it's likely that people like my parents, who are sick of tapping buttons to program everyday life, will adopt them. There are signs they're getting closer; my dad called the other day, clearly smiling through the phone. "Your mom and I are thinking about getting a Nest."

Critical Thinking

1. The article quotes Lorna Goulden saying "In some way, [Nest] is a first step in the right direction." If so, what steps do you foresee following in the near future? What are some problems you would like automated home technology to solve for you?

2. What unforseen big new idea (see Postman model in Unit 1 Introduction) might be enabled by automated home technologies?

3. Would you trust living in an automated home? If no or you aren't sure, what safety, privacy, or security concerns do you have? What would it take for a home technology to gain your trust?

Internet References

Amazon Wants Alexa to Take Control of Your Smart Home
https://goo.gl/VqjpJ2

Welcome To Privacy Hell, Also Known As The Internet Of Things
https://goo.gl/UjhQMH

We Can't Let Our Toasters Become Smarter Than We Are
https://goo.gl/Fzvcn6

ALISON BRUZEK is a science writer based in Cambridge, Mass.

Article

Prepared by: Daniel Mittleman, *DePaul University* and
Douglas Druckenmiller, *Western Illinois University*

The Murky Ethics of Driverless Cars

A new study explores a moral dilemma facing the creators of self-driving vehicles: In an accident, whose lives should they prioritize?

TOM JACOBS

Learning Outcomes

After reading this article, you will be able to:

- Recognize that there are ethical trade-offs we make doing routine activities in our everyday lives, such as driving.

- Recognize that the ethical choices we think we might make in abstract situations may or may not differ from what we would do if actually faced with the choice.

- Articulate the dilemma encountered if one is asked to make a decision that trades off one set of lives for another set of lives.

So you're driving down a dark road late at night when suddenly a child comes darting out onto the pavement. Instinctively, you swerve, putting your own safety in jeopardy to spare her life.

Very noble of you. But would you want your driverless vehicle to do the same?

That question, which can be found idling at the intersection of technology and ethics, is posed in the latest issue of *Science*. A variation on the famous trolley dilemma, it won't be theoretical for long: Self-driving vehicles are coming soon, and they will need to be programmed how to respond to emergencies.

A research team led by Iyad Rahwan of the Massachusetts Institute of Technology argues that this poses a huge challenge to their creators. In a series of studies, it finds people generally agree with the "utilitarian" argument—the notion that cars should be programmed to spare as many lives as possible.

However, when asked what they would personally purchase, they tended to prefer a vehicle that prioritized the safety of its riders. And a theoretical government regulation that would mandate a spare-the-greatest-number approach significantly dampens their enthusiasm for buying a driverless car.

"Figuring out how to build ethical autonomous machines is one of the thorniest challenges in artificial intelligence today," the researchers write. "For the time being, there appears to be no way to design algorithms that would reconcile moral values and personal self-interest."

Rahwan and colleagues Jean-Francois Bonnefon and Azim Shariff describe six studies, all conducted online via Amazon's Mechanical Turk. In the first, the 182 participants "strongly agreed that it would be more moral for autonomous vehicles to sacrifice their own passengers when this sacrifice would save a greater number of lives overall."

Another study found this still held true even when the passengers were described as "you and a family member," as long as it meant saving the lives of multiple pedestrians. The 451 participants, however, "indicated a significantly lower likelihood of buying the autonomous vehicle when they imagined the situation in which they and their family member would be sacrificed for the greater good."

In still another study, the 393 participants "were reluctant to accept government regulation" that would mandate programming the cars to ensure the fewest lives were lost. "Participants were much less likely to consider purchasing an autonomous vehicle with such regulation than without."

That suggests such regulations "could substantially delay the adoption" of driverless cars, the researchers write. That would be unfortunate, they note, since these cars are much safer than those driven by humans, and more lives will be saved as more of them are on the road.

Altogether, the results suggest people approve of self-driving cars "that sacrifice their passengers for the greater good, and would like others to buy them—but they would themselves prefer to ride in autonomous vehicles that protect their passengers at all costs."

A dilemma indeed. If you'd like to explore the specific ethical questions in more detail—which may or may not clarify your thinking—you may do so at http://moralmachine.mit/edu.

Or you can just give it some serious thought while you sit in traffic.

Critical Thinking

1. Should we be able to program ethical decision-making parameters into automated technologies? Why or why not?

2. Articulate how comfortable you are in permitting an automated technology to make a life or death ethical decision for you. Would you be more comfortable if you were able to give it instructional parameters ahead of time? If you are not comfortable, what is it about the situation that makes you uncomfortable?

3. Is there a way to avoid encountering the ethical dilemmas articulated in this article? [The third Internet Resource may assist you in answering this question.]

Internet References

Engineers Say If Automated Cars Experience 'The Trolley Problem,' They've Already Screwed Up
https://goo.gl/R13m5P

The Ethics of Autonomous Cars
https://goo.gl/YJuZxJ

When Should Your Driverless Car From Google Be Allowed To Kill You?
https://goo.gl/8bO3MA

Tom Jacobs is a staff writer with Pacific Standard magazine.

Prepared by: Daniel Mittleman, *DePaul University* and
Douglas Druckenmiller, *Western Illinois University*

Article

Your Smart Home Is Trying to Reprogram You

Murray Goulden

Learning Outcomes

After reading this article, you will be able to:

- Explain what the Internet of Things is and why its entry into people's homes worry some observers.

- Understand the trade-offs involved wtih home automation and personal agents.

- Articulate several ways home automation and personal agents breach the social order of the home.

A father finds out his daughter is pregnant after algorithms identify tell-tale patterns in the family's store card data. Police charge suspects in two separate murder cases based on evidence taken from a Fitbit tracker and a smart water meter. A man sues Uber for revealing his affair to his wife.

Stories such as these have been appearing in ever greater numbers recently, as the technologies involved become ever more integrated into our lives. They form part of the Internet of Things (IoT), the embedding of sensors and internet connections into the fabric of the world around us. Over the last year, these technologies, led by Amazon's Alexa and Google's Home, have begun to make their presence felt in our domestic lives, in the form of smart home devices that allow us to control everything in the house just by speaking.

We might look at stories like those above as isolated technical errors, or fortuitous occurrences serving up justice. But behind them, something much bigger is going on: the development of an entire class of technologies seeking to remake the fundamentals of our everyday lives.

Breaking the Social Order

These technologies want to be ubiquitous, seamlessly spanning the physical and virtual worlds, and awarding us frictionless control over all of it. The smart home promises a future in which largely hidden tech provides us with services before we've even realised we want them, using sensors to understand the world around us and navigate it on our behalf. It's a promise of near limitless reach, and effortless convenience.

It's also completely incompatible with social realities. The problem is, our lives are full of limits, and nowhere is this better demonstrated than in the family home, which many of these technologies target. From the inside, these places often feel all too chaotic but they're actually highly ordered. This is a world full of boundaries and hierarchies: who gets allowed into which rooms, who gets the TV remote, who secrets are shared with, who they are hidden from.

Much of this is mundane, but if you want to see how important these kinds of systems of order are to us, consider the "breaching experiments" of sociologist Harold Garfinkel in the 1960s. Garfinkel set out to deliberately break the rules behind social order in order to reveal them. Conducting the most humdrum interaction in the wrong way was shown to elicit reactions in others that ranged from distress to outright violence. You can try this yourself. When sat round the dinner table try acting entirely normal save for humming loudly every time someone starts speaking, and see how long it is before someone loses their temper.

The technologies of the smart home challenge our orderings in countless small ways. A primary limitation is their inability to recognise boundaries we take for granted. I had my own such experience a week ago while sitting in my front room. With the accidental slip of a finger I streamed a (really rather sweary)

YouTube video from my phone onto my neighbour's TV, much to the surprise of their four-year-old daughter in the middle of watching Paw Patrol.

A finger press was literally all it took, of a button that can't be disabled. That, and the fact that I have their Wi-Fi password on my phone as I babysit for them from time to time. To current smart home technology, those who share Wi-Fi networks share everything.

Of course, we do still have passwords to at least offer some crude boundaries. And yet smart home technologies excel at creating data that doesn't fit into the neat, personalised boxes offered by consumer technologies. This interpersonal data concerns groups, not individuals, and smart technologies are currently very stupid when it comes to managing it. Sometimes this manifests itself in humorous ways, like parents finding "big farts" added to their Alexa-generated shopping list. Other times it's far more consequential, as in the pregnant daughter story above.

In our own research into this phenomena, my colleagues and I have discovered an additional problem. Often, this tech makes mistakes, and if it does so with the wrong piece of data in the wrong context, the results could be disastrous. In one study we carried out, a wife ended up being informed by a digital assistant that her husband had spent his entire work day at a hotel in town. All that had really happened was an algorithm had misinterpreted a dropped GPS signal, but in a relationship with low trust, a suggestion of this kind could be grounds for divorce.

Rejecting the Recode

These technologies are, largely unwittingly, attempting to recode some of the most basic patterns of our everyday lives, namely how we live alongside those we are most intimate with. As such, their placement in our homes as consumer products constitutes a vast social experiment. If the experience of using them is too challenging to our existing orderings, the likelihood is we will simply come to reject them.

This is what happened with Google Glass, the smart glasses with a camera and heads-up-display built into them. It was just too open to transgressions of our notions of proper behaviour. This discomfort even spawned the pejorative "Glasshole" to describe its users.

Undoubtedly, the tech giants selling these products will continue to tweak them in the hope of avoiding similar outcomes. Yet a fundamental challenge remains: how can technologies that sell themselves on convenience be taught the complexities and nuances of our private worlds? At least without needing us to constantly hand-hold them, entirely negating their aim of making our lives easier.

Their current approach—to ride roughshod over the social terrain of the home—is not a sustainable approach. Unless and until the day we have AI systems capable of comprehending human social worlds, it may be that the smart home promised to us ends up being a lot more limited than its backers imagine. Right now, if you're taking part in this experiment, the advice must be to proceed with caution, because when it comes to social relationships, the smart home remains pretty dumb. And be very careful not to stream things to your neighbour's TV.

Critical Thinking

1. Murray Goulden calls the Internet of Things "an entire class of technologies seeking to remake the fundamentals of our everyday lives." Explain what he means. Do you agree with him? Why?

2. Personal agent technologies such as Alexa and Google Home listen to everything that is said waiting for their trigger word. What trade-offs does this convenience provide the user?

3. Murray Goulden suggests that personal agent technologies breach the social order of the home. What are some examples of how Alexa or Google Home does this? How might these changes to the social order impact other aspects of life at home (for better or worse)?

Internet References

Amazon Echo: The invisible platform
   https://www.recode.net/2016/3/15/11586992/amazon-echo-the-invisible-platform

Parents are worried the Amazon Echo is conditioning their kids to be rude
   https://qz.com/701521/parents-are-worried-the-amazon-echo-is-conditioning-their-kids-to-be-rude/

The Privacy Problem with Digital Assistants
   https://www.theatlantic.com/technology/archive/2016/05/the-privacy-problem-with-digital-assistants/483950/

MURRAY GOULDEN is a Senior Research Fellow at the School of Sociology, University of Nottingham. His work focuses on the role of digital technologies within social practices: on the changing patterns of life that result, and the implications for governance and design, specifically in the areas of energy, mobility, and digital data.

Unit 8

UNIT

Prepared by: Daniel Mittleman, *DePaul University* and
Douglas Druckenmiller, *Western Illinois University*

Social Networking and Identity

Social networking is not new. In fact, it predates the telephone! Of course, the earliest social networkers had to do it face to face, and coffee houses were the Facebook of the renaissance. Online social networking dates back to the advent of the telegraph. The telegraph operator of the 1840s was an active social networker, trading stories and gossip up and down the line during idle periods between serious messages.

Internet social media is not new. The earliest Internet-based social network message posting system, Usenet, was established in 1980, more than a decade before the WWW was introduced. Its function was limited to discussion board (called newsgroups) posts and responses, with no ability to establish a profile to supplement one's identity. There was established over time a hierarchy of many discussion boards, and an "alternate" hierarchy (newsgroups that began with the letters "alt.") where one could create their own boards on many nonstandard and counter-culture topics. Other Bulletin Board systems emerged on proprietary networks, such as The WELL in 1985, but Usenet was the only one readily available across the Internet for a long time.

Today, there are over two billion people active on Facebook. There are over 200 million active users in the United States alone, making Facebook the largest social media service at both levels. But it might surprise you to find out that Facebook is no longer the largest social media service in the United States for people under the age of 25. Since 2016, Facebook has actually been losing users under the age of 25 and, since 2017, has trailed Snapchat in total U.S. users under the age of 25. Facebook continues to grow in the overall—by 2.4 percent in 2017—but that growth is due to increased adoption by older users.

Why are younger users opting for services other than Facebook? There are likely several reasons. One, if you are looking for authentic, open communication with your peers, do you want to be friended so that your parents and grandparents are seeing your posts? As the median age of Facebook users has skewed older each year, quite obviously this means multigenerational families are all populating the same space.

Two, does Facebook have the features younger users want? Instagram (owned now by Facebook) and Snapchat both support photographic features and extension apps geared to a youth market. Snapchat contributions at their core are ephemeral (nonpermanent), unlike Facebook posts that exist forever—and when shared can carom out of control of the original poster.

Three, Facebook today is populated by content well beyond shared posts and photos of friends. Facebook has matured into a leading advertising channel populated by a significant component of paid and promoted content. Beyond that, it is populated by news (and fake news) as well as posts the Facebook algorithm suggests a user view that might be from a friend of a friend who has demonstrated a pattern suggesting compatible interests or political views. The content from actual preexisting friends has to compete with all of this. For teens not (yet?) focused on politics or other broader matters, this other content may be viewed as noise.

There seems to be a repeatable life-cycle pattern for successful social media services. Each year dozens to hundreds of new social media services launch. A few gain a foothold based on their ability to address something that has, to a particular market segment, frustrated users with the existing service choices. Facebook attracted users from MySpace in 2005 and 2006 because it—at that time—required a university e-mail address to register. So, its earliest users were college students who could talk to one another without anyone else around. Further, Facebook had a clean, easy to learn interface, while MySpace permitted so much customization, there was little standard look and feel from page to page. Instagram gained users because it better supported photos and videos at the time of its launch. Snapchat provided for ephemeral content. Each new platform mentioned here first attracted a youth market (college age or younger), but as its user base grew, so too did the advertising content to pay for the platform as well as an older demographic. The youth market, in each case, searched for the next best thing and fled the established platform as a new alternative emerged.

Fake news is a buzzword in popular use today. But in reality, fake news is simply propaganda—a concept that has been with us for centuries. It is the intentional mis-telling of information, often adding lies on top of a kernel of truth, in order to persuade an audience toward a desired point of view. One, perhaps new, feature of the fake news variant of propaganda is the meta-concept that there can be multiple conflicting versions of truth, which in itself is fake news.

Propaganda has been around as long as there has been argumentation (i.e., thousands of years). What is new these past few years is that social media has afforded most everyone the means to become a content publisher, and thereby has supported the viral propagation of fake news to millions of people over a short period of time. It appears, as of this writing, that several forces around the world have recognized the power of social media platforms to propagate fake news and have been undertaking intentional propaganda campaigns making use of these affordances. The scope and the impact of these efforts is not yet clear.

What is clear is that social media platforms have changed how we communicate with each other and how we discuss affairs of the day.

Article

Prepared by: Daniel Mittleman, *DePaul University* and
Douglas Druckenmiller, *Western Illinois University*

Caution: Identity under Construction

Pam Jarvis

Learning Outcomes

After reading this article, you will be able to:

- Describe the relationship between teenage social identity formation and use of social media.

- Identify and describe the four aspects of networked information surfaced by Danah Boyd. Can discuss benefits and drawbacks of each aspect when social network is used by teenager or young adult.

- Understand the concept of surveillance and how it applies to online social networking.

O ver the past decade technological advance has deeply impacted upon modes of human communication. In their September 2016 article for *The Psychologist*, Ian Tucker and colleagues explored the creation of what they term a "surveillance society," largely located within the information that people share through social networking. While this is clearly of concern to networked populations in general, psychological and neurological evidence suggests young people's personalities are more fledgling and fragile than those of mature adults. Might such interaction therefore be more damaging to children and young people than to mature adults?

In terms of its own lifespan development, the mass social networking phenomenon has not yet reached adolescence itself. The first iPhone was released in 2006, the same year as Facebook became generally available to anyone over 13. Due to such recency, there are as yet no definitive empirical findings to indicate whether social networking is harmful, only emerging findings (including from psychologists such as Mark Griffiths) that some users have reported symptoms of addiction.

In a 2014 book, *It's Complicated: The Social Lives of Networked Teens*, Danah Boyd identifies four aspects of networked information that may be viewed as either benefits or drawbacks, depending upon the purposes of the user:

- Persistence—durability of content
- Visibility—breadth of potential audience
- Spreadability—the ease with which content is shared
- Searchability—the ability to locate content through sophisticated search engines

All these features have the potential to create problems for the ongoing identity-formation processes of young people within the "glass box" of a socially networked environment. US psychologist Sherry Turkle, in her 2011 book *Alone Together*, reflected upon the classic psychoanalytic identity theory of Erik Erikson, who emphatically proposed that adolescence should be a period in which young people should be free to experiment with their identities without enduring consequence. She raised grave concerns about the lack of such provision for the current generation of young people in post-industrial societies.

Writing for the website Philosophy for Change in 2012, Tim Rayner went beyond the Foucaultian concept of the prisoner surveillance "Panopticon" in describing the surveillance experienced by young people: ". . . there are no guards and no prisoners in Facebook's virtual Panopticon. We are both guards and prisoners, watching and implicitly judging one another." Sherry Turkle writes that many of her research participants were painfully aware of such visibility, but were willing to sacrifice privacy for the sake of connectivity. In a pilot study carried out with a small sample of participants aged between 12 and 18, I have found a similar attitude, embodied in the participant comment that teenagers are compelled to regularly log on to social networks due to "a fear of missing out on things if they don't have it."

Why would this be? Danah Boyd proposes that contemporary Western teenagers experience highly organised and restricted lives due to heightened parental concern relating to environmental danger, and the focus upon academic and sporting achievement in highly competitive neo-liberal cultures; consequently young people deeply invest in social media as their major venue for simply "hanging out." I discussed the adult "colonisation" of children's lives in my co-authored 2014 article in the *International Journal of Play*; however, the suitability of the online environment as a forum for young people to engage in the intensive identity construction that takes place during adolescence has not yet been effectively explored by social scientists.

Footprints

Recent advances in biopsychology have offered some support to earlier psychoanalytic concepts of a fragile under construction' adolescent identity. It has been shown that in the neuronal sense, human beings are not fully adult until their mid-20s, with a great deal of biopsychological development occurring during the early adolescent period. The ways in which neuronal connections are made during this process are heavily dependent upon experiences encountered, as outlined in the 2014 *Annual Review of Psychology* article by Sarah-Jayne Blakemore and Kathryn Mills.

This builds a socially vulnerable model of the human adolescent. Blakemore and Mills cite additional empirical evidence that when adolescents find themselves in socially complex situations they are likely to make more risky decisions than both adults and younger children. The suggestion is that the adolescent period of development is concerned with building self-awareness in order to better integrate individuals' own self-judgements with peer evaluation. In order to do this, young people need to experiment with identity both alone and in interaction with each other. This process leads them to paradoxically become, on the one hand, hypersensitive to the opinions of others and, on the other, to take social risks that they would never consider during earlier and later stages of their lives. The learning that takes place through this process facilitates individuals' emergence into adulthood, as Blakemore and Mills say, "equipped to navigate the social complexities of their community."

Where such processes are carried out in the glass box offered by social networking sites, the unrelenting digital footprint created cements every misjudgement and social error, creating a range of social hazards for young people as they move through this stage of development. In his 2014 book *The End of Absence: Reclaiming What We've Lost in a World of Constant Connection*, Michael Harris cites the case of Amanda Todd, a 15-year-old Canadian who was blackmailed into uploading nude pictures of herself, and who subsequently killed herself in response to the deluge of peer censure and teasing that followed. Even moving schools did not curtail this, as her new peer group swiftly accessed online records created by her previous activities.

The persistence, visibility, and spreadability of Todd's networked activity meant that she would always be vulnerable

with respect to this digital footprint, and she likely viewed this from her highly socially sensitised adolescent perspective. While the young women in my pilot study did not cite such dramatic concerns, one commented that in using Facebook from the age of 15, she had presumed that "the default setting would be 'only your friends can see this stuff' but it's not, it's like friends of friends and that sort of thing." Three years later, at the age of 18, she had finally changed her Facebook settings to rectify the situation.

The "Tethered" Identity

The persistence of information committed to social networks also raises another issue for adolescents, which Turkle terms the "tethered" identity. Where individuals from previous generations typically formed a number of ephemeral friendships during adolescence which waxed and waned as an inevitable consequence of growing up and moving on, social networking provides an environment in which if nothing is actively done to cut such ties (the Facebook action referred to as "unfriending," which can have socially awkward implications), young people remain forever tethered through social networks to people who are no longer part of their everyday lives, and with whom they may have little in common. Turkle's participants described being unable to leave the person that they were in adolescence behind, with an ongoing sense of unease about embarrassing information that their teenage self may have left lurking in cyberspace. One commented: "I feel that my childhood has been stolen by the internet."

Additionally, as Turkle points out, equipped with a networked mobile device, support and direction from parents and friends to whom young people are digitally tethered is constantly available; therefore teenagers no longer routinely find themselves in situations in which they have only the self to depend upon; for example getting lost on unfamiliar streets or dealing with a difficult interaction with a stranger.

The deluge of information that arrives through social networking on mobile devices is a formidable challenge for a species which evolved to pay concentrated attention (see Daniel Levitin's 2005 blog on "how to better structure our time in the age of social media and constant distraction"). Again, this is of particular concern for those who are in the psychologically vulnerable stage of constructing the intricate neuronal architecture required to cope with adult social interaction, in which a relatively stable self-concept and considered prediction of potential responses from others is essential. In order to cope with a heavy volume of socially networked communication, we are led to reduce the depth and complexity of our messages. Michael Harris comments that this feature of social networking creates a paradox of "on tap" streams of connectivity that are highly appealing to deeply entrenched human social instincts, alongside a consequent lack of time for deep connection. This point is clearly not lost on some teenagers. One of the participants in my pilot study commented as she reflected upon her day-to-day social networking activities: "When you say it out loud, when you have to explain it, it sounds like the most narcissistic thing."

What Should We Do?

To thoroughly work through intricate identity-formation processes, teenagers need time and space for long, meaningful conversations with their peers and some amount of in-depth debate with parents and other emotionally bonded adults, interspersed with solitary reflection. It could be argued that instead they are immersed in a world that panders to more primal needs: writing in The Psychologist in September 2015, Ciarán Mc Mahon compared human responses to message notification sounds from networked devices to animal responses within operant conditioning contingencies. In Psychology Today in 2012 Eva Ritvo points out that the most powerful reinforcement for a highly social creature is a signal that others are seeking contact, raising levels of dopamine and oxytocin within the physical brain. As Danah Boyd poignantly comments, "most teens aren't addicted to social media; if anything, they are addicted to one another." Indeed, such effects may be heightened during adolescence, due to potentially enhanced effects of external stimuli during this life stage, and the compelling need for peer feedback.

While it is clearly prudent to warn young people about risky online behaviours, the nature of the adolescent stage of development means that they remain highly vulnerable to being drawn into incautious over-sharing; research from Blakemore and others suggests that during adolescence, the neuronal mechanisms that mediate social caution are muted in order to facilitate experiences that enhance social learning and, consequently, identity-construction processes.

The implication is that, over the past decade, young people have been recruited into a mass social experiment at a highly vulnerable stage of their development, which enticed them to commit a significant amount of highly personal information to a worldwide database, freezing their adolescent social experiments and errors within the most public forum imaginable. As Turkle notes: "While none of these conflicts about self presentation are new to adolescence . . . what is new is living them out in public, sharing every mistake and false step." This may have negative effects upon lifelong mental health, potentially creating an insidious anxiety from which, if no action is taken to permanently delete such data, they will never be free.

It is of course possible that future generations confronted with such a history may indeed be more cautious, possibly due to increased adult surveillance of their online activities. But if they continue to lack free time for "real-life" association, might this mean that they will never be free to construct a deep multifaceted, human identity due to fears of exposure; restricted by circumstance to experiencing the self and others through shallow, sterile online profiles? From this perspective, it could be argued that the worst may be yet to come. Indeed, the recent launch of a Facebook "lifestage app" marketed at young people was criticised by the BBC's technology reporter Zoe Kleinman due to its lax privacy settings.

The question that now arises for psychologists is whether the social networking environment can be empirically demonstrated to be a particularly inappropriate environment for young people and, if so, how they might subsequently be better protected in this respect. The instigation of such research is clearly supported by Article 36 of the United Nations Convention of the Rights of the Child, which states: "Children should be protected from any activity that...could harm their welfare and development." However, researchers would also need to be mindful of children and young people's rights under Article 13 (freedom of expression), Article 15 (free association), and Article 17 (accessing information).

Personally, I am reminded of Peter Kelly's comments back in 2001 that "youth is principally about becoming." The view from this developmentally informed perspective indicates that, in the light of existing and potential technological development, it is time to call for an international discussion that explicitly considers the creation of suitable physical, temporal and online spaces purposely designed to nurture this process.

References

Blakemore, S. & Mills, K. (2014). Is adolescence a sensitive period for sociocultural processing? *Annual Review of Psychology*, 65, 187–207.

Boyd, D. (2014). It's complicated: The social lives of networked teens. New Haven, CT: Yale University Press.

Ellis, D., Harper, D. & Tucker, I. (2016). Experiencing the 'surveillance society'. *The Psychologist*, 29(9), 682–685.

Ernst, M., Daniele, T. & Frantz, K. (2011). New perspectives on adolescent motivated behavior: Attention and conditioning. *Developmental Cognitive Neuroscience*, 1(4), 377–389. doi:10.1016/j.dcn.2011.07.013.

Foucault, M. (1979). Discipline and punish: The birth of the prison. New York: Vintage Books.

Griffiths, M. (2013). Social networking addiction: Emerging themes and issues. *Journal of Addiction Research & Therapy*, 4, 118. Available at: www.omicsonline.org/social-networking-addiction-emerging-themes-and-issues-2155-6105.1000e118.php?aid=22152

Harris, M. (2014). The end of absence: Reclaiming what we've lost in a world of constant connection. New York: Penguin.

Jarvis, P. (2017). Deconstructing the social network: Young people's rights and vulnerabilities within the online Omopticon. In I. Tshabangu (Ed.) Global ideologies surrounding children's rights and social justice. Hershey, PA: IGI Global.

Jarvis, P., Newman, S. & Swiniarski, L. (2014). On 'becoming social': The importance of collaborative free play in childhood. *International Journal of Play*, 3(1), 53–68. doi:10.1080/215949 37.2013.863440.

Kelly, P. (2001). Youth at risk: Processes of individualisation and responsibilisation in the risk society. *Discourse: Studies in the Cultural Politics of Education*, 22(1):23–33.

Kleinman, Z. (2016). Facebook launches lifestyle app for school teens. *BBC News*. Available at: www.bbc.co.uk/news/technology-37154458

Levitin, D. (2005). The organized mind: How to better structure our time in the age of social media and constant distraction [Blog post]. *LSE, British Politics and Policy*. Available at: http://blogs.lse.ac.uk/politicsandpolicy/the-organized-mind-how-to-better-structure-our-time-in-the-age-of-social-media-and-constant-distraction

Mc Mahon, C. (2015). Why do we 'like' social media? *The Psychologist*, 28(9), 724–728.

NSPCC (2016). A child's legal rights. Available online at: www.nspcc.org.uk/preventing-abuse/child-protection-system/legal-definition-child-rights-law/legal-definitions

Rayner, T. (2012). Foucault and social media: Life in a virtual panopticon. *Philosophy for Change*. Available at: https://philosophyforchange.wordpress.com/2012/06/21/foucault-and-social-media-life-in-a-virtual-panopticon/

Ritvo, E. (2012). Facebook and your brain. *Psychology Today*. Available at: www.psychologytoday.com/blog/vitality/201205/facebook-and-your-brain

Shurgin O'Keeffe, G. & Clarke Pearson, K. (2011). Clinical report: The impact of social media on children, adolescents and families. *Paediatrics*, 127, 800–804.

Turkle, S. (2011). Alone together: Why we expect more from technology and less from each other. New York: BasicBooks.

UNICEF (1989). Fact sheet: A summary of the United Nations Convention on the Rights of the Child. Available at: www.unicef.org/crc/files/Rights_overview.pdf

Critical Thinking

1. Is social netowrking interaction more damaging to teenagers than to mature adults? Explain your answer.

2. Define the term panopticon and explain the relevancy of the term to online social network participation.

3. Given what we know about teenage social identity development and what we know about social media, should we encourage or discourage teens from using social media? Or should we guide teens to use social media in a different way than most currently do?

Internet References

17 Apps and Websites Kids Are Heading to After Facebook
https://www.commonsensemedia.org/blog/16-apps-and-websites-kids-are-heading-to-after-facebook

Performing Identities in Social Media: Focusing on Language Learners' Identity Construction Online
https://alsic.revues.org/3005

The Online Self across Platforms and Realms: Multiple Social Media Platforms and Complex Identities Modes amongst Peripheral-urban Youth in Indonesia
http://networkcultures.org/blog/2017/07/04/the-online-self-across-platforms-and-realms-multiple-social-media-platforms-and-complex-identities-modes-amongst-peripheral-urban-youth-in-indonesia/

Dr Pam Jarvis, Reader in Childhood, Youth and Education at Leeds Trinity University, is a Chartered Psychologist and blogger.

Prepared by: Daniel Mittleman, *DePaul University* and
Douglas Druckenmiller, *Western Illinois University*

Article

Rules for Social Media, Created by Kids

Devorah Heitner

Learning Outcomes

After reading this article, you will be able to:

- Discuss the relationship of social identity formation with the choices of what to post to social media.

- Articulate how parents view social media differently than tweens or teens.

- Explain what the significant risks are for tweens and teens who use social media.

The challenge of growing up in the digital age is perfectly epitomized by the bikini rule.

"You can post a bikini or bathing suit picture only if you are with your siblings or your family in the picture," said one middle-school girl who was participating in a focus group on digital media. In other words, don't try too hard to be sexy and you'll be O.K. in the eyes of your peers.

By high school, the rules change. At that stage, a bikini picture often is acceptable, even considered "body positive" in some circles.

As an educational consultant, I lead workshops on digital media at schools around the country, giving me an unusual glimpse into the hidden world of middle and high school students. While parents sometimes impose rules for using social media on their kids, the most important rules are those that children create for themselves.

And these often unspoken rules can be dizzying.

Girls want to be sexy, but not too sexy. Be careful which vacation photos you share so you don't seem to brag. It's O.K. to post photos from a fun event, but not too many.

In one focus group I held recently with seventh-grade girls in an affluent suburb, all of the girls were avid Instagram and Snapchat users. It was clear that they understood the dynamics of presenting a persona through the images they posted. It was also clear that they had a definite set of rules about pictures.

Aware of their privileged socioeconomic status, they talked about how it would not be O.K. to share vacation pictures of a fancy hotel, using the example of a classmate who had violated this rule. Like many unspoken social codes, this one became vivid to these girls upon its violation.

As part of a school project the girl had displayed pictures from her vacation at a foreign resort. Her classmates considered it an immature form of "bragging," and said other kids had gone on even "better trips" or lived in "amazing houses" but "knew better" than to post about it.

The same girls identified another peer as "too sexual," a judgment some parents even encouraged. A few said their moms did not want them to hang out with a particular girl because she "acts too sexy." One of the girls expressed this sentiment in a group text that included the peer in question, leading to hurt feelings and conflicts.

Middle school can be an especially complicated time for girls. They are experimenting with social identity, even as their always-on digital world intensifies the scrutiny. Many want to be seen as pretty (even sexy, in some ways), but also as innocent and as "nice." This is an impossible balancing act. Parents can help by suggesting more empowering alternatives to posting bathing suit pictures.

Another group of seventh graders (of mixed gender and in a different community) told me the rules regarding how many pictures to post from an event. There was a sense of what was acceptable and what was not. Posting one to three images was fine, they said, but all agreed it was "obnoxious" to "blow up people's phones" with a huge stream of images from a party or event.

These kinds of images can lead to feelings of exclusion as well. Imagine watching a party unfold, in real time, on Snapchat or Instagram, when you aren't there. The experience can be absolutely devastating to tween and teenage children. When

I asked these seventh graders about it, they said that it happened all the time, and that it can be hard to deal with.

With their lives constantly on display, it's a challenge for even well-intentioned tweens to avoid making others feel excluded. The "rule" was that it is "better not to lie or make excuses" if you are with one friend and another friend wants to hang out. Better to be honest and say, "I have plans," than to lie and say, "I have too much homework," then take a risk when sharing images of yourself out with friends later.

Parents often feel as if their children's smartphones are portals to another world—one that they know little to nothing about. A study released last month found that fewer than half of the parents surveyed regularly discussed social media content with their tween and teenage children.

But parents need to know that their child's peers have created their own set of rules for social media, and that they should ask their kids about them. What are you "allowed" to post, and what seems to be off-limits? Are the rules the same for boys and girls? Why or why not? Can you show me an example of a "good" post, or a "bad" one? Does social media ever stress you out (and can you give yourself a break)? How can kids in your group make group texts or social media nicer for everyone?

In a study published last summer, researchers at the University of California, Los Angeles, found that the pleasure centers in teenagers' brains respond to the reward of getting "likes" on Instagram exactly as they do to thoughts of sex or money. And just as parents try to teach children self-control around those enticements, they must also talk to them about not falling victim to behavior they will regret when craving those "likes."

As parents, we don't want our kids to make a big mistake online: writing something mean in a group text, posting a too-sexy picture or forwarding one of someone else. According to a Pew Research Center survey, 24 percent of teenagers are online "almost constantly," so it's essential that they know how to handle themselves there.

Getting your children to articulate the unspoken rules can be the first step in helping them be more understanding of their peers. When we observe our children harshly judging others who have a different sensibility about the use of social media, they need us to set aside our judgments about their world, and help them cultivate empathy for one another.

Critical Thinking

1. How do rules of what is socially acceptable on social media get formed? How do they get communicated among peers?

2. The article cites a PEW Research survey that found almost a quarter of teens aged 13–17 use the Internet "almost constantly" and another 56 percent use it "several times a day." What do you think of these findings? What implications (positive or negative) does this Internet use have on their lives?

3. The author writes, "Parents often feel as if their children's smartphones are portals to another world—one that they know little to nothing about." Should parents know more about their teen's social media world? If so, how should they learn? If parents learn more, how will the their teen's social media world change because of that?

Internet References

How Girls Use Social Media to Build Up, Break Down Self-Image
http://www.cnn.com/2017/01/12/health/girls-social-media-self-image-partner/index.html
How to Supercharge Your Online Dating
https://www.cnet.com/how-to/online-dating-profile-pictures-okcupid-services-tips/
The Link Between Selfies and Self-Delusion
https://psmag.com/news/the-link-between-selfies-and-self-delusion

DEVORAH HEITNER is the author of "Screenwise: Helping Kids Thrive (and Survive) in Their Digital World."

Article

Prepared by: Daniel Mittleman, *DePaul University* and
Douglas Druckenmiller, *Western Illinois University*

Twitter's New Order

Inside the changes that could save its business—and reshape civil discourse.

WILL OREMUS

Learning Outcomes

After reading this article, you will be able to:

- Describe Twitter's post selection algorithm and its intended impact on user experience.

- Discuss the issue of fake news, and the impact of post selection algorithm on the spread of fake news.

- Contrast the social networking experience between a chronological post timeline and a post selection algorithm timeline.

What do you see when you open Twitter? Until a year ago, the answer was straightforward: With minor exceptions, you'd see every tweet from every person you followed, in chronological order, with the most recent at the top.

In February 2016, word leaked to *BuzzFeed* that Twitter was planning a move that would change everything. The company was introducing what insiders called an "algorithmic timeline." It meant that tweets would no longer appear in the order they were posted. Instead, a complex, opaque software program would decide which tweets you'd see when you opened the app.

It sounded nefarious. Worse: It sounded like Facebook, the older, more mainstream social network that Twitter's cool kids shun. Longtime users revolted, channeling their indignation into a bitter hashtag: #RIPTwitter. Meanwhile, a handful of techies, investors, and contrarian pundits countered the gloom with sunny predictions. An algorithm, they argued, was just what Twitter needed to reverse its fortunes and join Facebook in the ranks of social media giants.

But a funny thing happened when Twitter launched the new feature a month later: nothing. So it seemed, at any rate, to casual users of the service. Implemented in a surprisingly modest form, the algorithm so far has neither saved nor killed Twitter but wrought effects so subtle that they've passed almost without mention. After all the outrage, fewer than 2 percent of all users opted out of the algorithmic timeline.

Yet the changes to Twitter's underlying structure run much deeper than outsiders realize. At a critical moment in the company's history—and that of our body politic—the algorithm is quietly starting to reshape both Twitter's business and the way people experience it. That includes the president of the United States, his 25 million followers, the activists opposing him, and the media that must make sense of it all.

For this article, Twitter offered a glimpse into the workings (and continued evolution) of the algorithm for the first time since it was launched a year ago. On the most immediate level, the new timeline has clearly made the service a little friendlier and livelier. It ensures that you see more tweets from the people you interact with the most and more of the most popular tweets from others you follow. It has also ensured that the most popular tweets are far more widely seen than they used to be, enabling them to go viral on an unprecedented scale.

The company says the effect has been to draw in new users and make the old ones more active. In a time of crisis for Twitter's business, it has driven desperately needed increases in key metrics such as monthly active users, impressions, and time spent on the site. Those gains have yet to reverse the company's overall slump, but they offer a beam of hope amid the gloom—especially since Twitter is only beginning to tap the algorithm's potential.

But you can't see more of some kinds of tweets without seeing less of others, and the hidden consequences of that equation could affect us all. As it gradually tightens the loops in Twitter's social fabric, the algorithm risks further insulating its users from people whose viewpoints run counter to their own—a phenomenon, already rampant on Facebook, that has contributed to the polarization of the American electorate and the Balkanization of its media.

Facebook has taken the brunt of the blame for the fake news and sensationalism that polluted political news in the 2016 U.S. presidential election, both because it is bigger and because its more potent algorithm lends itself to those pitfalls. But Twitter played a role, too, and with the world's most powerful person setting national policy via tweets on a daily basis, the service has never been more influential than it is today.

The question now for Twitter is whether a service that doubles as a global news ticker and water cooler can seize this moment to regain its business footing. The rest of us need to ask a different question: Should we hope that Twitter succeeds?

Despite insisting that the algorithm is working, Twitter declined to share its precise impact on key metrics with me. This reticence suggests that the effects, while positive, are not yet impressive enough to comfort the company's restless investors. Its latest earnings report, covering the fourth quarter of 2016, showed modest gains in active users and engagement, which CEO Jack Dorsey attributed to "better relevance in both the timeline and notifications." Yet the company's revenue flatlined, and its stock dropped.

Twitter's engineers are constantly probing how well the service is engaging its users, running tests that quietly enable tweaks for a small fraction of Twitter accounts, then studying the effects on their behavior. Those tests generate much richer insights now that Twitter can toy with the ordering of users' feeds. "Everything we are doing, we are measuring if it's working or not," said Deepak Rao, the product manager who oversees the company's home timeline. "We run dozens of experiments every month."

I spoke in depth with Rao to better understand this process and the thinking behind Twitter's algorithm. In our conversation, Rao described a system that is still in its nascent stages yet is already far more complex and subtle than most users realize. It is a system so finely personalized that no two users will experience it in the same way yet rudimentary enough that its engineers are still struggling to ensure that it doesn't show you the same people's tweets every time you open the app.

The company told me that its own data show that the algorithm has boosted users' engagement along every major yardstick it watches. Not only are people spending more time reading, favoriting, and retweeting as a result, but they're actually tweeting more themselves—an outcome that surprised

Twitter's own product managers. "Every possible engagement and attention metric went up" when the algorithm took effect last year, Rao told me. By exactly how much, the company declined to disclose, although a spokesperson called it "one of our most impactful product launches."

As a result of the experiments made possible by the algorithm, Twitter knows more about its users than it ever did before, such as how much they value recency or how they react to seeing multiple tweets in a row from the same person. The company has tried out new features that group tweets about a given topic or hashtag within your feed. It has even experimented with showing you occasional tweets from people you don't follow, if Twitter's ranking system shows that you're likely to want to see them. Twitter can now evaluate the efficacy of such new features by comparing their effects on user behavior to the effects of the ranked timeline and "In case you missed it," another newish feature. "Our algorithm changes on an almost daily to weekly basis," Rao said.

All these tweaks have yet to bear much fruit, from investors' perspectives. The good news for the company is that, when managed properly, machine-learning algorithms can be radically improved with time. Likewise, upticks in user engagement have a way of gaining momentum, as engagement begets engagement. Muted as its impact has been to the business so far, the algorithm may still power future product changes that both lure and retain new users—and, ultimately, get Twitter growing again in a meaningful way.

Twitter is sometimes accused by its loyalists of making changes too rashly. In fact, the company has treated its core product with excessive caution. The failure of former CEO Dick Costolo, pushed aside in 2015, was not that he ruined the product, as so many feared. It was that he accorded it too much reverence. The business evolved on his watch, but the user experience stagnated. The timeline when he left looked and functioned much the same as it did when Costolo arrived in 2010.

His successor, Dorsey, approved the timeline algorithm in 2015, and its success or failure will probably be attributed to him. But the minds who developed and championed the idea within the company included former CTO Adam Messinger, former head of engineering Alex Roetter, and former head of product Kevin Weil. (That all three have since left is a sign of the long-running dysfunction atop Twitter's org chart.)

To understand why they saw the algorithm as vital to Twitter's future, it helps to recall what preceded it. The reverse-chronological timeline stemmed from the site's origins as a way to blast brief, real-time "status updates" via text message to friends and acquaintances. But over the years Twitter morphed into something more like a public platform for news, opinions, jokes. As the user base and its follow lists grew, the chronological feed's limitations became clear. You'd log in and find yourself thrust into the middle of dozens of unrelated, often insider-y conversations, and the good stuff required tedious scrolling to unearth. For the ordinary internet user, it simply wasn't worth the trouble.

This led to Twitter's most existential and enduring problem as a business: its inability to retain a large proportion of the new users who sign up. In December 2012, Twitter announced that it had 200 million monthly active users. CEO Costolo predicted that Twitter would hit 400 million within a year. Instead, the company filed to go public in late 2013 with only 218 million monthly active users. More than three years later, that active-user number is still just 319 million, and growth has slowed to a trickle. Though the comparison isn't perfect, the company plateaued at roughly the age at which Facebook took off. A crucial difference between the two services: Facebook's news feed algorithm, which the company implemented early on and has been aggressively improving ever since. Whereas right now Twitter's algorithm affects only the tweets at the very top of your feed, Facebook's automatically orders every post according to a highly sophisticated formula that is personalized to each user's habits, tastes, and relationships.

Part of Twitter's problem has been its struggle to define the timeline's precise purpose. Rao told me that this has become clearer since the algorithm launched, that the company now sees the timeline's function as "helping users to stay informed with what's going on in the world." Twitter, in other words, is no longer a social network, at least by its own reckoning. It's a real-time, personalized news service. And since there are no human editors, it falls to Twitter's algorithm to determine which tweets will lead the news each time you open it.

Of all Twitter's efforts to address its retention problem—and there have been many—the algorithm is its boldest. But what *is* the Twitter algorithm, and how does it work? The short version is that it's a software program that evaluates tweets according to various criteria, then chooses a handful to show each user at the top of his or her timeline upon opening the app. The rest of the timeline remains reverse-chronological, at least for now. For the curious (and the confused), here is the long version— the first public peek into the algorithm's workings.

As soon as you open it, Twitter quickly collects and assesses every recent tweet from every person you follow and assigns each one a relevance score. This score is based on a wide array of factors, ranging from the number of favorites and retweets it received to how often you've engaged with its author lately.

At the same time, the algorithm is assessing a variety of other variables—including how long you've been away from the site, how many people you follow, and your individual Twitter habits—to determine exactly how those scores will affect what you see in your feed. (All of this happens in the background.)

The algorithm's output can take different forms in your feed, but the "ranked timeline" and "In case you missed it" are the most notable additions. The ranked timeline is what was supposed to herald the end of Twitter as we know it. Visit the site or open the app after a few hours away, and the top of your feed will look much the same as it did a year ago, with a series of tweets listed in reverse-chronological order. But examine the time stamps and you'll notice that these tweets aren't quite as recent as you might expect. The top one might have been posted 10 or 15 minutes ago. Scroll just a few tweets down, and you might see something published an hour ago or more. Together, these are the tweets that Twitter's algorithm has "ranked" for you to see first.

While Twitter won't disclose all the signals involved in the ranking—"thousands," a spokesperson told me—the company did specify a few of them. They include:

- A tweet's overall engagement, including retweets, clicks, favorites, and time spent reading it
- A tweet's engagement relative to other tweets by the same author
- How recently the tweet was published
- How often you engage with the tweet's author
- How much time you spend reading tweets by that author, even if you don't engage.
- What kind of attachment the tweet includes (e.g., link, image, video, none), and what kind of attachments you tend to engage with.

The tweets that appear in this ranked section of your timeline constitute a tiny subset of the tweets you missed since the last time you were active on Twitter. So if you keep scrolling, soon enough you'll reach a tweet that was published even more recently than the one that appeared at the very top of your feed. From that point on, your Twitter is back to normal, displaying every tweet from every person you follow in reverse-chronological order. And when you refresh your timeline, the ranked tweets will sink out of view.

That the ranked tweets are easy to miss, Rao told me, is by design. The company has tried at several junctures in its history to cordon off a batch of algorithmically selected tweets from the rest of the timeline. But these efforts were mostly stumbles because they didn't feel like part of the core experience. (Remember the #Discover tab? Neither do most people.) They were "too module-y," in Rao's words. He said the company ultimately decided to incorporate the ranked tweets directly into the timeline so that they wouldn't detract from the "liveliness" of the Twitter experience.

The ICYMI feature, which used to be called "While you were away," predates the ranked timeline and remains under a separate label from the rest of your feed. Given its move away from self-contained modules, many assumed Twitter would dispense with ICYMI when the ranked timeline was launched, but the company has retained it as a complementary feature. Whereas the ranked timeline will appear at the top of your feed after just an hour or two away, ICYMI typically enters your feed only when it's been several hours or a few days since you last opened Twitter. The tweets that appear there are less recent, and they don't appear in chronological order at all. Rather, they're ordered according to their ranking scores. The tweet at the top of your ICYMI box, then, will be the one that ranked highest out of all the possible tweets from everyone you follow since the last time you logged on. It's Twitter's equivalent of the top post in your Facebook feed.

From a design standpoint, Twitter's use of both the ICYMI box and the ranked timeline is a clunky arrangement. But if people find it confusing, Rao said no one has told him so. The goal, in his mind, is for users not to have to think about which set of ranked tweets they see at what time, or how many, or why. Twitter's algorithm is supposed to do that thinking for them.

Twitter, the technology and media writer John Herrman once wrote, is a truth machine. The network's inherently public structure made it relatively easy to debunk the sorts of viral rumors and misinformation that tend to spread unchecked on Facebook. But as Twitter gets better at showing users the tweets that most resonate with them, the risk is that it's also getting better at reinforcing their biases and abetting their construction of alternate realities—not a marketplace of ideas, but a battlefield pocked with foxholes. This past election cycle, those searching for truth on Twitter could still find it, but for others the service doubled as a lie machine—a place where falsehoods and fake news flourished among isolated ideological subcommunities that dwell in divergent realities. The same social network that had helped to call the world's attention to Tahrir Square and Ferguson became a breeding ground for conspiracy theories such as Pizzagate. The same service that gave Trump's critics a platform to counter his rhetoric with facts also gave his supporters the power to drown them out in a cacophony of abuse and invective.

The reason for this self-reinforcing dynamic is unsurprising: When you draw on users' past habits to shape their future experiences, you risk enclosing them in bubbles of their own making—what Eli Pariser called a "filter bubble." The term has often been applied to Facebook, due to its heavy reliance on a personalization algorithm that weights each post according to, among other metrics, how likely you are to hit "like." Old-school Twitter could be a bubble of sorts, too, depending on who you followed. But the chronological timeline at least gave equal weight to every tweet, regardless of whether it was likely to please or upset you.

The ranked timeline, even in its modest present form, has changed that. You're now far more likely to see certain types of tweets than others when you log in. The question is: What types of tweets are you seeing more of?

While social media ranking algorithms are incredibly difficult to perfect, it actually isn't that hard to improve on a purely chronological approach when it comes to generating engagement. Without an algorithm, users might log in and see at the top of their timeline a random thought from technology writer Farhad Manjoo that got far less engagement than his typical tweets. But even a rudimentary ranking system could ensure that users are more likely to see a viral joke from comedy writer Dan Amira, playing off a popular meme, which generated far more engagement.

The question, though, is how an algorithm alters the overall playing field—whose tweets tend to flourish, and whose wither on the vine. One person who has almost certainly benefited from Twitter's ranked timeline is Donald Trump. Trump may not have won the presidency because of Twitter, but it's hard to imagine his campaign strategy succeeding without it. Mocked and disdained by the mainstream media, Trump used the platform as his megaphone, bypassing editorial filters to address voters directly, in his own words—and with his own facts. With each tweet gaining tens of thousands of shares, and some far more than that, Trump's Twitter account became a major media organ in its own right, helping to dictate the political news of the day. While no data are available on exactly what role the algorithm played, it's a safe bet that Trump's tweets regularly topped his followers' ranked timelines, ensuring that the missives reached a much wider audience than they would have under the old system.

And it's not just his fans. Before the algorithm, I used to see Trump's tweets only when he happened to publish while I was online or shortly beforehand. They would trigger a sudden cavalcade of retweets and commentary in my feed, but it would quickly die down. Now the president's tweets—in their original, unfiltered form—appear routinely near the top of my feed, even if he published them hours ago. I see at least one of them most weekday mornings when I log in as I prepare to board the subway to work. It's often joined there by one or two of the cleverer or more trenchant responses from people I follow. (Twitter has also recently begun using an algorithm to order the replies to popular tweets, giving rise to a cottage industry of "first replies" that reach a substantial portion of the original tweet's audience.)

Has this improved my Twitter experience? On the whole, I'd argue it has. Trump's tweets and the commentary around them, for better or worse, are part of what I come for now. Twitter's algorithm has successfully detected that, even though I almost never favorite them myself. (It may be because I occasionally quote-tweet or reply to them, or it may be because so many other people on Twitter interact with them.) By making sure I see Trump's tweets without having to seek them out, Twitter's timeline software is doing the job Rao asked of it. It's telling me what's going on in the world, or at least that portion of the world that generally concerns me.

On the other hand, the commentary it shows me about Trump's tweets—and about politics in general—almost always comes from the left. No doubt that's largely a function of the people I've chosen to follow: Most of them are liberal. Yet I've also taken care over the years to follow a number of pundits whose politics I disagree with. They tend to skew toward the moderate, #NeverTrump side of the spectrum, although some do support the president.

Their tweets often irk me, sometimes upset me, and occasionally infuriate me. But I've always continued to follow them because it's important to me that my Twitter feed not insulate me altogether from opposing viewpoints. I rarely favorite or rebroadcast their tweets, or even click their links. But I do read them, and on the whole I find them indispensable.

Interestingly, Twitter's timeline algorithm seems not to have picked up on this. For whatever reason, conservatives' tweets virtually never seem to crack my ranked timeline or my ICYMI box.

This has implications far beyond my own attempts to consume a balanced media diet. If you're a right-winger who watches Fox News and reads *Breitbart*, you might still follow a handful of mainstream news outlets on Twitter. But if you tend not to favorite or retweet their tweets, Twitter's software could decide that you don't really care to see them in your feed after all. To boost your engagement, it might instead serve you ever more tweets from the same few people whose tweets you favorite and retweet the most. Within that subset, it might further emphasize the tweets that are getting most widely favorited and retweeted by others who already think like you do. Stoking a few Pizzagate embers might cause the conspiracy theory to flourish on your feed.

The good news is that Twitter is not in denial about them, as Facebook CEO Mark Zuckerberg seemed to be about his own platform's shortcomings in the election's immediate wake. Twitter assures me that it's both concerned by and actively working to mitigate the algorithm's potential to reinforce biases.

Taking more into consideration than retweets and favorites is part of this effort. A Twitter spokesperson explained to me that a Bay Area resident might never interact with the Caltrain account she follows for its service updates. But Twitter's software can learn over time that she tends to stop scrolling long enough to read a Caltrain tweet before moving on. It could then make sure to show her a noteworthy Caltrain update in her ranked timeline during commute hours.

Rao told me Twitter also runs qualitative surveys meant to complement its data on users' behavior, to help distinguish between what the team thinks of as "salad" (like Caltrain's tweets) and "doughnuts" (such as an ideological exhortation that plays to your preconceptions). Still, it's clear to anyone who uses Twitter regularly that the viral "doughnut" tweets now go more viral than before and that you tend to see more tweets from the people whose accounts you engage with most frequently. In our polarized political climate, the potential implications could be dire—not because of Twitter's sheer scale, but because the people in power in Washington, Hollywood, and the media are among those who use it the most.

Rao said the company has noticed this homogeneity in the rankings and has already tweaked its software to try to address it. So far, he said, the data suggest that injecting more diversity into users' ranked timelines might actually be good for engagement. If that's true, it could be good news for both the company and its users. Then again, recent history is rife with examples of tech companies' interests not aligning with society's quite so neatly.

At a time when Twitter is still clawing desperately for traction—it has launched multiple live-streaming products and overhauled its harassment policies in a bid to budge its stagnant user growth and clean up the more noxious and abusive discourse in its commons—giving the algorithm more control over users' feeds would be a logical next move. It would be risky, sure. But for Twitter, at this juncture, the risks of inaction may be greater.

Yet if ever-greater personalization is the answer to Twitter's business woes, it's unlikely to be the answer to the woes of a media ecosystem in which all news has become "fake news" to someone. Presenting people with contrary viewpoints simply isn't a recipe for massive gains in engagement, for reasons that may run too deep in human nature to change.

On the other hand, the main alternatives to Twitter as a news source—Fox News, CNN, Facebook, et al.—all have their own crises of credibility and perception, driven in part by the perverse incentives of their respective business and audience models. If Twitter is right that its users value at least some diversity of viewpoints in their feeds—and if it's serious about being a place people come for information rather than just entertainment or endorphins—we'll be better off with a more automated Twitter than we would be with no Twitter at all.

Critical Thinking

1. Is the use of an algorithm to select which social media posts you see first an appropriate or inappropriate manipulation of your experience? Why?

2. Does the use of an algorithm increase or decrease the likelihood fake news memes will be widely spread? Why do you think this?

3. Twitter and other social media platforms are tweaking their algorithms to increase "engagement." What is engagement? Why is increasing engagement a good thing for the platform? For the user?

Internet References

What Do Social Media Algorithms Mean For You?
https://www.forbes.com/sites/ajagrawal/2016/04/20/what-do-social-media-algorithms-mean-for-you/#2ba94c35a515

Why Instagram Is Becoming Facebook's Next Facebook
https://www.nytimes.com/2017/04/26/technology/why-instagram-is-becoming-facebooks-next-facebook.html

Your Social Media News Feed and the Algorithms That Drive It
https://www.forbes.com/sites/quora/2017/05/15/your-social-media-news-feed-and-the-algorithms-that-drive-it/#309118b4eb8c

WILL OREMUS is Slate's senior technology writer.

Unit 9

UNIT

Prepared by: Daniel Mittleman, *DePaul University* and
Douglas Druckenmiller, *Western Illinois University*

Politics and Social Media

Almost every American college student knows the First Amendment to the Constitution guarantees the right to practice any religion and to exercise free speech. What many may not know are the other rights specified by the First Amendment: the right to peaceably assemble and the right to petition the government. The founders of the American government recognized that to establish and maintain a free and open society, not only must the ability to speak be protected but the ability to gather in groups, form associations, and network must also be protected. Without these latter protections, citizens would not be able to form the critical mass necessary to feel safe standing up and petitioning the government.

A French social observer, Emile Durkheim (1858–1917), argued that a vital society must have members who feel a sense of community. Community is easily evident in preindustrial societies where kinship ties, shared religious beliefs, and customs reinforce group identity and shared values. Not so today in the United States, where a mobile population commutes long distances and retreats each evening to the sanctity and seclusion of individualized homes. Contemporary visitors to the United States are struck by the cornucopia of cultural options available to Americans. They find a dizzying array of religions, beliefs, philosophical and political perspectives, models of social interaction, entertainment, and now, digital gadgets. Today, we have the technical means to communicate almost instantly and effortlessly across great distances. And with that, the bounds of traditional association are being abandoned and replaced by online interactions on Facebook, Tumblr, LinkedIn, and other social media.

On the positive side, social media is a vehicle for people to express their views, connect with others, and learn about the world around them. On the negative side, however, it has also become a place where shaming and bullying occur, sometimes out in the open and other times behind a cloak of anonymity. The most famous instance of public shaming by social media might have been the firing of Justine Sacco, a corporate communications director who tweeted during layovers en route from New York to South Africa. The worst of her tweets, "Going to Africa. Hope I don't get AIDS. Just Kidding. I'm White!" was posted moments before the last leg of her journey from London to Cape Town. While she slept on the flight, the tweet went viral and more than 10,000 people responded. Those watching live on Twitter knew she'd been fired before her plane landed.[1]

In June 2016, the United Kingdom voted to leave the European Union. Those for and against campaigned vigorously on social media and given that most of us see views similar to our own across our social media feeds, it was easy to believe one's own side held a large majority when in fact it was a very close vote. It turns out that those who wanted to leave the EU were more engaged on social media and had more money behind their campaign.[2] What we did not know at the time (and are only beginning to learn as of this writing) was that there were well organized "fake news" campaigns impacting that UK referendum—and by extension the existence of the European Union.

Fake news, or—more conventionally: propaganda—has been around since the rise of democracy. But given the immediacy and the indeterminacy of authorship social media provides, the use of partially to wholly untrue messaging has been turbocharged. We live at a crossroads of time where we can no longer be certain of the legitimacy of much of what we read. Nor can we be certain the majority outcome of any election was based on an honest discourse of ideas and information. Perhaps we never should have been certain, but only now the machinations are more obvious.

Today anyone can be a publisher simply by creating a Facebook page or Twitter account. The lines between citizen commentator and professional journalist have blurred. News is reported instantly on any number of social media platforms that supplement, complement, and feed the traditional media outlets. By the time the nightly news airs on a late weekday afternoon, most of what is shared is a rehashing of information that has already been transmitted and digested as it was unfolding live throughout the day. Newspapers—at least in their print versions—are reporting historical record by the following morning.

---

[1] http://www.nytimes.com/2015/02/15/magazine/how-one-stupid-tweet-ruined-justine-saccos-life.html?_r=0
[2] http://marcom2.com/blog/brexit-and-social-media-6-things-you-should-know/

In 2016, 62 percent of U.S. adults surveyed by the Pew Research Center reported obtaining news on social media. While this did not exclude news from other sources, only 46 percent reported receiving news from local TV and only 20 percent from print newspapers.[3] As social media became a primary news source, not only was traditional journalism affected, but our entire discourse about current events was affected as well.

Some questions to consider in this unit:

- How does social media impact our sense of community and shared identity?
- Who decides what is newsworthy? Who decides what is real news and what is fake news?
- If elections around the world are being impacted by fake news, how to address it?

---

[3] http://www.journalism.org/2016/05/26/news-use-across-social-media-platforms-2016/#fn-55250-1

Article

Prepared by: Daniel Mittleman, *DePaul University* and
Douglas Druckenmiller, *Western Illinois University*

What's Propaganda Got to Do with It?

Calling out news—whether real or fake—as propaganda expresses anxieties over media power, but is it helping us a get a grip on the media landscape?

CAROLINE JACK

Learning Outcomes

After reading this article, you will be able to:

- Define propaganda and fake news.

- Understand online media's role in the creation, propagation, and validation of propaganda.

- Articulate an opinion about the impact of propaganda on online public discourse.

Amid the "fake news" controversies in the aftermath of the 2016 United States Presidential election, the notion of propaganda surged back into popular consciousness. Across the political spectrum, online conversations about propaganda bloomed like a thousand flowers of media anxiety.

For example, shortly after the election, futurist Alex Steffen garnered thousands of retweets and likes with a tweet that declared, "Fake news is propaganda. The powerful demanding apologies from artists is censorship. Business dealings while in office are corruption." To underscore the anti-authoritarian thrust of the message, a follow-up *Medium* post featured an image of *1984* author (and dedicated democratic socialist) George Orwell, invoking the thought-limiting qualities of that novel's Newspeak. Although Steffen did not name the President-Elect in his short text, the post is tagged, "Donald Trump."

While some social media users were using the notion of propaganda to critique both the President-Elect and clickbait masquerading as journalistic content, others were labeling cable news networks and newspapers of record both "fake news" *and* propaganda, thus enfolding both terms into longstanding critiques of the media establishment.

Propaganda, in other words, is having a moment. People are turning to propaganda as a media epithet because it helps to express discomfort with media—and the "fake news" controversy is just one part of this discomfort. The epithet gets its sting, in part, from popular imaginings of propaganda as bombastic, deceptive mass communications from an overreaching or abusive state. But this cultural imaginary can also limit our perceptions of how power and meaning move through society. State actors are involved in the current media moment, but so are a variety of other collectivities, with a variety of motives.

What Is Propaganda?

Propaganda is notoriously difficult to define. Beyond the generally agreed upon principle that propaganda involves some effort at persuasion, it's hard to settle on clear boundaries on what counts as propaganda. Communication scholar Philip M. Taylor briefly defines propaganda as "the deliberate attempt to persuade people to think and behave in a desired way" (2003, p. 6). Philosopher Jason Stanley lists a variety of definitions, including the "classical" sense of "manipulation of the rational will to close off debate" (2015, p. 48). Stanley focuses in particular on *supporting* propaganda, which bolsters certain favored ideals but does so by nonrational means, and *undermining* propaganda, which presents itself as bolstering favored ideals but in fact "tends to erode those very ideals" (p. 53). These are only two examples, differing on many points but tied together in their attention to power and persuasion.

"We could quote definitions for pages on end," Jacques Ellul wrote in his 1965 treatise on the topic, and the situation hasn't improved much since then. But even if we leave aside the thorny question of definition, the fact of use-in-practice remains. People are using the term "propaganda" to express their discomfort with the media in this moment.

I want to ask what the resurgence of propaganda as a topic of conversation reflects about popular understandings of the media in this moment. What itch does this nebulous term scratch for the people who are using it? And what does it draw attention away from?

Holding the Media to Account . . . Kind of

Most obviously, calling news propaganda expresses a suspicion that the leading media are affected by powerful interests, either directly or indirectly. It speaks to a sense of boundaries transgressed: democratic citizens want news to be trustworthy and dedicated to the public interest. Calling a news story or news outlet propagandistic suggests that it is anything but.

The prevalence of "propaganda" as a media epithet reflects a variety of sentiments about the shortcomings of American journalism. The recent discussions of "fake news" and propaganda issue from many points on the political spectrum. We saw, during the recent election cycle, how news-like items of questionable or outright false web content, designed to garner maximum clicks and likes, sowed confusion within our national discourse.

Concerns about these new developments have been added to longstanding objections from the left that include the corporate dominance of the fourth estate and the perpetuation of social injustice, and objections from the right that include what it sees as attacks on traditional values and undue protection of partisan political figures and projects. Add to these positions the many emergent strains of anti-institutionalism, nationalism, and populism in current American political discourse, and you get a sense of how the discourse about propaganda runs far beyond typical lines of partisanship.

The popular revival of "propaganda" as a media epithet expresses misgivings about media power and media practices. But even as it helps to focus popular misgivings, it also creates a frame. And that frame brings assumptions with it that can make it hard to see some of the cultural aspects of the present moment.

State-controlled Media?

For one, the epithet of "propaganda" raises the spectre of state control, but governments are only one of the types of collectives that can exert influence over media. The most egregious historical cases of propaganda—ones everyone agrees were propagandistic—were media productions that issued from, or were driven by, state (or would-be state) actors. Scholarly treatments, of propaganda, too, tend to focus on state (or would-be state) actors. When coordinated, persuasive messages issue from non-state entities, we tend to use gentler terms like *public relations*, which shifts matters from the civic sphere to the

seemingly separate sphere of commerce, or *activism*, which conjures images of grassroots, bottom-up persuasion. But these bright-line divisions are not as reliable as they seem.

Consider, for example, the online discussions that culminated in Edgar Welch firing an assault rifle inside Comet Ping Pong. Discussions on user-driven sites such as Reddit and 4chan helped propel conspiracy theories about a possible child sex abuse ring headquartered in the DC-area pizzeria (#Pizzagate) into popular consciousness. Subsequently, some social media users (and the *New York Times*) condemned the Pizzagate conspiracy theory itself as fake news. Meanwhile, other users leveled charges of propaganda at *New York Times* for its coverage of these events, alleging that the powerful were banding together to protect one another.

A Matter of Perspective

The Pizzagate conspiracy theory itself was far-fetched, to say the least; even Welch conceded that the "intel" was "not 100%." Depending on your perspective, though, discussions of Pizzagate on such sites could be described, variously, as propaganda or (misguided) activism. This is an admittedly extreme example, but it speaks to a broader issue in American culture.

The boundaries between education, entertainment, and propaganda are blurry. This is a problem with a long history in the United States, as I have argued elsewhere. And amidst an ideologically and epistemologically divided population, agreement on the boundaries between categories like activism and propaganda are especially hard to find. Colloquial understandings of propaganda—narratives about strategic manipulation of leading media outlets by governments and or para-governmental groups—don't capture this categorical contingency.

It's Not (Necessarily) a State Actor

If "propaganda" is a useful as a media epithet because it expresses concerns about media persuasion and power, then we must allow that a variety of actors, not just states or would-be states, can influence the television networks, newspapers of record, and leading online news sources.

Our understanding of media power (and of what it means to call something propaganda) must make room for a *variety* of potential collective and individual influences. This includes corporations, interest groups, activist groups, and other traditional collectives; it should also include the new forms of individual and collective presence that digital communications facilitate. This includes state-sponsored online actors *and* ad-hoc user collectives.

It's Not Always Entirely Serious, Although the Outcomes Can Be

Turning to the specific dynamics in play with Pizzagate, there's another way that an observer could have categorized the conspiracy theories about Comet Ping Pong that flourished as users dug through John Podesta's leaked emails, and it's one that prior conceptions of propaganda don't account for: play.

A sense of absurd play—of trolling—prevails in some corners of user-driven online spaces. Trolling involves a kind of social playfulness that, if done correctly, is undetectable to the objects of the ruse; folklorist Whitney Phillips has written brilliantly and at length on this matter. There is no way to know for certain what motivations, in which proportions, drove users to participate in the conspiracy discussions on 4chan and Reddit. It may have been sincere concern, absurd play, curiosity, nihilism, boredom, or some mixture of all of these.

Our understandings of media persuasion and power need to be capacious enough to acknowledge that some users participate in online projects such as this to gain a particular outcome, while others participate to enjoy the engaging or absurd play of the process. The resulting media texts can spur serious outcomes. Some of these may have been intended (e.g., entrenching negative sentiment against Clinton and her associates); others may not have been (as, seemingly, was the case with Welch).

Shifting the Frame

Americans will be grappling with these novel contexts of media persuasion and power for some time. And the use of "propaganda" as a media epithet will likely continue. As these conversations unspool over the coming months and years, one way to avoid getting mired in is-it-or-isn't-it debates that serve as proxies for a fractured civic sphere is to ask what people get from using the epithet. People are referencing a disconcerting set of realizations about how media and power function in our society. In some cases, those realizations challenge the foundational beliefs of our constitutional democracy.

While definitions of propaganda may vary, they generally have to do with power and persuasion. But propaganda (versus entertainment, versus education, versus activism...) is a matter of perspective. Almost any communication can be interpreted as propagandistic in nature. Outside of the most blatantly egregious, demagogic or hateful cases, attempting to stifle propaganda won't work. The emergence of propaganda as a media epithet, in practical use, isn't a cause but a symptom of deeper fissures in American culture.

Critical Thinking

1. What is propaganda? How is it similar or different from "fake news"? Or from and argumentation essay?

2. How might one go about validating whether news is factually correct or fake? Stated another way, how can you tell if something is propaganda?

3. How does propaganda impact the way we use social media? How does it impact the way we form opinions about public issues?

Internet References

How to Spot Fake News (and Teach Kids to Be Media-Savvy)
 https://www.commonsensemedia.org/blog/how-to-spot-fake-news-and-teach-kids-to-be-media-savvy

Pay To Sway: Report Reveals How Easy It Is To Manipulate Elections With Fake News
 https://www.theguardian.com/media/2017/jun/13/fake-news-manipulate-elections-paid-propaganda

Samantha Power: Why Foreign Propaganda Is More Dangerous Now
 https://www.nytimes.com/2017/09/19/opinion/samantha-power-propaganda-fake-news.html

CAROLINE JACK is a media scholar whose research focuses on media history and the public communication of economies. She holds a PhD in Communication from Cornell University, and is currently a Postdoctoral Scholar at Data & Society.

Article   Prepared by: Daniel Mittleman, *DePaul University* and
                                             Douglas Druckenmiller, *Western Illinois University*

The Filter Bubble Revisited

A new study suggests online media aren't to blame for political polarization—yet.

WILL OREMUS

Learning Outcomes

After reading this article, you will be able to:

- Describe what the filter bubble is, and posit what effects it might be having on online discourse.

- Articulate an opinion on whether social media is tearing us apart or bringing us together.

- Understand the role social media plays in informing us about politics and social issues.

In 2011, with Facebook and Google growing in influence, liberal activist and entrepreneur Eli Pariser wrote a best-selling book that coined a term: *The Filter Bubble.* Personalized news feeds and search results, he warned, would undermine civic discourse by steering people toward information that appeals to their preconceptions. We would search for, like, and retweet the ideas we already agreed with, and algorithms optimized for engagement would serve us more of the same—crowding out anything that might trouble our worldview.

Five years later, Pariser's work was hailed anew. The electoral triumphs of Brexit and Donald Trump, which germinated in the online warrens where like-minded declinists congregate, seemed to validate his theory, at least to the establishment pundits who failed to see them coming. The *Guardian* profiled him as a sort of social media prophet; Bill Gates weighed in; a *Wired* headline chided, "Your Filter Bubble Is Destroying Democracy." Liberals and moderates, suddenly more aware of their own cozy echo chambers, resolved to better understand what the other side was thinking.

But if filter bubbles are destroying democracy, a new study suggests they aren't doing it in quite the ways you might expect—or to the extent you might assume.

We know that the American electorate has become more polarized in recent decades in multiple ways. But a new working paper from economists at Brown University and Stanford University, which studies the relationship between polarization and the use of the online media in American adults from 1996 to 2012, suggests the self-refining contours of your Facebook feed are not to blame. There are lots of ways to measure polarization, so the authors split the difference by combining nine different plausible metrics from the academic literature into a single index.

Their counterintuitive finding: Polarization has been driven primarily by the demographic groups that spend the *least* time online.

Specifically, the researchers find that Americans older than 75 experienced by far the greatest ideological divergence of any age group over the time period studied. Yet just 20 percent of this group reported using social media as of 2012. In contrast, the vast majority (80 percent) of Americans aged 18 to 39 used social media. Yet according to the study's findings, this younger group was hardly any more polarized in 2012 than it had been in 1996, when online media barely existed.

"These facts argue against the hypothesis that the internet is a primary driver of rising political polarization," conclude authors Levi Boxell and Matthew Gentzkow of Stanford, and Jesse Shapiro of Brown.

That doesn't mean there's zero filtering at work in online media, of course. The phenomenon Pariser described is real, and polarization is just one of its putative effects. There are also some important limitations in this paper's data and methodology that might help to explain why it found so little correlation between polarization and reading the news online.

For instance, while the authors' macroscopic approach captures differences *between* age groups, it may obscure trends *within* age groups along lines such as party affiliation, income and education level, or intensity of engagement with social media. And, importantly, while the study covers the period in which online media grew from infancy to near-ubiquity, the data capture only the first few years of the algorithmic personalization trend that Pariser described. Facebook introduced the "like" button in 2009; Google began personalizing search results the same year. Twitter launched in 2006 and introduced a ranking algorithm just last year.

Even so, if the authors' polarization index is to be trusted, it's noteworthy that so much of our country's rise in partisanship transpired offline among people who didn't even have Facebook accounts. The finding is consistent with a previous body of work by Gentzkow, Shapiro, and others, who have found little evidence for the hypothesis—advanced by legal scholar Cass Sunstein—that the internet is tearing us apart. In 2011, for instance, they reported that people were actually more likely to encounter opposing views in online media than they are in their day-to-day interactions with neighbors, co-workers, and family.

Less controversially, this newest study is a useful reminder of a simple fact that media pundits are prone to overlook. As central as Facebook and Twitter are to the news consumption habits of certain groups—like, cough, the media—most Americans still get their news through more traditional channels. Even as nearly half of Americans now read at least some news on Facebook, the majority still cite television as their primary news source. And while Facebook took the brunt of media criticism in the wake of the 2016 election, Pew found that voters relied more heavily on Fox News and CNN.

Pariser himself is well aware of that, as he told me this week when we discussed Boxell, Gentzkow, and Shapiro's paper. "I'm not surprised," he said of their findings on polarization and social media, though he added that finer- grained research would be needed to properly interpret their results. "I've always been worried about overclaiming what social media is doing to us now based on the way that people actually consume media."

Yet Pariser noted that the influence of social media on the news continues to grow, and he believes the filter bubble problem is growing with it. Facebook and Google today are already quite different from Facebook and Google in 2012, when the Boxell et al. study ends, and the Facebook and Google of 2020—or whatever platforms complement or displace them— are likely to look different still. "We haven't yet reached the event horizon where social media is the primary driver of how we consume things," he said. "I still believe that across that event horizon are strange and scary phenomena."

Meanwhile, Pariser highlighted a different way in which filter bubbles may be contributing to polarization. Some of the people who rely most heavily on social media for news, he pointed out, are members of the media itself. If journalists' own filter bubbles are influencing what news they cover, and how they cover it, that could help explain the vast and still-growing partisan divide between the audiences of more traditional outlets such as Fox News and CNN. Those cable news networks are especially popular among older Americans—the same ones who are leading the polarization trend, according to the study.

And then, of course, there's the reality that the political media have only so much power, and they tend to reflect public opinion at least as much as they shape it. As Trump's rallies reminded us, a lot of politics still happens at the local and interpersonal levels: if not at a strip mall, then in a small arena.

But if social media isn't driving polarization as much as we might assume, then what is? I put that question to Shapiro, one of the study's authors, and he demurred: "I honestly don't know. I would think, given how demographically broad we find the polarization trend to be, whatever is driving it is also likely to be something that's very demographically broad."

Shapiro acknowledged that more research is needed to fully understand the relationship between social media and polarization. "I think part of it is, traditional media remain very important," he said. "And part of it is that, although the internet does provide some scope for people to have really segregated news diets, they're not as segregated as people imagine them to be. The notion that people are out there reading only really extreme sources and no mainstream sources just didn't wash with the data we looked at" in 2011. "That's not to say the opportunities for it aren't changing. It's just not as powerful a factor as it might seem."

In other words, whatever future our online media habits will bring has yet to fully arrive. And it's not a foregone conclusion that it will be a hyperpartisan dystopia—at least, not any more than the one that's already reflected on cable news.

Critical Thinking

1. Are filter bubbles destroying democracy? Explain your reasoning.

2. Is, as Cass Sunstein suggests, the Internet tearing us apart? Explain your reasoning.

3. How, if at all, does the post selection algorithm used by Facebook, Twitter, and other sites affect our online discourse?

Internet References

Could Social Media Be Tearing Us Apart?

https://www.theguardian.com/media-network/2016/jun/28/social-media-networks-filter-bubbles

Is Communication Technology Tearing Us Apart?

https://www.15five.com/blog/communication-technology-tearing-us-apart/

Maybe The Internet Isn't Tearing Us Apart After All

https://www.wired.com/2017/05/maybe-internet-isnt-tearing-us-apart/

WILL OREMUS is Slate's senior technology writer.

Article   Prepared by: Daniel Mittleman, *DePaul University* and
                             Douglas Druckenmiller, *Western Illinois University*

Are There Limits to Online Free Speech?

When technologists defend free speech above all other values, they play directly into the hands of white nationalists.

ALICE TIARA

Learning Outcomes

After reading this article, you will be able to:

- Articulate multiple points of view regarding major online free speech issues.

- Understand the history of online social media and how it influences both law and accepted practice for political discourse.

- Discuss the merits of CDA 230 "safe harbor" provisions and their importance to guaranteeing free speech.

In November 2016, Twitter shut down the accounts of numerous alt-right leaders and white nationalists. Richard Spencer, the head of the National Policy Institute and a vocal neo-Nazi, told the *LA Times* it was a violation of his free speech. "[Twitter needs] to issue some kind of apology and make it clear they are not going to crack down on viewpoints. Are they going to now ban Donald Trump's account?"

Old and new media organizations are scrambling to define acceptable speech in the era of President Trump. But Twitter is in a particularly poor position. The prevalence of hateful speech and harassment on the platform scared off potential acquisitions by both Disney and Salesforce. The company has dealt with one PR disaster after another, from *Ghostbusters* star Leslie Jones temporarily leaving the platform after being harassed and doxed, to a viral video of obscene and abusive tweets sent to female sports journalists, to pro-Trump accounts sending *Newsweek* reporter Kurt Eichenwald animated gifs

designed to induce epileptic seizures. A site once touted as " the free speech wing of the free speech party" is now best known for giving a voice to Donald Trump and #gamergaters.

At the same time, attempts by Twitter and sites with similar histories of free speech protections to regulate the more offensive content on their site have been met with furious accusations of censorship and pandering to political correctness. This enables the alt-right to position themselves as victims, and left-wing SJWs ("social justice warriors") as aggressors. Never mind that private companies can establish whatever content restrictions they wish, and that virtually all these companies already have such guidelines on the books, even if they are weakly enforced. When technology companies appear to abandon their long-standing commitment to the First Amendment due to the concerns of journalists, feminists, or activists, the protests of those banned or regulated can seem sympathetic.

How did we get to the point where Twitter eggs spewing anti-Semitic insults are seen as defenders of free speech? To answer this question, we have to delve into why sites like Reddit and Twitter have historically been fiercely committed to freedom of speech. There are three reasons:

1. The roots of American tech in the hacker ethic and the ethos that "information wants to be free"
2. CDA 230 and the belief that the internet is the last best hope for free expression
3. A belief in self-regulation and a strong antipathy to government regulation of the internet

But a commitment to freedom of speech above all else presumes an idealistic version of the internet that no longer exists.

And as long as we consider any content moderation to be censorship, minority voices will continue to be drowned out by their aggressive majority counterparts.

To better understand this, we need to start with the origin story of the modern internet. Like many technology stories, it takes place in Northern California.

The Secret Hippie Hacker Past of the Internet

The American internet was birthed from a counter-culture devoted to freedom, experimentation, transparency and openness. While the internet originates with the military—ARPANET was commissioned and funded by the Department of Defense—the early hardware and applications that helped technology to thrive were mostly created by academics, geeks, hackers and enthusiasts.

For instance, in post-hippie Berkeley, early microcomputer aficionados formed the Homebrew Computer Club, freely sharing information that enabled its members to create some of the first personal computers. When Steve Wozniak and Steve Jobs built the first Apple Computer, they gave away its schematics at the Club. (Woz regularly helped his friends build their own Apples.) In the 1980s, people at elite universities and research labs built on ARPANET's infrastructure to create mailing lists, chat rooms, discussion groups, adventure games, and many other textual ancestors of today's social media. These were all distributed widely, and for free.

Today, it boggles the mind that people would give away such valuable intellectual property. But the members of this early computing culture adhered to a loose collection of principles that journalist Steven Levy dubbed "the hacker ethic":

> As I talked to these digital explorers, ranging from those who tamed multimillion-dollar machines in the 1950s to contemporary young wizards who mastered computers in their suburban bedrooms, I found a common element, a common philosophy that seemed tied to the elegantly flowing logic of the computer itself. It was a philosophy of sharing, openness, decentralization, and getting your hands on machines at any cost to improve the machines and to improve the world. This Hacker Ethic is their gift to us: something with value even to those of us with no interest at all in computers.

Early technology innovators deeply believed in these values of "sharing, openness, and decentralization." The Homebrew Computer Club's motto was "give to help others." Hackers believed that barriers to improving technology, contributing to knowledge, and innovating should be eliminated. Information should instead be free so that people could improve existing systems and develop new ones. If everyone adhered to the hacker ethic and contributed to their community, they would all benefit from the contributions of others.

Now, obviously, these ideals only work if everyone adheres to them. It's easy to take advantage of other people's work—economists call this the "free rider problem." And it doesn't take into account people who aren't just lazy or selfish, but people who deliberately want to cause harm to others.

But these beliefs were built into the very infrastructure of the internet. And they worked, for a time. But regulation was always necessary.

Regulating the Early Internet

On April 12, 1994, a law firm called Canter and Siegel, known as the "Green Card Lawyers," sent the first commercial spam e-mail to 6,000 USENET groups advertising their immigration law services. This inspired virulent hatred. Internet users organized a boycott, jammed the firm's fax, e-mail, and phone lines and set an autodialer to call the lawyers' home 40 times a day. Canter and Siegel were kicked off three ISP's before finally finding a home and publishing the early e-marketing book *How to Make a Fortune on the Information Superhighway.* Despite these dubious successes, the offense was seen as so inappropriate that Canter was finally disbarred in 1997, partially due to the e-mail campaign; William W. Hunt III of the Tennessee Board of Professional Responsibility said, "We disbarred him and gave him a one-year sentence just to emphasize that his e-mail campaign was a particularly egregious offense."

Early internet adopters were highly educated and relatively young with above average incomes, but, more importantly, many of them were deeply invested in the anti-commercial nature of the emerging internet and the "information wants to be free" hacker ethos. Any attempted use of the network for commercial gain was highly discouraged, particularly uses that violated "netiquette," the social mores of the internet. Netiquette was a set of community-determined guidelines that were enforced though both norms (people explicitly calling each other out when they violated community standards) and technical means (software that allowed users to block other users). Most USENET groups had lengthy Frequently Asked Questions documents where they spelled out explicitly what was encouraged, tolerated, and disallowed. And users who broke these rules were often sharply reprimanded.

The extent of the backlash against Canter and Siegel spam shows not only how egregious a violation of netiquette their messages were, but that their actions *threatened the very utility of USENET.* If the newsgroups were cluttered with spam, useful messages would be drowned out, interesting discussion would end, and key members would leave.

Fast forward a few years and email spam had taken over the inbox. Many internet users used dial-up connections, and resented having to pay to download useless messages about Rolexes and Viagra. By the mid-aughts, email, long a backbone of online communication, had become less useful. So technology companies and computer scientists worked together to develop sophisticated email filters. They don't work all the time, but people who use commercial email services like Gmail or Hotmail rarely see a spam message in their inbox. The problem was solved technically.

In both of these situations, there was no argument that technical and normative ways to circumvent spam violated the free speech rights of spammers. Instead, internet users recognized that the value of their platforms was rooted in their ability to foster communication, and spam was a serious threat. It's also worth noting that these problems were solved not through government regulation, but through collective action.

But today, we face a different set of problems related to free speech online. On one hand, we have aggressive harassment, often organized by particular online communities. On the other, we have platforms that are providing spaces for people with unarguably deplorable values (like neo-Nazis) to congregate. And this is particularly true for sites like Twitter and Reddit, which prioritize freedom of expression over virtually all other values.

Free Speech and a Free Internet

In 1997, the Supreme Court ruled in the landmark *Reno v. ACLU* case that internet speech deserved the same free speech protections as spoken or written speech. Justice John Paul Stevens wrote in the majority opinion that the internet's capacity to allow individuals to reach (potentially) mass audiences, made it, perhaps, even more valuable than its broadcast equivalent:

Through the use of chat rooms, any person with a phone line can become a town crier with a voice that resonates farther than it could from any soapbox. Through the use of Web pages, mail exploders, and newsgroups, the same individual can become a pamphleteer.

The implication is that it was even *more* important to protect free speech online than offline because of the internet's wide accessibility. While few people could publish in the *New York Times* or air their views on *60 Minutes*, almost anyone could post their ideas online and make them immediately accessible to millions. Stevens, and many technologists, imagined that the internet would be a powerful check on entrenched interests, especially given the deregulation and consolidation of corporate media begun by Reagan and solidified by Clinton.

Such ideals meshed perfectly with the hacker ethic. Rather than corporations or governments having proprietary access to ideas and information, the internet would break down such barriers. These are the ideals behind Wikipedia—"a free encyclopedia that anyone can edit," and Wikileaks—"we open governments." Protecting internet speech became a primary value of technology communities. Organizations like the ACLU and the EFF dedicated themselves to fighting any encroachment on internet free speech, from over-zealous copyright claims to the jailing of political bloggers.

This was furthered by CDA 230: the so-called "safe harbor" provision of the Digital Millennium Copyright Act. CDA 230 holds that "online intermediaries"—originally ISPs, but now including social media platforms—aren't responsible for the content that their users produce. If I write something libelous about you on Facebook, you can't sue Facebook for it. If someone writes a horrible comment on a blog I write, that's not my problem. Basically, CDA 230 enabled user-contributed content (aka social media) to exist. YouTube doesn't have to review a zillion hours of content before it's posted; it doesn't have to censor unpleasant opinions. As a result, CDA 230 is beloved by the tech community and free-speech advocates. The EFF calls it "one of the most valuable tools for protecting freedom of expression and innovation on the Internet."

Now, free speech and progressive ideas have always co-existed uneasily. The ACLU has been attacked from both the left and the right for defending the American Nazi party's right to march in Skokie, Illinois. In Margaret Atwood's *The Handmaid's Tale,* it's an unholy alliance between anti-pornography feminists and anti-pornography fundamentalist Christians that leads to the creation of an explicitly patriarchal state. But today, for both liberals and libertarians, the solution to bad speech is more speech. Rather than banning, for instance, racist speech, most First Amendment advocates believe that we should expose its inaccuracy and inconsistencies and combat it through education. (Lawyers call this "the counterspeech doctrine.")

For the most part, this makes sense. Usually, when the government does attempt to regulate internet speech, we end up with poorly conceived legislation. The EFF found that across the Middle East, laws that attempt to shut down terrorist recruiting usually end up being strategically applied to commentary and expression that doesn't favor the government. And in the United States, the Digital Millennium Copyright Act prevents virtually all internet users from using copyrighted content of any kind. A young activist could post an intricate, creative, political video on YouTube—typically the type of speech that's highly protected—and it would automatically be taken down if it used a copyrighted song. Few of us want people who refer to the internet as a "series of tubes" or "the cyber" making decisions about how the rest of us should use it.

If Not the Government, Then Who?

The problem is that many tech entrepreneurs are still guided by utopian views of the early internet and create products that presume that people are good actors, ignoring considerable evidence to the contrary. The strong antipathy to government regulation and the legal precedent set up by CDA 230 mean that tech companies rely on self-regulation, and when this fails, they are often left scrambling.

Let's take Reddit. Originally a community for geeks to upvote geeky things, Reddit's current reputation has been tarnished by communities devoted to the alt-right, men's rights advocacy, and illicit photos of underage girls wearing yoga pants. In 2014, Reddit was heavily criticized for hosting the Fappening, a subreddit devoted to organizing and discussing stolen nude photos of female celebrities. Then-CEO Yishan Wong wrote a blog post called "Every Man is Responsible for His Own Soul" where he defended Reddit's choice to continue hosting the subreddit. Wong claimed that Reddit would not use technical means, like banning users or deleting subreddits, to shut down unpleasant content. Instead, they planned to highlight good actors on the site, like Reddit's popular Secret Santa. (Confusingly, later that day Reddit deleted the subreddit anyway. Pressure and DMCA requests from deep-pocketed celebrity lawyers were apparently enough to outweigh such lofty ideals.) He wrote:

> The reason is because we consider ourselves not just a company running a website where one can post links and discuss them, but the government of a new type of community. The role and responsibility of a government differs from that of a private corporation, in that it exercises restraint in the usage of its powers.

Well, that's all well and good, but Reddit is *not* a government. It is a corporation. **In the United States, the right to free speech applies only when the government attempts to limit what people say,** not when private citizens critique media or when websites limit what words people can use in comments. For instance, if Congress passed a bill banning negative comments on Reddit about the President, that would be a legitimate threat to free speech and would be unconstitutional.

But if Twitter decides to ban neo-Nazis or terrorist propaganda, that's perfectly within their right. Sites like Facebook and Instagram aggressively moderate content, which cuts down on the types of organized brigading that happens on Twitter and Reddit. But of course, free speech isn't just about what's legal, but about upholding values that are expressed in many places in society.

Companies like Twitter and Reddit that have stayed true to hacker ideals of information as free, and of the internet as a haven of free speech, continue to struggle with this balance. ISIS has been extremely effective at using digital media to spread propaganda. The same tools that let people collaborate on awesome projects like Wikipedia also let them collaborate on crazy theories like Pizzagate. Given Reddit's upvote/downvote infrastructure, it's hardly surprising that a community devoted to naked pictures of hot famous chicks became the fastest-growing subreddit of all time, regardless of how those pictures were obtained. And Twitter's feature set is fantastic for people to organize and mobilize quickly, even when those people are virulent anti-Semites.

The internet was explicitly founded on idealism. Even though most people *are* good actors, there are several very vocal minorities who want to use the internet for various Bad Things. Now, this wouldn't really matter if it was just a matter of counterspeech. If we could end sexism just by pointing out its flaws, then we'd all be in debt to Gender Studies majors. But the type of organized brigading that contemporary social media affords has the intended consequence of deterring other people's speech—specifically, the speech of women, especially queer women and women of color. And it gives rise to organized movements that want to diminish community trust and belief in institutions. This has very real and very negative consequences.

What do we do when tools founded on openness and freedom are used by straight-up bad actors? And what do platforms committed to those ideals do when their technologies are used to harass and suppress others?

Who Brought the Alt-Right Into This?

When technologists defend free speech above all other values, they play directly into the hands of white nationalists.

The rise of the alt-right, a fusion of white nationalists, Russian trolls, meme enthusiasts, men's rights activists, #gamergaters, libertarians, conspiracy theorists, bored teenagers, and hardcore right-wing activists has been well-documented by others. Suffice to say that the alt-right has been extraordinarily effective at using digital technologies, from Reddit to 8chan to Twitter to Google Docs, to collaborate, mobilize, and organize. They've also been very effective at co-opting the language of left-wing activism to paint themselves as victims. And they've done this through claiming the value of free speech.

To Milo Yiannopolous and his army of Breitbart commentators, safe spaces, inclusive language, and "political correctness" are not attempts to right wrongs, but incursions on free speech. Sexism and racism are lies that feminists, "social justice warriors," and others have come up with in order to suppress the truth (or insert your favorite conspiracy theory here). If feminist criticism of sexist imagery in video games functions as censorship, then people who enjoy such games can position themselves as the victims of Big Brother. Not only that, but it allows them to portray feminists as weaklings who can't handle the harsh realities of everyday life, and need to be coddled and handled carefully—which diminishes very real concerns.

They've already been extremely successful at positioning college campuses as the worst violators of free speech. Both Yiannopolis and Richard Spencer have garnered great publicity by booking invited talks at college campuses and then delighting in the uproar that typically follows. Campus anti-hate-speech policies have long been targets of the right; add to that anti-bullying and anti-harassment campaigns and you have an environment where Nina Burleigh writes in *Newsweek,* hardly a bastion of right-wing thought, that "American college campuses are starting to resemble George Orwell's Oceania with its Thought Police, or East Germany under the Stasi." (As someone who works in higher ed, this could not be further from the truth.) The idea that college campuses regularly censor and violate the free speech rights of people who aren't politically correct has become a mainstay of think pieces and Twitter, to my dismay. It's also given rise to the Professor Watchlist, a directory of "college professors who discriminate against conservative students and advance leftist propaganda in the classroom." (Leftist propaganda, in this case, indicates any anti-capitalist tendencies or acknowledgment of white privilege.)

So when tech companies like Reddit and Twitter, who have always been strong supporters of internet free speech, begin carefully moderating content, the alt-right sees it as full-scale censorship. Ironically, they co-opt the language of the left to portray their critics as aggressive SJWs, and themselves as powerless victims. Content moderation by private technology companies is not a First Amendment violation; in most cases, it's just a matter of enforcing pre-existing Terms of Service. But this victim/bully dichotomy allows them to garner sympathy from many who truly believe that the internet should be a stronghold of free speech.

We need to move beyond this simplistic binary of free speech/censorship online. That is just as true for libertarian-leaning technologists as it is neo-Nazi provocateurs. Sometimes the best way to ensure diverse voices is to make it safe for people to speak up who'd otherwise feel afraid. In his studies of Wikipedia, Northeastern Communication professor Joseph Reagle found that the classic liberal values of the internet—openness, transparency, and freedom—prioritize the voices of combative or openly biased community members over the comfort of female members, leading to male domination even in high-minded online communities. Aggressive online speech, whether practiced in the profanity and pornography-laced environment of 4Chan or the loftier venues of newspaper comments sections, positions sexism, racism, and anti-Semitism (and so forth) as issues of freedom of expression rather than structural oppression.

Perhaps we might want to look at countries like Canada and the United Kingdom, which take a different approach to free speech than does the United States. These countries recognize that unlimited free speech can lead to aggression and other tactics which end up silencing the speech of minorities—in other words, the tyranny of the majority. Creating online communities where all groups can speak may mean scaling back on some of the idealism of the early internet in favor of pragmatism. But recognizing this complexity is an absolutely necessary first step.

Critical Thinking

1. Should social media companies be permitted to restrict comments or restrict who can be a user of the site? Why or why not?

2. Are postings and speech from hate groups acceptable discourse on social media sites? Who gets to decide boundaries, if boundaries are to exist?

3. Social media posts are available for viewing world wide. Which country's laws should apply to posts on these sites?

Internet References

Defending Crucial Protections For Internet Platforms
http://thehill.com/blogs/congress-blog/judicial/345195-defending-crucial-protections-for-internet-platforms

Germany's Social Media Law May Force Facebook To Be Judge, Jury, And Executioner Of Free Speech
https://qz.com/1090825/germanys-new-social-media-law-analysis-facebook-twitter-youtube-to-remove-hate-speech-in-24-hours-or-face-fines/

The Secret Rules of the Internet
https://www.theverge.com/2016/4/13/11387934/internet-moderator-history-youtube-facebook-reddit-censorship-free-speech

---

ALICE TIARA is former Director of the McGannon Communication Research Center and Assistant Professor of Communication and Media Studies at Fordham University. She is a 2016–2017 fellow at Data & Society.

THE WITCH'S HAT

by

TONY JOHNSTON

pictures by

MARGOT TOMES

G.P. PUTNAM'S SONS
NEW YORK

Text copyright © 1984 by Tony Johnston.
Illustrations copyright © 1984 by Margot Tomes.
All rights reserved. Published simultaneously in
Canada by General Publishing Co. Limited, Toronto.
Printed in the United States of America.
Library of Congress Cataloging in Publication Data
Johnston, Tony.
The witch's hat.
Summary: A witch's hat causes its owner some problems
when it turns into a bat, then a rat, then a cat,
and still won't behave after that.
1. Children's stories, American.
[1. Witches—Fiction. 2. Hats—Fiction]
I. Tomes, Margot, ill. II. Title.
PZ7.J6478Wi   1984   [E]   84-9948
ISBN 0-399-21010-5

Third Impression

For Ashley, my porkus,

my hamus, in pink pajamas —TJ

For Frith, the cat —MT

A witch was stirring her brew in a big, fat, magic pot.

She stirred and stirred.

Then she bent to taste, and — oops — her hat fell in.
"My hat!" she screeched in a voice as thin as she was.
"I'll have to fish it out."

She fished

and fished.

Then, when she felt a nibble, she pulled up the soggy hat.

"My hat!" she cackled happily.

But when she reached for it—the hat turned into a bat.

(It was a magic pot, in case you forgot.)

"My hat is a bat!" cried the witch. "Hat! Stop, I say!"
But did it stop?

No. It flew away.

It settled in the attic.

The attic was dark. Was the witch brave?

Would she go inside? Yes.

She squinted. And what did she see?

A whole flock of bats hanging from a rafter.

"Oh, fine," she grumbled. "Which one is mine?"

She called out, "Hat, come down!"

Nothing moved. Not one bat. Not one hat.

"Grrrrrrrr," said the witch, grinding her teeth. She mumbled a magic spell, "Porkus, hamus, pink pajamas," and — *all* the bats fluttered down and piled around her knees.

"Which one are you?" asked the witch in a grouchy voice. Did anyone answer?

No. Not one bat. Not one hat.

So she began to pinch the bats to find her very own.

"Squeak!" went a bat.

"Bat," said the witch.

"Squeak!" went a bat.
"Bat," said the witch.

"Ouch!" went a bat.
"HAT!" cried the witch.
She grabbed for it, but—

it turned into a rat.

(It was a magic pot, in case you forgot.)
"My hat is a rat! Stop, I say!"
But did it stop?

No. It scrambled into a hole in the wall.

The hole was dark.

Was the witch brave? Yes.

Would she go inside? No. She wouldn't fit.

"We'll see about that, hat," muttered the witch.

She fetched a cheese, big as you please, and —

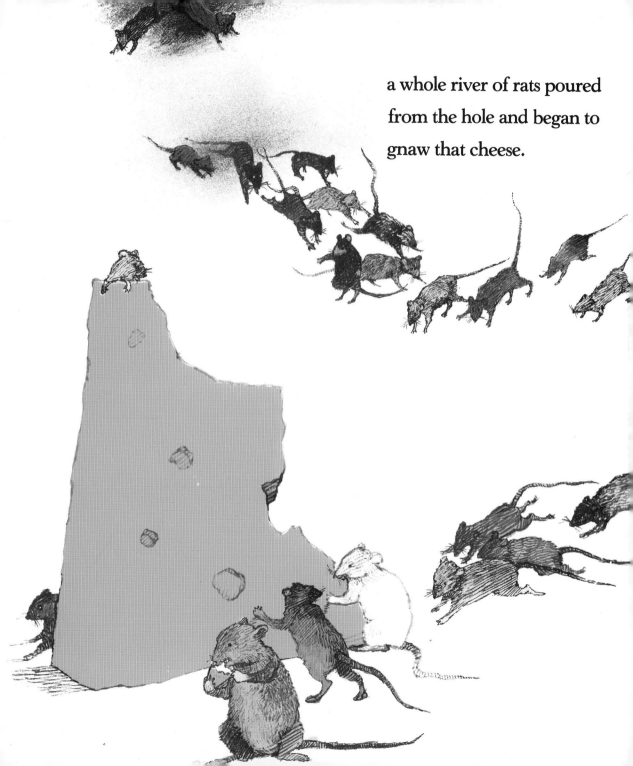

a whole river of rats poured
from the hole and began to
gnaw that cheese.

The witch began to poke the rats to find her very own.

"Oooh," went a rat. "Rat," said the witch.

"Oooh," went a rat.

"Rat," said the witch.

"Boo!" went a rat.

"HAT!" cried the witch.

She grabbed for it, but—

now it wasn't a rat. Now it was a cat.

(It was a magic pot, in case you forgot.)

The cat ran downstairs
like an inky streak.

The witch ran after it.
But when she reached
the last stair, what was there?

Twenty-seven cats from who-knows-where,

purring on the hearth.

The witch wasn't purring. She was roaring.

"I'm going to get you, hat!"

She tickled the cats to find her very own.

"Meow," went a cat. "Cat," said the witch.

"Meow," went a cat.

"Cat," said the witch.

"Tee-hee-hee," went a cat.

"HAT!" cried the witch,
pouncing on it with both hands
and popping it on her head.

The witch went back to stir her brew.
All was well. She had her very own hat.

The witch went back to stir her brew.
All was well. She had her very own hat.

"Meow," went a cat.
"Cat," said the witch.

"Tee-hee-hee," went a cat.
"HAT!" cried the witch,
pouncing on it with both hands
and popping it on her head.

She was smiling now. And—

the magic pot was smiling too.